AF526886

MAO ZEDONG and SOCIAL RECONSTRUCTION

Mao Zedong and Social Reconstruction

EDITORS
GIRIN PHUKON, DHIREN BHAGAWATI
Dibrugarh University, Dibrugarh 786004

SOUTH ASIAN PUBLISHERS * NEW DELHI

This volume is an anthology of papers presented at the seminar on "Mao Zedong and Social Reconstruction" held in the Department of Political Science Dibrugarh University, Dibrugarh 786004 in November 1994.

Copyright © Dibrugarh University, 1996

All rights reserved. No part of this publication may be reproduced in any form or aby any means, without the written permission of South Asian Publishers Pvt. Ltd. 50 Sidharth Enclave, P.O. Jangpura, New Delhi 110014.

Typeset at

ANJALI COMPUTER TYPESETTING
50 Sidharth Enclave, P.O. Jangpura
New Delhi 110014. Phone: 6925315

ISBN 81-7003-198-2

SOUTH ASIAN PUBLISHERS PVT. LTD.
50 Sidharth Enclave, P.O. Jangpura
New Delhi 110014. Phones: 6835713 6925315

Published by South Asian Publishers Pvt. Ltd., 50 Sidharth Enclave, P.O. Jangpura, New Delhi 110014 and printed at Mehra Offset Press, Chandni Mahal Daryaganj, New Delhi 110002. Printed in India.

A Tribute
to
MAO ZEDONG (1893-1976)
on his
Birth Centenary

Contents

Preface

This volume is a compilation of a set of papers presented at a national seminar, organized by the Department of Political Science, Dibrugarh University on 14-15 November, 1994 to mark the birth centenary of Mao Zedong. The papers covers a wide-range of aspects of Mao's thought and activity. "Mao Zedong and Social Reconstruction" being the frame work of the seminar, the papers concern with Mao's thought, perspectives on reconstruction, foreign policy initiatives, military strategies, impact of Mao's thought in Afro-Asian countries and Mao's literary thought. It is a critique of Mao with a positive but non-dogmatic outlook which appreciates progress with enrichment of human values.

In compilation of this volume, we have received generous help from many sources which we take the pleasure to acknowledge here. The University Grants Commission, Indian Council of Social Science Research and Dibrugarh University jointly sponsored the seminar at which the papers were presented. We express our profound gratitude to the authorities of these institutions. It is the contributors of various papers who constitute the soul of this volume. We would like to record our appreciation and gratefulness for their admirable cooperation. We are also indebted to our colleagues in the Department of Political Science, Dibrugarh University for their valuable help in this effort.

In regard to the publication of this work, we thank the authorities of Dibrugarh University for extending a part of the publication grant. But for the constant encouragement and inspiration received from Prof. M.M. Sarmah, Vice-Chancellor, Dibrugarh University, the volume would not have seen the light of day. So, we have a debt of gratitude to him. Our grateful thanks are also due to Mr. B.C. Saikia. Registrar and Mr. N.K. Koch, Deputy Registrar (F&A) for their assistance in this task. We would also like to thank Mr. Nityananda Gogoi and Mr. Kalyan Kumar Gogoi who took much pain in typing out the manuscript of this volume.

Dibrugarh
February 1996

Girin Phukon
Dhiren Bhagawati

Contributors

ABU NASAR SAIED AHMED
Department of Political Science, Dibrugarh University

DHIREN BHAGAWATI
Department of Political Science, Dibrugarh University

BUDHADEVA BHATTACHARYYA
Surendra Nath Banerjee Professor of Political Science, Calcutta, University

MIRA SINHA BHATTACHARJEA
Institute of Chinese Studies, Centre for the Study of Developing Societies, Delhi

NEERA CHANDHOKE
Department of Political Science, University of Delhi

GIRI DESHINGKAR
Institute of Chinese Studies, Centre for the Study of Developing Societies, Delhi

MAQAITUL HUSSAIN
Department of Sociology, Dibrugarh University

TILOTTOMA MISRA
Department of English, Dibrugarh University

MANORANJAN MOHANTY
Department of Political Science, University of Delhi

GIRIN PHUKON
Department of Political Science, Dibrugarh University

ASISH K. RAY
Department of South & Southeast Asian Studies, Calcutta University

SAMIRENDRA N. RAY
Department of Political Science, University of North Bengal

NAGEN SAIKIA
Department of Assamese, Dibrugarh University

SHANTI SWARUP
Lala Lajpat Rai Professor of Political Science (Retired), Punjab University

1. Introduction

Mao's was a multi-faceted personality – a thinker, a revolutionary, a strategist, a statesman and a poet. But he liked to call himself a teacher. His life and activity were an epitome of his philosophy.

Mao was twenty four years younger than our Gandhi. Whatever contrast is made between the two leaders, yet they have certain common characteristics. Both of them were leaders of the masses, they had the same vision of creating a new society, they had similar aversion to the Western arrogance but respect for Western human values, and both of them were equally bound by their respective traditions. But Gandhi died the most unhappy and disillusioned man. Mao initiated and completed the task of building China as a great nation according to his own ideological vision. Moreoever, Mao's model of social reconstruction cast a spell all over the Third World countries. In view of this, Mao's thought, ideas and approach to social transformation are quite relevant for a serious debate.

Mao's success lies in his ability to keep off bureaucratization of the power structure, to keep the masses in the centre of politics which prevented estrangement of the masses from the leaders. Mao did not achieve his success by imposing a monolithic unity on the party, by coercion and by propaganda alone. He preferred educating his opponents to exterminating them. Mao was certainly not adept at bargains, compromises and manipulation. Indeed, he proved that a system of thought and a system of institutions do not have any intrinsic value of their own. They are important to the extent that they serve the masses and help in realization of a secured life for the common man in the society.

Just after assuming power in 1949, Mao directed his partyman to guard against corruption and wastage and exhorted them to live a simple life. He himself set the model by living a modest life and growing his own vegetables till his death. When Mao discerned a tendency of degeneration in the party and the state structure he initiated and launched the great Cultural Revolution to rectify the evil tendencies. Unless this was done, he visualized, revisionism might arise and the high wave of consumerism and profiteering would wash away whatever he had achieved for the common man of China. This is how he rightly predicted the fate of the erstwhile USSR.

In view of all this, it is imperative to reassess and evaluate the words and deeds of this great figure. Although the populist writings on Mao are abundant, scholarly and serious works, based on objective perspective are scant. This volume is an endeavour to fill this gap.

Delivering the keynote address to the seminar, Manoranjan Mohanty developed Mao's contributions into a creative theory of knowledge and practice, and of knowing and doing. The creative theory of Mao is rooted in historical practices – tradition, law and convention of people and at the same time it possesses enormous power to respond to the conditions of time and space and to create and reconstruct reality. While the creative theory of Mao takes stock of the historical traditions of knowledge, it breaks new grounds for the process of knowing. It discovers the nature of knowledge in the course of practice and discerns the governing conditions of knowledge. More importantly it liberates knowledge from its feudal, parochial and bourgeois roots, and makes knowledge more true and more democratic. In India, for example, creative theory can liberate knowledge from the Brahmanical roots and orient it towards the toiling masses, Mohanty suggests. Though located in history, Mao' creative theory aims at reconstruction of contemporary history; it is oriented towards action for changing the environment. Mao's creative theory is concerned with pre-occupations of our time. We seek liberation, autonomy, self-determination and all these are engrossed in Mao's creative theory.

Mohanty takes note of two large, though contradictory, streams of the present history of human kind and shows how dialectics of Mao in his creative theory can be applied to analyse them, and to resolve them. On the one hand, there is an upsurge of democracy and freedom in the twentieth century. The Bolshevik Revolution, the Chinese Revolution, the national liberation struggle against colonialism were a continuous process of freedom. Another trend of democratic upsurge, often unnoticed though it goes, is the movement of oppressed groups like women, tribals, dalits for expanding the horizon of freedom.

On the other hand, there is the persistence of the oppressive trends of domination, technology, capital, elite structure, neo-colonial patterns of structural adjustments of economy, new modes of domination by forces of fundamentalism and authoritarianism. Reality of the twentieth century is the dialectical contradiction of these two streams. Gandhi spelt out the contradiction in his idea of *Swaraj* and the idea of liberty. Mao's struggle against imperialism, Soviet revisionism, sources of degeneration of the modern society which he exposed through the Cultural Revolution revealed the same contradictions of this era. Dialectics of Mao not merely exposes power relations but also expands the forces of freedom by liberating knowledge from power of reactionary forces.

No doubt Mao was a product of history – and historical forces shaped Mao's ideas and actions but that is not the whole truth for Mohanty. Rather he insists on understanding how an individual, a member of a movement or a leader of a movement intervenes in the process of history. To understand how the gap between individual and history is bridged in Mao, Mohanty draws attention to three aspects.

1. First is the dialectics involving the individual, the movement and history. There may be several sets of relations like individual and the movement, individual and the organization and individual and a collectivity, all placed in the process of history.
2. Second is to grasp how did Mao apply dialectics to grasp the process of history. The answer is Mao's method of application of historical materialist dialectics to comprehend the conditions of history. Mao's principal occupation was analysing sets of contradictions, applying it to understand reality of both overall history and particular phase of history. It is not enough to know that Mao applied Marxism-Leninism but how he applied it through his creative theory, his method of dialectical analysis which is to be emphasized.
3. Then comes the role of human capacity or will to respond to a situation. It is not merely human consciousness, rather consciousness is to be transformed into action. It is the human power to intervene in the face of the strongest adverse situation. It is not a subjective formulation of individual power. Rather, it is the power of a subject and weaker people to intervene, to change and to create new conditions. Power is to be interpreted as capacity to change and to create conditions.

Mao's dialectics and Mao's emphasis on practice provided him the basic perspectives in his struggle against imperialism, colonialism, feudalism and capitalism and in building socialism. Mohanty mentions four formulations of Mao's dialectics. The first formulation of dialectics is the unity of knowing and doing. It means not only inheriting tradition of knowledge and applying known theories of knowledge but to test them through practice.

What has happened in China today is to hold practice as sole criterion of truth and if any policy cannot deliver the good, it has to be changed. Mohanty argues that a distinction must be made between practice in a wide time frame and space on the one hand and practice interpreted in terms of specific utilitarian objectives on the other. Objective of Deng Xiaping was to achieve China's economic prosperity. The objective of Mao was to create a socialist society in China in which human relations were egalitarian, and not based on consumerism as in a capitalist society – it was based on ethical human values of solidarity, love, sacrifice, exploring nature and developing human potentialities, inheriting people's cultures and developing them – what Mohanty terms socialism with socialist freedom at its core. Capitalism in its initial centuries promised equality and freedom. However, in the second half of the nineteenth century Marx discovered and proved how capitalism had created new conditions of alienation and exploitation. Therefore, capitalism's early promise of enlarging freedom and fulfilling it was belied. Socialism's goal was to generate conditions of freedom. For Mao's dialectics the method was to emphasize the objectives of socialism in terms of these human values. Marx's socialist revolution was in the framework of industrial revolution whereas Mao differentiated the Chinese path of revolution from the Soviet path. The Soviet path under Stalin and also under Khurushchev and Brezhnev was oriented towards the same kind of growth targets as in capitalism. The Chinese path under Mao had the freedom-centred, liberation-centred notion of socialism. Practice is to be judged in terms of those objectives not economic prosperity alone. After the reforms China is successful as an economic power but consumerism, crime, corruption are on the rise, degeneration of society, inequality among groups in the same area and different areas are rising. Assessment of practice is to be dialectical. Law of analysis meant grasping the essential character of a thing to find out what contradictions were present in a situation. Law of synthesis meant resolving by transformation of them through struggle and seeing it as a continued process of affirmation and negation. Law of particularity was a clue to finding out the principal contradiction so that one could order the contradiction in a particular time period to chalk out the focus of one's strategy.

Dialectics unites different contradictions by ordering them. Law of particularity today redefines liberation in terms of multi-dimensional approach to freedom. While aiming at the ending of class oppression, caste oppression, patriarchical oppression, ethnic oppression, it relates them all in the present context to what capitalism at global as well as national, regional scale is doing to these sets of contradictions. For example how capitalism protects patriarchy, how capitalism protects ethnic domination, how capitalism relates class struggle with other forms of struggle or subdues class struggle or creates artificial class struggle delinked from the other struggles of society. Mohanty continues that law of particularity in its application of dialectics enables us to analyse relationship among different sets of contradictions and order them and translate them into action programme against a principal enemy in the particular context of time and space and orient them to larger agenda of struggle. Mao in 1959 appealed to popularize the dialectics and to develop the dialectics so that China had six hundred million dialecticians, the whole population, pursuing creative theory. Mohanty felt the need of five billion dialecticians in today's world.

Though the papers included in this volume are within the parameter of "Mao Zedong and Social Reconstruction" they deal with diverse aspects of Mao's personality and action. To knit them together a thread of logic encompassing a broad range of themes is developed. Starting with Manoranjan Mohanty's paper as a critical evaluation of Mao by leaders succeeding him, we go on to deal with Mao's thought as expressed in the papers of Girin Phukon, Dhiren Bhagawati and Maquitul Hussain; Mao's role in socialist construction is analysed by Ashis Kr. Roy, Budhadeva Bhattacharyya, Samirendra N. Roy and Shanti Swarup; Mao's formulation of international relations is discussed in the papers of Meera Sinha Bhattacharjya and Abu Nasser Syed Ahmad; Mao's influence in the Afro-Asian countries is narrated in the papers of Tillotoma Misra and Neera Chandoke; and also a divergent aspect of his life, i.e. his poetic interests, is discussed by Nagen Saikia.

Mohanty's paper is in outline, an evaluation of Mao by his successors. He calls it a discriminating evaluation which is contrived to maintain a linkage with Mao's legacy in the face of de-maozisation policies initiated by the present leadership of China. Deng's approach to Mao distinguishes between Mao's personality cult and Mao's thought, it affirms Mao's contributions to revolution and reconstruction, including Mao as the core in a collective leadership, and selects certain traits of Mao's thought emphasizing particularly Mao's dictum of seeking truth from facts. Mao's mistakes during the Great Leap Forward and Cultural Revolution are considered mistakes of a great leader, which means that class struggle and politics finds secondary importance with the present leadership. Ultimately Mohanty concludes that the distinction between Mao and Deng is to be found in the fact that for Deng material production and prosperity is the primary objective; while creation of a socialist human being with moral, political consciousness was the basic objective of socialism.

There are three papers concerning certain aspects of Mao's thought. Girin Phukon in his paper brings forth Mao's concept of contradiction as Mao developed it in two of his essays. He analyses the basic characteristics of contradiction in Mao's use of the concept. In elaborating the concept of contradiction Mao included elements like universal and particular contradictions, principal and the principal aspects of contradiction. Arguing on the role of given conditions in transformation of opposites Phukon quotes Mao as asking "Why can an egg, not a stone, be transformed into a chicken"? Distinguishing antagonism from contradiction, Mao talked of antagonistic and non-antagonistic contradiction. In the post revolutionary period Mao emphasized the role of non-antagonistic contradiction in Chinese society and supported methods other than revolutionary war for resolving them. Phukon concludes that Mao's assertion of contradictions persisting in socialist society is a remarkable contribution to Marxist theory.

Dhiren Bhagawati in his paper analyses the epistemological basis of Mao's article "On Practice". Marx's material basis of knowledge means knowledge as a part of labour and productive process. Engels made development of knowledge and development of nature of the material world inter-dependent. Alteration of nature by man is the measure of human intelligence. Materialist dualism of Lenin, however, made knowledge subjective. Drawing heavily from Lenin, Mao made subjective knowledge dependent on practice which for Marx and Engels was social and productive context of knowledge, for Lenin it was following theory in revolutionary action. But for Mao truth and utility of a theory was to be tested in practice and even to be modified and developed in the light of practice. It means more than blending theory with practice.

Mao's "On Practice" has evoked another paper. M. Hussain in his paper looks at the problem from a sociology of knowledge framework and makes a comparative analysis of Mao's and G.H. Mead's theory of knowledge Hussain infuses Mead's "role taking" of other in the process of socialization of the individual into Mao's leap of perception to conception and conception to rational knowledge to identify the two processes as a societal interaction process in the formation of the individual self. Hussain argues that integration of Mead's social psychology with Mao's theory of knowledge will provide a sociological framework to analyse society. He applies Berger's model of sociology of knowledge framework to juxtapose Mao's and Mead's ideas of knowledge.

The role of Mao in leading the Chinese revolution and in the reconstruction of post-revolutionary China is viewed from certain angles in four papers. Shanti Swarup in his paper wants to explain the shifts in Mao's strategy and ideas from greater revolutionary fervour to moderation at different times. Swarup implies that shifts can be explained in terms of Mao's attempts to grapple with certain dilemmas in the light of changing empirical reality. Mao faced two problems and tried to resolve them. The first problem was his realization that it was possible to have small scale, slow and piecemeal revolution in China but such a revolution had its implication. This concept of revolution was not to be found in Marxist thought and tradition. Mao opted for it. Once it was started Mao had to initiate the process of transformation and reconstruction which could not wait till the revolution was to be complete. Mao's revolution therefore was required to continue the revolutionary momentum through continuous mobilization and to see that socio-economic development was not drastically affected. Consequently Mao felt that he required for his revolution the skill, capacity and capital of the middle class. He wanted to win the middle class, to soothe the middle class when there were excesses, to fulfil their nationalist urges. Mao's "Hundred Flowers Bloom" emanated from such a desire. Shocked at the response of the middle class, Mao hit back with his rectification campaign.

Buddhadeva Bhattacharyya's paper analyses the distinction between Lenin's and Mao's approaches to the two stages of revolution – bourgeois-democratic stage and the socialist stage. His basic assertion is that Mao distinguished himself from Lenin by incorporating elements other than proletariat and peasantry in the structure of state and government in his New Democracy. The possibility of the elements obstructing socialist revolutionary process from within the state structure came to the surface in 1956 over the division within the CPC leadership between Maoist and Liu Shao Chi groups on economic policies. In 1964 Mao tried to correct the situation but perhaps without success as the present happenings in China demonstrate. Bhattacharyya concludes with the observation that Chinese experience establishes the importance and priority of political superstructure in socialist transformation and negates the productionist view of Stalin.

S.N. Ray assesses Mao's contributions to the agrarian and rural reform measures of China. He counts the positive contributions of Mao as (1) the concept of mass line which involved an element of democratic participation; (2) Mao's stress on human change accompanying economic and technical progress; (3) attack on bureaucracy; (4) centre of gravity in the country-side and active role for the peasantry. Mao's success depended on the recognition of the facts that (1) vast majority of the Chinese people were poor and illiterate; (2) China's greatest reservoir of creative energy lay in the majority; (3) political leadership belonged to the persons who organized the majority; (4) capital for China's prosperity lay in the labour power of the vast majority. Ray considers several phases of China's economic development and finds that the establishment of people's communes in 1959 was the culmination of land reform process initiated in 1950. Mao's communes were extraordinary at the social level, since they brought together workers, peasants, shopkeepers, soldiers and students creating a full and clear image of an egalitarian society, he argues. Communes were the framework in which people functioned politically to voice their interests, economically to produce and consume and socially to form a community beyond family. Ray enumerates the deficiencies which weakened the communes. The Cultural Revolution that Mao initiated sought to realize certain ideals like narrowing gap between city and country-side, between mental and manual labour, and workers' control over workplace and the society as a whole. But it almost disrupted the economy and created near anarchy condition.

A.K. Roy in his paper emphasizes that the revolution Mao completed in China and the order he created was peasant communism as distinguished from industrial communism of Marx (though Roy did not call it so). Marx's Asiatic mode of production with its nuclear village and oriental despotism could not provide for a revolution unless an industrial proletariat in the line of Europe could be developed in Asia. Lenin was the first Marxist theoretician to emphasize the role of national liberation struggle of the colonies in war against imperialism. At the intervention of M.N. Roy and Lenin, their differences notwithstanding the Comintern endorsed the role of communists in national revolutionary movements.

Consequently Lenin justified revolution in a large country, like Russia with underdeveloped industries and communications by applying his theory of the weakest link. Lenin also recognized the revolutionary potential of the peasantry but he ruled out the possibility of peasants leading a revolution. Mao began where Lenin had left off, Roy argues. By adopting the traditional Chiness pattern of peasant revolts and by developing a strategy and tactics around it Mao developed his peasant communism. Mao's report on Hunan peasant condition was the origin of the revolutionary way Mao applied it to China. Mao replaced the leadership of the proletariat by his concept of the broad alliance of the masses; the dictatorship of the proletariat by the people's democratic dictatorship. In place of mere reliance on poor peasants, Mao developed the peasant military force to conduct the revolution. Contrasting it with the October Revolution Lin Piao held that the Chinese Revolution won victory through encirclement of the cities from the rural areas and final capture of the cities.

Mao's role in formulating China's relation with other countries and his ideas on international relation in general are assessed in three papers. Mira Sinha Bhattacharjea in her paper describes how Mao determined the objectives and strategies and made analysis of Chinese foreign policy, which was for Mao a part of a holistic strategy for making revolution. The core of the holistic approach of Mao consisted of anti-imperialism and making revolution. Mao sought the answers to the questions of what making revolution was, who would make revolution and how it was to be made. He got its clear answer only in his Hunan experience which led him to understand the objective world of China consisting of revolutionary peasantry and threat of Japanese imperialism . On the basis of this formulation Mao developed his strategy of national liberation struggle under the leadership of CCP and national and international United Front. Since this period Mao made insightful assessments of the global balance of power and forces. Bhattacharjea considered eight interventions of Mao in response to developments in China and also the entire world which brought about a change of strategy and methods of Mao. Referring to India, Bhattacharjea argues that Mao offered a pivotal role to India in international united front and the 1962 war was a purposive action of Mao with the desire of demonstrating China's ability of independent decision and action in comparison to India.

A.N.S. Ahmed in his paper deals with the infinite risk taking ability of Mao in foreign policy initiatives particularly in confrontation with the USA and the

Soviet Union. Being a nationalist patriot Mao was never unaware of his international obligations. From his early experience Mao became aware of the emergence of a revolutionary force in China and its role in cleaning China of all imperialist forces and bringing about her economic and industrial development. He refers to the fact that Mao emerged from a collective leadership of pre-1949 era and rose to a single unassailable position in the subsequent years. Ahmed traced Mao's attitude towards the US since the revolutionary days and his distrust of Stalin. Inspite of it Mao aligned China with the Soviet Union and benefitted from it. Mao could not afford to displease Stalin in the face of American threat and rather tried to disprove Stalin's fear of Mao as another Tito through the Chinese participation in the Korean War. Since the death of Stalin, particularly from the Camp David talks, the hostility between Mao and the Soviet leadership came to the surface. Result of it was development of China's nuclear capability. Initial possibility of good relations with the USA was stalled by the Korean War but subsequent development with the Soviet Union explains Mao's move towards the USA.

Giri Deshingkar assesses Mao's military thought, Mao learned the craft of war during his confrontation with the Guomindang and the Japanese Army. He had to wage a war against vastly superior enemies both in terms of number as well as weaponry. Mao raised his experience to the level of a theory of warfare. Besides the experience on the ground, Mao also drew on the Chinese classics. Major concepts of Mao's theory of war were, war as a social product not merely a product of human nature; war as a form of politics, concept of protected war, involving the entire population in war; treating the enemy as supplier of weapons; party control of the armed forces; three phases of war; namely strategic defensive, strategic consolidation and strategic offensive; emphasis on man over weapons. Mao did not modify his view that man was primary not weapons except that he had to think about the impact of nuclear weapons. His initial response that atom bomb was a paper tiger underwent change but he continued to insist that nuclear war would not annihilate the human race and those who would survive would establish a glorious socialist revolution. Mao's military theory was considered to be important even after 1949 as it was completely internalized by the Peoples Liberation Army (PLA) and was applicable where the PLA was weak and the enemy was strong. Mao, of course felt the need of a strategic nuclear deterrent against the enemy as the first step before launching a people's war. Deshingkar finds several inconsistencies in Mao's theory and practice. In spite of the dominance of the people's war doctrine, the PLA did not fight a people's war during Korean War and the Indo-China War. Mao believed that US imperialism intended only to frighten others but it could not use nuclear weapons. Still Mao backed down in the face of an American nuclear threat in 1958. Deshingkar admits that many questions about Mao's military thought cannot be answered due to lack of authentic documentation. Mao's military theory was a brilliant exposition but it was time-bound and became obsolete in the technological changes and nuclear weapons of the present time.

There are two representative papers on Mao's influence on third world countries. Neera Chandoke's paper depicts the liberation war of Amilcar Cabral in Guinea Bisau. Amilcar Cabral provided a matching parallel to Mao in this small Protuguese colony of Africa though there were certain basic differences in their approaches to revolution and organization of the peasantry. Initially Amilcar Cabral's party made an abortive attempt to capture power by striking the urban centres with the help of port and dock workers. Cabral learnt two lessons from it, first that success of liberation depended on the armed struggle and secondly armed struggle was to be organized in the country-side by mobilizing the peasantry. Cabral visited China in 1960 and since then he pursued the strategies of Mao in his country like building a national bloc to fight imperialism and creating liberated zones, developing social and political arrangements in those zones. Chandoke argues that it testifies to the relevance of Mao's strategy and ideology in rural societies and technologically under-developed countries who became the subjects of imperialism. Amilcar Cabral's emphasis on political control over militarization of the struggle and his formation of the village committee with extensive economic and social functions and democratic participation much resemble Mao's reconstruction activities in post-revolutionary China. Chandoke's analysis unfolds several points of differences also between Mao and Cabral in their approaches to class mobilization and ideology.

Tilottoma Misra in her paper recollects how Mao's thought stirred the minds of Indian youths particularly those of Calcutta and Delhi and steered them towards students agitation in the years between 1966 to 1971. Students agitation in Calcutta started in the wake of Naxalbari uprisings and the thought of Mao dominated the mind of the students. A prominent feature of the agitation was call for boycotting the union elections and for joining the masses in the armed struggle. In Delhi University also a group of students and teachers formed Maoist group with the aim of carrying forward the cause of armed struggle. However, the Delhi group was more cautioned and disciplined and less violent perhaps due to their affluent social background. Misra also refers to the creation and functioning of a Marxist league at Dibrugarh University at that time. Total disquiet and disillusionment with the prevailing socio-political situation and inspiration from the Chinese Cultural Revolution were the main factors behind creation of Maoist groups among Indian students. The New Left of the West and Che Guevara's heroism also inspired the Indian youths. The students agitation could not make a headway because for them Mao Zedong's thoughts remained a fashionable gospel of rebellion rather than a guide to understanding concrete reality of this country. Snobbish high-brow attitude of the elitist students also could not appeal to the other students and Marxist political leaders. Distortion of Maoist thought by leaders like Charu Majumder exposed the students to state terrorism and belied their hope.

Mao's literary and poetic contributions are appreciated by Nagen Saikia. Mao, like Lenin, emphasized the effect of literature in inspiring people to change society from feudalism to socialism. Anything that did not serve the interest of the people was rejected by Mao and mythology was an example of it. Saikia mentions how Mao drew from the history and rich cultural heritage of China to build a new democratic culture. Mao rejected pure literature and like Lenin he was more concerned with the immediate social need than universality of literature. However, the poet in Mao reacted to the appeal of time and nature.

The discourse initiated at the seminar to critically review the contributions of Mao to human civilization and enrich knowledge with the innovation of the great genius should continue for generations to come. This volume is a humble effort in that direction.

2. Power of History
Mao Zedong Thought and Deng's China

MANORANJAN MOHANTY

Method of Discriminating Evaluation

Successor generations have several options to define their relationship with the leaders of their social movements. One is to raise the leader into a cult figure and ritually pay respect. In such cases, the values and goals of the leader are put on a high pedestal in an abstract form and commitment to them is reaffirmed by the new leaders. This probably has been the way Gandhi was treated by Nehru and his successors. Another way is to over-generalize the ideas of a leader so as to generate a large spectrum of interpretations. Thus besides maintaining a cult, the successors continue to affirm their adherence to the founder's principles. This is how Lenin was treated by the later Soviet leaders and many communists in different parts of the world. A third mode is to sharply break with the earlier leader and after denouncing the predecessor announce a new line. Khrushchev's denunciation of Stalin belonged to this category.

Deng Xiaoping's assessment of Mao Zedong did not adopt any of the three approaches. He followed what can be called the method of discriminating evaluation – a method that Mao applied to analyse Stalin's role and his ideas. This method identifies the criteria of judgement, particularly the vantage point of the observer and after having a total view of a leader, proceeds to find the positive and negative aspects of the leader's role and ideas. The total view presents the summary perspective as to whether the leader ought to be on the whole admired or condemned. Accordingly, the positive aspects would be primary or secondary. This is how Mao assessed Stalin to be "70 per cent right and 30 per cent wrong."[1] Similarly Deng Xiaoping has stated that Mao's "contributions were primary and his mistakes were secondary."[2] In some cases the mistakes of the great leaders are either not discussed at all or explained away in terms of contingencies of the prevailing situation. Analysing Gandhi's mistakes is a taboo in many quarters in India as is critical scrutiny of Sun Yatsen's role in China. The popular adoration of such national figures is so widespread that discriminating evaluation becomes difficult except as deliberate exercises.

In the application of this method, the vantage point of assessment is critical. Mao viewed Stalin both when the latter was alive and after his death, from the standpoint of the leader of the Chinese revolution and socialist construction. Mao was engaged in finding a Chinese path for a democratic and a socialist revolution and that influenced his judgement on Stalin. Even though Stalin's directives to the CPC in the 1920's and 1930's caused considerable harm to the communist movement and several of Stalin's policies in the 1940's and early 1950's offended China's nationalist sentiments, still Mao paid homage to Stalin for his leadership of the USSR during the World War II. Mao actually traced Soviet revisionism to Stalin's "walking on one leg" or one-sided policies and violation of democratic centralism. While proposing "mass line" as the alternative to Stalin's bureaucratic centralization and political terror, Mao however, refused to totally denounce Stalin.[3] Whether the later events exposing the fragility of the Soviet state and its collapse would warrant a further evaluation of Stalin is another important question.

Deng Xiaoping's vantage point was China's economic construction. The context was passing away of Zhou Enlai, Zhu De and Mao in quick succession in 1976, the arrest of the Gang of Four and the formal termination of the Cultural Revolution. A cult of Mao had been built up during the Cultural Revolution (CR). In the two years following the fall of Gang of Four when Hua Guofeng was the CPC Chairman and Premier there was an intense debate on various ideological and political issues in China. Hua's line of defending the basic orientation of the CR while pushing for a strategy of four modernizations was finally defeated and Deng's line of "reform and open door" achieved victory at the Third Plenum of the Eleventh Central Committee in December 1978. After that Deng and his colleagues decided to orient every policy to serve the needs of economic development.

The official denunciation of the CR was so strong and it seemed to have so much public support that it could have engulfed a total condemnation of Mao Zedong. In fact, many posters on the Democracy Wall in February-March 1979 called for deMaoization like Khrushchev's deStalinization in Russia. Many leaders who had been harassed by Mao – these included Deng Xiaoping and Chen Yun – could have taken that line. But Deng himself took the initiative to stem that tide and called for a careful assessment of Mao Zedong Thought. The CPC Central Committee appointed a Group headed by General Secretary Hu Yaobang in 1980 to formulate a document on this question. After much deliberations and many revisions in which Deng himself participated the *Resolution on Certain Questions in the History of Our Party* was adopted at the Sixth

Plenum in June 1981.

The 1981 Resolution spelt out the perspective of discriminating evaluation relating to Mao which guided the public discussion on Mao during the reform period right upto the celebrations of the Mao Zedong Birth Centenary on 26 December 1993.

"Upholding and developing"

When one of the drafts of the Resolution on Party History was brought before Deng Xiaoping in 1980 he was upset by the fact that Mao Zedong's contribution to the Chinese revolution was not adequately acknowledged. He said that the vast masses of the landless and small peasants of China and the veteran cadres will not forgive the Party for this lapse.[4] This frank admission of the social basis of Mao's legacy was significant in itself. At the same time Deng knew the tremendous political advantages of maintaining a linkage between his reforms drive with Mao's historical role.

The most important linkage was the continuity of Chinese nationalism. Mao's declaration on the occasion of the proclamation of the PRC on 1 October 1949 was: "Chinese people have stood up". Deng's 1980 call to double China's GNP in ten years and quadruple it by the year 2000 so as to build a strong, prosperous modern and socialist China also had an electrifying effect. The themes of nationalism, modernization and democracy have dominated Chinese intellectual discourse for a century since the reforms debate of the 1890's. How to unite China, liberate it from colonial domination, build a strong and prosperous country to cope with Western challenges and eradicate poverty have been the common threads connecting the Sun Yatsen, Mao Zedong and Deng Xiaoping and their respective generations of leaders. These goals and the movements for realizing them created widespread popular support for their organizations. Hence the fund of legitimacy that was associated with the name of Mao Zedong could not be thrown away. Deng mobilized the party to affirm the contributions of Mao, but at the same time launched an altogether, new line for socialist construction.

What would have appeared to be a delicate task, Deng made unambiguously sharp. His method consisted of the following:

(a) Distinction between Mao Zedong and Mao Zedong Thought, (b) Defining the essence of Mao Zedong Thought as Seeking Truth from Facts, (c) Affirming Mao's contributions and criticizing Mao's mistakes and (d) Selectively stressing specific principles form Mao Zedong Thought. It was such a composite approach that the present generation of leadership could "uphold", i.e. adhere to and at the same time "develop", i.e. alter in the light of changed circumstances the principles advocated by Mao Zedong. This was methodologically comparable to what Mao did to Marxism-Leninism by "creatively applying it to the concrete conditions of China." This is how the legacy of Mao was related to the reform programme under Deng's leadership. For this purpose a clear criticism was also made of Mao's policies during his last years, particularly relating to the Great Leap Forward (1958-60) and the Cultural Revolution (1966-76).

How Deng himself took the lead in evolving a "correct appraisal" of Mao Zedong was acknowledged by CPC General Secretary Jiang Zemin in his speech on the occasion of the Mao centenary at the Great Hall of the People in Beijing.

Mao and Mao Zedong Thought

A crucial distinction was made by Deng between Mao Zedong, the individual leader and the system of ideas associated with his name. Almost as the distinction between Marx and Marxism, this exercise allows a continuous development of the ideological system with contributions from later leaders and movements. In fact, Deng Xiaoping's Theory of building socialism with Chinese characteristics was acclaimed in 1992 as the latest component of Mao Zedong Thought.

The Seventh Congress of the CPC in 1945 had for the first time adopted the political ideas of Mao Zedong as part of its ideology along with Marxism-Leninism. At the First Session of the Eighth Party Congress in 1956 the reference to Mao's ideas was removed from the CPC Constitution. During the CR the leader and the thought got merged and were put at a high pedestal. The Ninth Congress Constitution of the CPC referred to Mao Zedong Thought as the "Marxism of the era in which imperialism was heading towards total collapse and socialism was advancing towards worldwide victory."

That Deng was opposed to such a cult-building is evident from one of his speeches of 1960.[5] He strongly criticized vulgarization of Mao Zedong Thought by attributing heroic deeds to it in day to day life. Secondly, he asserted that Mao Zedong Thought should not be separated from Marxism-Leninism. Thirdly, Mao Zedong was part of a collective leadership and its leader.

This approach was further articulated by Deng during 1978-1980 in course of the transition to the new framework. To begin with there was a campaign against "Two whateverisms" This aphorism referred to the claims by Hua Guofeng's supporters that "principles" laid down by Chairman Mao should be adhered to and "instructions" on specific matters be carried out. Since Mao had personally appointed Hua as his successor, these claims had a great deal of political implications. Deng advocated a complete break with the theory, ideology and policies of the CR and any effort to defend any of those had to be opposed. Hence a campaign to "emancipate the mind" (*jiefang sixiang*) was launched to free the Party cadres from being guided by the policies of the CR. As a consequence Hua was also criticized for his "leftist" views and was replaced by Hu Yaobang in 1980.

While distinguishing Mao the leader from Mao Zedong Thought, Deng stressed the fact that there were many other leaders such as Zhou Enlai, Zhy De and Liu Shaoqu whose contributions should also be emphasized. The CR campaign against Liu had been denounced and his honour was restored by a special decision of the Party in 1979. But within the collective Mao Zedong was the most prominent leader. As Jiang Zemin put it in the Centenary speech, ..."it was the first generation of the Party's central collective leadership with Comrade Mao Zedong at its core, that made pioneering and indelible contributions to building a new and modern socialist China."

Mao's contribution is recognized in terms of his "integration of the basic principles of Marxism-Leninism with China's reality". The effort to seek a Chinese path to revolution in conditions of semi-colonialism and semi feudalism was Mao's historical contribution.[6] He formulated the theory and strategy of new democratic revolution and evolved a series of policies and tactics to carry forward the liberation struggle. Jiang lists them saying this: "He opened up a revolutionary road of building rural revolutionary base areas, encircling the cities from rural areas and seizing political power with armed force." It is interesting to note that in his "Long Live the Victory of People's War", celebrating the 20th anniversary of the victory over Japan in 1965 Lin Biao too had summed up Mao's contribution in similar terms. Jiang Zemin described Mao as "a great Marxist, a proletarian revolutionary, a military strategist and a theoretician, . . . a great patriot and a national hero in contemporary China."

Acknowledging the influence that Mao's ideas had outside China, Jiang said: "Comrade Mao Zedong, as a great historical figure not only belongs to China, but also to the world." This is important because the same was not claimed for Deng Xiaoping's ideas. Deng's theory itself was christened with particular reference to China.

As distinct from the leader or person Mao Zedong, Mao Zedong Thought has been understood by the Deng leadership as the collective wisdom of the Party. As Jiang Zemin put it: "CPC members, with Comrade Mao Zedong as their chief representative, theoretically summed up China's experiences . . . in accordance with the basic tenets of Marxism-Leninism, moulding them into a scientific guiding ideology suited to China's conditions." Calling it as "a complete, scientific ideological system" with "original theories on a wide range of ideas, Jiang identified three basic aspects of Mao Zedong Thought as "seeking truth form facts, the mass line and maintaining independence and keeping the initiative in one's own hands".

This formulation linked Mao's ideas with Marxist tradition at the samc time stressing the principles emerging from Chinese revolutionary experiences.

Mao's role in this process is acknowledged, but other Chinese leaders too have contributed to the "theoretical treasure house" of the CPC. It is a body of crystallized principles, but it is always subject to further enrichment. Thus the distinction between Mao and Mao Zedong Thought became an important political device to proceed on a new road of development with the reforms package while paying homage to Mao Zedong.

In fact, "The one focus and two points" framework of Deng's modernization programme had "Marxism-Leninism Mao Zedong Thought" as one of the Four Cardinal Principles. (Economic construction is the focus. One point is reform and open door. The other point is adherence to four cardinal principles: socialist road, Peoples's Democratic Dictatorship, Leadership of the CPC and Marxism-Leninism Mao Zedong Thought.)

Seeking Truth From Facts

The theoretical device which Deng adopted for purposes of relating Mao's legacy with his reforms programme was the doctrine of "seeking truth from facts". This essentially meant accepting those principles which delivered results in practice and rejecting those which did not work. What is more, this doctrine, Deng asserted, was the essence of Mao Zedong Thought. Thus Deng derived a method and legitimacy from Mao to unfurl a new path of development.

Mao had inscribed "shishi qiu shi" (seek truth from facts) while laying the foundation for the party school at Yan'an in 1942. Those were the days when Mao was attacking dogmatic interpretation of Marxism and Leninism, especially the Russian path of revolution. Earlier, in 1930 he had attacked "book worship".

In 1940 he had articulated the ideology and strategy of the Chinese revolution in his essay *On New Democracy*. That the CPC under his leadership had found its own path to fight colonialism and feudalism and unite China after going through a process of trial and error had become clear. Through political practice the CPC had tested various ideas and had arrived at "correct knowledge."

This method had been dealt with by Mao in his 1937 essay, *On Practice*. One starts with existing concepts and ideas and in course of practice they get tested, confirmed or disproved. Again those ideas are put to practice. A long process of such exercises gives rise to rational knowledge. There is, however, no end to this process of interaction between knowledge and practice. Knowledge is constantly refined and enriched through practice.[7] As the 1981 Resolution on CPC History put it, "... truth is inexhaustible and that truth of any piece of knowledge, namely, whether it corresponds to objective reality, can ultimately be decided only through social practice."[8]

With this philosophical weapon Deng launched a drive in 1979 for "taking practice as the sole criterion of truth". After all Mao himself pursued this line while evolving a new path of revolution in China. So his successors were called upon to apply the same method to Mao's policies especially of the preceding decade. This political strategy was used to accomplish a sharp break with the Cultural Revolution and eliminate the influence of even moderate leaders of the transitional period such as Hua Guofeng.

"Seeking truth form facts" or testing knowledge through constant practice makes every idea dynamic and developmental and injects a pragmatic outlook to policy making. It is an extremely useful notion that every leader will love to propagate. But there is a complex dimension of this principle which may reduce it to a crude utilitarian doctrine. What is the span of experience in time and place which decides the validity of a principle? What is the procedure for aggregating the experiences and evaluating a principle? Are not alternative judgements possible for the same set of empirical evidence if vantage points and criteria are different?[9] In fact, the debate on Deng's reform policies has precisely raised these questions. But undoubtedly, this formulation served a serious political purpose of Deng for openly pointing out Mao Zedong's mistakes and proposing an alternative line of modernization of China.

Mao's Mistakes

The 1981 Resolution on CPC History traces Mao's mistakes to the launching of the Great Leap Forward in 1958. Prior to that besides acknowledging Mao's theory of new democratic revolution and series of policies and principles which consolidated the newly established People's Republic, it underlined the significance of two of Mao's works, *On Ten Great Relations* (1956) and *On the Correct Handling of Contradictions among People* (1957). The first article stressed the need for balanced development of various sectors of the economy and society. The second sought to unite maximum social forces or "people", i.e. excepting the small number of enemy forces, to build socialism. For the current programme of socialist modernization Deng advocated a similar scale of united efforts of popular forces including the national bourgeoisie.

According to Deng's assessment Mao's errors started when he tried to reverse the programme of the Eighth Congress of the CPC of 1956. That Congress had announced the establishment of a socialist system and had declared that the principal contradiction now was between productive forces which were still backward and people's material needs. But Mao took the view that the contradiction was between working class and the bourgeoisie. In other words, while the former view implied a focus on economic construction, the latter led to continuing class struggle through political mobilization. That divide persisted for the next two decades and Mao initiated the Cultural Revolution to emphasize politics of class struggle. After Mao's death and the fall of the Gang of Four, Deng essentially mobilized those members of the Eighth Central

Committee and Politbureau who has been persecuted in course of the CR and inaugurated the drive for four modernizations.

The two errors of Mao that the 1981 Resolution highlighted were the error of "broadening the scope of class struggle" and "undermining the principle of collective leadership."[10] The former led to the "catastrophe of the Cultural Revolution" creating anarchy in Chinese society and disrupting production. It also violated, according to Deng, the basic principle of historical materialism which stressed the primacy of material or productive forces. The letter led to the building up of a Mao cult which violated the principle of inner-Party democracy. As the coup attempt of Lin Biao and manoeuvres of the Gang of Four proved, this situation was taken advantage of by several factional leaders to settle scores with their critics.

The 1981 Resolution decrees thus: "Chief responsibility for the grave left error of the 'Cultural Revolution', an error comprehensive in magnitude and protracted in duration, does indeed lie with Comrade Mao Zedong. But it was the error of a great proletarian revolutionary."[11]

Despite this sharp critique much care was taken to point out as to how Mao protected many cadres during the CR, rehabilitated several senior leaders and frustrated some of their designs and kept administration and the economy going during the decade of the CR. The Resolutions stated: ". . . if we judge his activities as a whole, his contributions to the Chinese revolution far outweigh his mistakes. His merits are primary and his errors secondary."[12] The same was echoed by Jiang Zemin in his centenary address as well.

Once the Deng leadership worked out a method of inheriting Mao's legacy and at the same time repudiating his model of socialist construction it was easy to proceed with the new economic policies of "reform and open door". On specific occasions Mao's formulations were invoked selectively. On inviting foreign capital, for example, the principle of "maintaining initiative and independence" was cited in defence of national dignity. To curb the spread of values such as greed, selfishness, money-making, Mao's writings "Serve the People", "Learn from Lei Feng" were recalled. To check bureaucratism in Party and Government references would be made to Mao's stress on Mass Line. In other words, this framework allowed empirical utilization of Mao's ideas on particular problems, despite the clear rebuttal of Mao's theory and policies on class struggle in socialist society.

This perspective served the reform process of the fifteen years rather well. But every time there was a crisis, Mao's alternative perspective inevitably formed part of the discourse. For example, there were some elements among the wide spectrum of forces of youth and students in Tiananmen Square in April-June 1989 who recalled Mao's participatory socialism.[13] But on the whole the economic success of the reforms and China's rising status in the world provided a degree of vindication to Deng's approach to Mao. Yet the politics of the centenary celebrations brought forth some interesting questions.

Politics of Centenary

The preparations for the celebrations of the birth centenary of Mao Zedong clearly indicated that Mao Zedong Thought had become an object of political and ideological struggle in China. The nature and scale of celebrations had to be oriented in the right direction lest they had adverse effects on the course of Deng's reforms.

As the centenary approached there was a sudden upsurge in the appearance of mementoes on Mao in 1992. Buttons, posters, sketches and artefacts flooded the streets all over China. Songs of the 1950's and 1960's including the ones which were most popular during the CR such as "East is Red" and "Ode to the Helmsman" were rerecorded by prominent singers of present-day China. Audio and video cassettes were sold in million. The "Kara OK" (dance halls) in most restaurants presented Mao songs with film clips from the earlier years to the tune of which men and women danced. By early 1993, the onset of the centenary year, the popular wave of paying homage to Mao Zedong was so widespread that there were reactions in several quarters.

Messages were sent to the CPC leaders that some people may use the occasion of the centenary to revive "ultraleft" ideas. So the Party was asked to take precautionary steps to ensure that the reforms were not derailed. Already in the wake of the Tiananmen uprising, after the collapse of the Soviet Union some leaders had tried to slow down the process of marketization and opening to foreign capital during 1990-91. Deng's visit to Shenzhen and other Special Economic Zones in January-February 1992 reversed that trend and resumed the pace of development. In April 1993 there was reportedly a meeting of the Party leaders in which Deng Xiaoping, Peng Zhen and Wan Li were present where it was decided that the Mao birth centenary celebrations should be "moderate and not excessive".[14]

Among the pressures exerted on the Party to monitor the scale of celebrations, some came from the All China Federation of Industry and Commerce (AFIC). In a letter to the CPC Central Committee in August 1993 the AFIC opposed the tendency to "revive the Mao cult" pointing out that it might seriously undermine the confidence of non-Party personnel and industrialists in the programme of four modernizations. Around the same time thirty two writers including the famous novelist Ba Jin and historian Zhou Gucheng signed a petition calling for a halt to the building of the Mao cult.[15]

One of the indications of the low key official stance was the absence of a national committee for the centenary celebrations with representations from the Party, State and Army. In order that sensitivity of the non-communist forces was not hurt there was an attempt to project some of the main activities as party level activities. Three Department of Party, namely, the Propaganda Department, Institute of Party Literature and Department of Party Archives; The General Political Department of the PLA and the State Education Commission – these five bodies were responsible for the celebrations at the national level.[16] A controversy arose as to whether Bo Yibo's book, *A Review of Several Major Policy Decisions and Events* Vol.II covering the period of the Great Leap Forward should be recommended to Party cadres. Apparently it did not sufficiently criticize Mao for his mistakes. The Party School thought that whereas the book should be available to the public it need not be part of the curriculum in Party study circles.[17]

However, eventually the scale of celebrations did not appear small at all. Numerous bodies, universities, institutes and associations in various provinces and cities had their own programmes. In Shaoshan, Mao's birth place in Hunan, a new copper statue of Mao was installed and a museum was inaugurated. Mao's poems were engraved on stone.

Memorial meetings were held all over China with a great deal of fanfare. Hundreds of new publications appeared in the market. A new multi-volume anthology of Mao containing many items unpublished so far was launched by the Central Institute of Party Literature. A collection of Mao's writings on military affairs and another on diplomatic work were brought out on this occasion. A new detailed chronicle of Mao's life, a picture album of reminiscences on Mao by veteran revolutionaries were some other highlights. Films on Mao attracted full houses in China and were screened by Chinese missions abroad. Finally, the centenary meeting at the Great Hall of the People on 23 December 1993 which was televised live gave a grand finale to the centenary celebrations. CPC General Secretary Jiang Zemin spoke and Premier Li Peng presided over the meeting.

Power of History

Politics of the centenary celebrations acknowledged the power of history and the need to cope with the legacy of Mao Zedong. This was done by the Party's theoreticians working hard to piece together a theory on the reforms which could perhaps match with Mao's contributions. This came in the form of Deng Xiaoping's theory of building socialism with Chinese characteristics.

In October 1992 at the Fourteenth Congress of the CPC the concept of "socialist market economy" was spelt out and so was Deng's theory. Originally, however, Deng's theory was announced by Jiang Zemin in his speech celebrating the fortieth anniversary of the foundation of the PRC in 1989. The "socialist market economy" entailed treating "market", "management" and "technology" as instruments of transition from traditional economy to modern economy rather than features of capitalism. And China was developing its productive forces by using these instruments. Thus the concept of "primary stage of socialism" which was articulated at the Thirteenth Party Congress in 1987 was further developed through this exercise. On the foundation of these premises Deng was credited to have formulated his "theory of building socialism with Chinese characteristics". Without having gone through a process of capitalist industrialization China had to pursue a comprehensive programme of economic development with the help of capital and technology from all over the world. It also involved utilizing multiple forms of ownership, public and private and pursuing a distribution system based on production responsibility. Through the maintenance of macroeconomic control and Communist Party leadership this course of development was to be pursued. This is how the "one focus and two points" framework mentioned earlier was put in the form of a theory.

Referring to Deng's theory, Jiang Zemin said in his centenary speech: "this epitomizes another new historical leap for our Party of integrating Marxism with the realities of China". Calling it "the Marxism of contemporary China", Jiang described it as "an unprecedented brand-new creation in the history of the development of socialism". Deng was described to have "inherited and developed Mao Zedong Thought". Jiang said: "He (Deng) proves himself to be Comrade Mao Zedong's loyal comrade-in-arms, as well as the most prominent heir to and developer of Mao Zedong Thought."[18]

It may be recalled that the personal treatment that Deng had got from Mao was in the extremes. In 1957 Mao reportedly told Khrushchev that Deng was the brightest (zui congming) among his colleagues. But Deng was twice dismissed from his posts during the CR. Mao and Zhou Enlai had restored Deng to take charge of the Central Committee in 1973-74. All that was part of history.

Building up the political and theoretical image of Deng was heightened during 1992-93 in China. Deng's "statements" in his southern tour in early 1992 became the stimulus and reference point for cadres and managers of enterprises to speed up production with great enthusiasm. Many cadres believed that the best way to avert a Soviet type of collapse in China was to achieve economic development, satisfy material demands of people and maintain stability under party control. The economic successes therefore provided the basis for Deng's popularity among Chinese people. The release of the third volume of Deng's Selected Works was marked by a campaign to study Deng's Theory.[19] The Party propagated the view that just as Mao contributed an innovative path of revolution, Deng presented an innovative path of socialist development.

History, however, is a difficult terrain full of tough tests. Deng's definition of socialism represents one model of society while Mao's another. For Deng "the essence of socialism is to emancipate and develop productive forces, eliminate exploitation and polarization and finally realize common prosperity."[20] This is no doubt a grand enough vision to excite the imagination of people to build a new society. For Mao, however, there was something more in the agenda for socialism in addition to this – the creation of a socialist human being with a moral-political consciousness. Achievement of this was historicized, in a long but defined period for a stage-by-stage movement towards goals of equality and freedom progressively distinguishing such a society from the alienated and atomized capitalist society. Even newer questions have emerged from the aftermath of the collapse of Soviet Union. Deng may have addressed some and found some economic and political answers. Mao had raised some questions earliers through his stress on class struggle. Perhaps history would demand further creative responses in future to the growing urges of socialist freedom.[21]

REFERENCES

1. Manaranjan Mohanty, "Mao's Portrait of Stalin", *China Report*, XI:4 (July-August 1975)
2. Deng Xiaoping, "Uphold Mao Zedong Thought", *Selected Works of Deng Xiaoping (1975-1982)* (Beijing: Foreign Languages Press, 1984).
3. "On the Historical Experiences of Dictatorship of the Proletariat", *The People's Daily*, Editorial of 5 April 1956 which dealt with this question is generally attributed to Mao. Another on the same theme appeared on 29 December 1956.
4. Deng Xiaoping, op.cit.
5. Deng Xiaoping, "Correctly disseminate Mao Zedong Thought" (March 25, 1960), *Selected Works of Deng Xiaoping (1938-1965)* (Beijing Foreign Language Press, 1992).
6. Manoranjan Mohanty, *The Political Philosophy of Mao Tse-tung* (New Delhi: Macmillan, 1978).
7. Mao Zedong, "On Practice" in *Four Essays on Philosophy* (Beijing: Foreign Languages Press, 1968). See also Chapter on "Four Laws of Materialist Dialectics" in M. Mohanty, *The Political Philosophy of Mao Zedong*, op.cit.
8. *Resolution on CPC History (1949-81)* (Beijing: Foreign Languages Press, 1981), p.68.
9. For a discussion of these issues see M. Mohanty "Between Truth and Revolution", *China Report* XVII:1 (Jan-Feb 1981).
10. *Resolution on CPC History*, op.cit, pp.44047
11. Ibid., p.41.
12. Ibid., p.56.
13. M. Mohanty, "For Socialist Freedom", *Economic and Political Weekly* (16 June 1989).
14. *Daily Report: Foreign Broadcasting Information Service (FBIS): China – 93-198* (15 October, 1993), p.22.
15. *Daily Report: FBIS: China* (6 October 1993), pp.24-25.
16. Some of this information is based on the author's discussions at the Institute

of Marxism-Leninism Mao Zedong Thought at the Chinese Academy of Social Sciences in Beijing in August 1993.

17. *Daily Report: FBIS: China* (9 September 1993), quoting Cheng Ming.
18. Jiang Zemin's speech, *Daily Report: FBIS: China* (29 December 1993), pp.G7-8.
19. Apparently Deng himself disallowed use of the term "thought" (*sixiang*) for his ideas and approved the term "theory" (*lilun*). It may be recalled that Mao had preferred *sixiang* to *zhuyi* (ism). This construction is based on the author's discussions at the Shanghai Academy of Social Sciences in August, 1993.
20. Jiang's Speech, op.cit. p.G/5.
21. Manoranjan Mohanty, "Mao, Deng and Beyond: Dialectics of Early Stage of Socialism", *China Report* Special Number on "New Course in China" XX: 4 & 5 (July-October, 1984).

3. Dialectics of Scientific Socialism A Study of Mao "On Contradiction"

GIRIN PHUKON

Materialist dialectics is the core of scientific socialism. The law of contradiction in things is the basic law of materialist dialectics. In fact, law of contradiction is the "essence of dialectics". Marx and Engels created the great theory of Dialectical Materialism critically absorbing the rational elements of Hegalian dialectics. This theory was further developed by Lenin and Stalin. Similarly, Mao Zedong, the greatest Marxist and Leninist of our time, gave new emphasis to, and expanded this legacy. His famous essays, *On Contradiction* (August 1937) and *On the Correct Handling of Contradictions among the People* (February 1957) are the major contributions in this direction. As is well-known, in Marxist Theory, contradictions are resolved by the dialectical process of negation of the negation and the restoration of the whole on a new and higher level of synthesis. The negation of this negation is reproduction of the old on a higher plane which in contrast with the past, finds its theoretical conclusion in scientific socialism. Mao has further developed this theme in his essay – *On Contradiction.*

It seems to be assumed that Mao was a genius political organizer and a guerrilla leader. This paper is, however, intended to focus on his "Philosopher Genius" which made him to be a successful political organizer. For this purpose, in this paper an endeavour has been made to review Mao's "On Contradiction" which has great philosophical value in scientific socialism.

II

The materialist dialectics asserts that contradiction in things is the law of development. But development of a thing does not take place automatically; a condition needs to be created to develop the existing contradiction so as to have a desired change of a thing. For this purpose, Mao realized that it was necessary to determine the nature and different aspects of contradiction of a thing. As such, without proper understanding of the contradiction of society, no revolutionary can lead a revolution successfully. In view of this, Mao dealt with a number of philosophical problems of contradiction. In his writing – *On Contradiction* (1937) he enumerated these problems as:[1]

i. The two world outlooks.
ii. The universality of contradiction.
iii. The particularity of contradiction.
iv. The principal contradiction and principal aspect of a contradiction.
v. The identity and struggle of the aspects of a contradiction; and
vi. The place of antagonism in contradiction.

Mao strongly reiterated the view of materialist dialectics that throughout the history of human knowledge, there have been two opposing world outlooks concerning the law of development of the universe, i.e. metaphysical and dialectical. "The metaphysical world outlook," Mao said, "sees things as isolated, static and one-sided" and "all things in this universe increase or decrease in quality due to external causes only." Mao wrote:

> Metaphysicians hold that all the different kinds of things in the universe and all their characteristics have been the same ever-since they first came into being. All subsequent changes have simply been increases or decreases in quantity. They contend that a thing can only keep on repeating itself as the same kind of thing and cannot change into anything different.[2]

As opposed to this metaphysical world outlook, Mao was of the firm opinion that all things in the universe are dynamic and inter-related. Materialist dialectics holds that development arises from the contradictions inside a thing. The fundamental cause of the development of a thing is not external but internal. Similarly, Mao believed that social development is due mainly to internal but not to external causes. Thus Mao argued:

> Changes in society are due chiefly to the development of the internal condition in society, that the contradiction between the productive forces and the relations of production, the Contradiction between classes, and the contradiction between the old and new; it is the development of these Contradictions that pushes society forward and gives the impetus for the supersession of the old society by the new.[3]

Materialist dialectics, however, Mao asserted, does not exclude external causes absolutely. Indeed, external causes are the condition of change and the internal causes are the basis of change and the external causes become operative through internal causes. In support of this argument while putting an example Mao said: "In a suitable temperature an egg changes into a chicken but no temperature can change a stone into a chicken – because each has a different basis."[4]

Mao reaffirmed his predecessor's view that contradiction has been a universal phenomenon of all things of this universe. The interdependence of the contradictory aspects present in all things and struggle between them determines the life of all things and push their development forward. There is nothing that does not contain contradiction. As such, universality of contradiction implies that – (i) Contradiction exists in all processes of development of all things; and (ii) Movement of opposite exists through the process of development of things from beginning to end. Thus Mao maintained:

> Contradiction is universal and absolute, it is present in the process of development of all things and permeates every process from beginning to end . . . . The old process ends and the new process begins. The new process contains new contradiction and begins its own history of the development of contradiction.[5]

While asserting these points, Mao referred to Engel's and Lenin's explanation to universality of contradiction. According to Engel, motion itself is a contradiction and is the basis of all forms of motion. Engel further opines that life is also a contradiction which is present in things. As soon as the contradiction ceases, life too comes to an end, and death steps in."[6] Similarly Lenin illustrated the universality of contradiction as follows:

> In mathematics: + and –, differential and integral.
> In mechanics: action and reaction;
> In physics: positive and negative electricity;
> In chemistry: the combination and dissociation of atoms; and
> In social science: the class struggle.[7]

In a similar vein, Mao argued that in war, offence and defence, advance and retreat, victory and defeat are all mutually contradictory – one cannot exist without the other. Difference in man's concept, he believed, represents an objective contradiction which is the reflection of subjective thinking. This process constitutes the contradictory movement of concept and pushes forward the development of thought which solves the problem in man's thinking. In this connection, Mao even went to the extent of saying that if there were no contradiction in the party and no ideological struggles to solve them, the party's life would come to an end.[8] Thus Mao emphatically asserted that contradiction exists universally and in all processes, whether in the simple or in the complex forms of motion, whether in objective phenomena or ideological phenomenon.

Besides universality of contradiction, Mao was concerned with the particularity of contradiction. Lenin's formula of the – "concrete analysis of condition" was the basis of the idea of particularity of contradiction. However, Marx and Engels were the first to provide an excellent model of such "concrete analysis". In conformity with this principle of Marxism, Mao analysed the particularity of contradiction. Every form of motion in thing, Mao assumed, contains within itself its own particular contradiction which constitutes the particular essence distinguishing one thing from another. The particular essence of each form of motion is determined by its own particular contradiction. Every form of society and ideology has its own particular contradiction and particular essence. In view of this, Mao argued that positive and negative number in mathematics, class and class struggle in social science, offence and defence in military science; idealism and materialism in philosophy are the objects of study of different branches of science precisely because each branch has its own particular condition and particular essence.[9] It follows from the fact that while the universality of contradiction implies the general character of contradiction, the particularity of contradiction implies the individual character of contradiction. The general character is contained, Mao asserted, in every individual character and without general character there can be no individual character. Individual character, Mao believed, exists conditionally and temporarily.[10] Thus, it is obvious that universality as well as particularity of contradiction is inherent in everything. And all contradictions cannot be resolved in the same way since each has its own particularity and characteristics. In this connection, Mao maintained:

> Qualitatively, different contradictions can only be resolved by qualitatively different methods. For instance, the contradiction between the proletariat and bourgeoisie is resolved by the method of socialist revolution; the contradiction between the great masses of the people and the feudal system is resolved by the method of democratic revolution; the contradiction between the colonies and imperialism is resolved by the method of national revolutionary.[11]

The other two points are connected with the problem of particularity of contradiction what Mao called, the principal contradiction and principal aspect of a contradiction. There are many contradictions, Mao said, in the process of development of a complex thing and one of them is necessarily the principal contradiction which influences the development of the other contradictions. Mao made this point clear when he said that in a capitalist society, the contradiction between the proletariat and the bourgeoise form the principal contradiction; the other contradictions such as between feudal class and bourgeoisie; the petty bourgeoisie and bourgeoisie; the proletariat and the peasant petty bourgeoisie are determined by this principal contradiction.[12] Thus it appears that the principal aspects of contradiction plays the leading role in the contradiction which gains the dominant position. Mao however, realized that this situation is not static; the principal and the non-principal aspect of a contradiction transform themselves into each other and nature of things change accordingly.[13] The moment the new aspect gains dominance over the old, the old things change qualitatively into new things. Thus the role of principal and non-principal aspect of contradiction becomes reverse. In view of this, in studying the particularity of contradiction of Mao's thought, unless one examined these two facts of contradiction, one would be unable to find the correct method of resolving it. Therefore Mao claimed: "once the principal contradiction is grasped all problems can readily be resolved."[14] As the particularity of this facet of contradiction represents the unevenness of the forces that are in contradiction, the study of various states of unevenness in contradiction, Mao believed, constituted an essential method by which a revolutionary political party can correctly determine its strategic and tactical policies both in political and military affairs.[15]

Further, Mao has extensively dealt with the problem of identity and struggle of the aspect of a contradiction. In this connection, he was influenced by the principle of materialist dialectics as explained by Lenin who said:

> Dialectics is the teaching which shows how opposites can be and how they happen to be, [how they became] identical: Under what conditions they are identical, transforming themselves into one another, – why the human mind should take these opposites not as dead, rigid, but as living, conditional, mobile, transferring themselves one another.[16]

On the basis of this statement made by Lenin, Mao had defined the identity as: (i) all contradictory things are interconnected and both the aspects of a contradiction co-exist in a single entity; and hence no contradictory aspect can exist in isolation. Without its opposite aspect, each loses the condition for its existence; (ii) in a given condition each of the two contradictory aspects transform itself into its opposite. This is what Mao meant the full meaning of the identity of opposite and he explained this with the following example:

> Without life, there would be no death, without death there would be no life; without misfortune there would be no good fortune; without good fortune, there would no misfortune, without landlord there will be no tenant peasants; without tenants peasant there will be no landlords; without bourgeoisie there will be no proletariat, without proletariat there will be no

bourgeoisie . . . .[17]

Thus Mao argued that all these opposites are opposed to each other and at the same time they are interrelated and inter-dependent. In regard to the second meaning of identity, i.e. transformation into each other, Mao convincingly argued when he said that by means of revolution the proletariat, at one time the ruled, is transformed into the ruler while the bourgeoisie, the erstwhile ruler, is transformed into the ruled and changes its position to that originally occupied by its opposites.[18] The transformation into opposites is the inevitable consequence of the dialectical process of "negation of the negation". Mao substantiated this process when he argues that violent seizure of state power and the establishment of the dictatorship of the proletariat, the building up of a strong communist party, armed insurrection and war are all negation of negation paving the way for a new synthesis. In his own words:

> To consolidate the dictatorship of the proletariat is in fact, to prepare the condition for abolishing this dictatorship and advancing to the higher stage when all state systems are eliminated, to establish and build the communist party is in fact, to prepare the condition for the elimination of communist party, to carry on revolutionary war is in fact, to prepare the condition for the permanent elimination of war. These opposites are at the same time complementary.[19]

Mao further asserted that transformation takes place only in a given condition; because the identity of opposites exists only in necessary given condition without which there can be no identity. That is how Mao posed questions like – why can an egg not a stone be transformed into a chicken? Why can human beings give birth only to human beings and not to anything else?[20] Since the identity of opposites, i.e. transformation of each other obtains in a given condition, identity is conditional and relative. More importantly, it is the *struggle of opposite*, Mao believed, that permeates process from the beginning to end and makes one process transform itself into another. The struggle is, therefore, obviously unconditional and absolute. While explaining the relation between identity and struggle, Mao invariably referred to Lenin who said:

> The unity of opposite is conditional, temporary, transitory, relative. The struggle of mutually exclusive opposites is absolute, just as development and motion are absolute.[21]

This idea of Lenin led Mao to assert that (i) all processes have beginning and an end; (ii) all processes transform themselves into their opposites. But there are two states of motion in the process of transformation of all things – one is *relative rest* and other is conspicuous change. Both the motions are caused by the struggle between the two contradictory elements contained in a thing. While under the first state of motion only quantitative changes occur in a thing, under the second state of motion the quantitative change reaches its culminating point and a qualitative change takes place. To quote Mao:

> Things are constantly transforming themselves from the first into the second state of motion; the struggle of opposites goes on in both states but the contradiction is resolved through the second state. This is why we say that the unity of opposites is conditional, temporary and relative while the struggle of mutually exclusive opposite is absolute.[22]

Thus it appears that the combination of conditional, relative identity and unconditional, absolute struggle constitutes the movement of opposites in all things. Similarly, in identity there is struggle, in particularity there is universality and in individuality there is generality.

Finally, Mao deals with the question of antagonism in contradiction, Lenin said: "Antagonism and contradiction are not all one and the same. Under socialism, the first will disappear, the second will remain."[23] In pursuance of this, Mao observed: "Antagonism is one form, but not the only form, of struggle of opposite."[24] In fact, antagonism is a particular manifestation of the struggle of opposite. Contradictory classes co-exist, Mao argued in the same society for a long time and they struggle with each other until the contradiction between the two classes reaches a certain stage assuming the form of open antagonism which finally develops into revolution. This point was well explained by Mao when he said:

> Before it explodes, a bomb is a single entity in which opposites co-exist in given conditions. The explosion takes place only when a new condition is present. An analogous situation arises in all those natural phenomena which finally, assume the form of open conflict to resolve old contradictions and produce new things.[25]

What Mao really wanted to focus was that one must make a concrete study of the circumstances of each specific struggle of opposite and should not arbitrarily apply a formula of antagonism. Although contradiction and struggle are universal, Mao argues, the method of resolving contradictions that is the form of struggle "differs according to the difference in the nature of contradiction. In accordance with the concrete development of thing, Mao believed, contradictions which were originally non-antagonistic develop into antagonistic ones, while others which were originally antagonistic develop into non-antagonistic."[26] He however, dealt with this problem of antagonistic and non-antagonistic contradictions in the context of post-revolutionary Chinese society which culminated in his writing "On the correct handling of contradiction among the people"

Thus it appears that during the period of revolution, Mao gave a theoretical orientation to the concept of "contradiction" in the light of materialist dialectics as advocated by his predecessors – Marx, Engels, Lenin and Stalin. In fact, he acquired the knowledge of "On Contradiction" from social practice. He applied the theory of materialist dialectics into practice to understand the contemporary Chinese society and developed it further. Indeed, Mao realized that it was a pre-condition for revolution as Lenin said: "Without revolutionary theory there can be no revolutionary movement."[27] Similarly, Stalin stated that "theory becomes purposeless if it is not connected with revolutionary practice."[28] Mao precisely put importance on these ideas and therefore, he emphasized "knowledge begins with practice, and theoretical knowledge is acquired through practice and must then return to practice."[29]

III

In the new historical period since the founding of the People's Republic of China, Mao consistently upheld the principle of integrating the universal truth of Marxism-Leninism with concrete practice of revolution. During this period his greatest contribution to theory was to sum up systematically and historically the experience of the dictatorship of proletariat in China and abroad. More importantly, he analysed the contradiction and class struggle in socialist society by means of fundamental concept of materialist dialectics – "the unity of opposites." Mao wrote:

> Marxist philosophy holds that the law of unity of opposite is fundamental law of the universe. This law operates universally whether in the natural world, human society or men's thinking. Between the opposites in a contradiction there is at once unity and struggle and it is this that impels things to move and change. Contradiction exists everywhere, but their nature differs in accordance with the different nature of different things.[30]

In the period of post-revolutionary China, Mao made "Concrete analysis of the concrete problems" and sought to resolve contradiction among the people. Generally, contradictions among the people are non-antagonistic; but if they are not handled properly, Mao affirmed, antagonism may arise.[31] During the period of socialist construction, therefore, he was mainly concerned with the problems of contradiction. In his essay "On correct handling of contradiction among the people", Mao had brilliantly dealt with a number of such problems which he stated as:[32]

i. Two types of contradictions differing in nature;
ii. The question of eliminating counter-revolutionaries;
iii. The question the cooperative transformation of agriculture;
iv. The question of industrialists and businessmen;
v. The question of intellectuals;
vi. The question of minority nationalists;
vii. Overall consideration and proper arrangement;
viii. On "Let a hundred flowers blossom, let a hundred schools of thought contend" and "Long term coexistence and mutual supervision";
ix. On the question of disturbance created by small numbers of people;
x. Can bad things be turned into good things;
xi. On practicing economy;
xii. China's path to industrialization.

Basically, there are two types of contradictions differing in nature which Mao called: (1) contradiction between the people and their enemies; and (ii) contradiction among the people. While the first type of contradiction is antagonistic, the second is non-antagonistic. For instance, the contradiction between the proletariat and the bourgeoisie; between the colonies and the imperialist powers are antagonistic. On the other hand, the contradiction between the working class and the peasantry; between leadership and the led, between democracy and centralism, among the members of the communist party are non-antagonistic. In the words of Mao:

> The contradictions between ourselves and the enemy are antagonistic, contradictions within the ranks of the people, contradictions among the working people are non-antagonistic, while those between the exploited and the exploiting classes have a non-antagonistic as well as an antagonistic aspect. There have always been contradictions among the people; but they are different in content in each period of the revolution and in the period of building socialism.[33]

In fact, domestic contradictions which are rooted in class conflict and those between colonies and imperial powers are antagonistic while other contradictions are generally non-antagonistic. But whether a particular contradiction could be operationally regarded as antagonistic or non-antagonistic is contingent of a historically relative tactical consideration For example Mao argued: during the long Sino-Japanese War, the external contradiction between China and Japan became principal and therefore antagonistic. Similarly, the contradictions which are antagonistic when the communist party is in opposition became non-antagonistic after it seizes power. Indeed, Mao developed the Leninist theme that contradictions in a pre-revolutionary class society are antagonistic, while those in the post-revolutionary socialist society are non-antagonistic. Thus he maintained:

> Contradictions in a socialist society are fundamentally different from those in old societies, such as capitalist society. In capitalist society, contradictions find expression in acute antagonism and conflict, in sharp class struggle; they cannot be resolved by the capitalist system and can only be resolved by the socialist revolution. On the contrary, the case is different with contradictions in socialist society where they are not antagonistic and can be resolved one after another by the socialist system itself.[34]

The obvious implication of this statement was that antagonistic contradiction can be resolved through the use of armed force, while the non-antagonistic contradiction may be resolved through organizational agitational method. Although the argument that class contradiction can be resolved only through violent revolution is central to Marxism, Mao believed that non-antagonistic contradictions may be resolved through methods other than revolutionary war. Mao explained some of these methods when he said that:

> The contradiction between the working class and peasant class in socialist society is resolved by the method of collectivization and mechanization in agriculture, contradiction within the communist party is resolved by the method of criticism; contradiction between the society and nature is resolved by the method of developing the productive forces.[35]

Along with these methods the periodic mass campaigns are obviously related to what Mao called the – "Mass line" – an important technique of mass mobilization under the leadership of the communist party for the political, economic and social transformation.

Another problem of contradiction among the people during the period of socialist construction in China was regarding the question of eliminating counter-revolutionaries. The elimination of counter-revolutionaries, Mao believed, was a struggle of opposites as between the people and the enemy. But there was difference between the people with "Right" and "Left" deviation in identifying the real counter-revolutionaries forces. Indeed, both of them followed, Mao complained, wrong method in doing so and he emphasized on the correct handling of the contradiction to eliminate the counter-revolutionaries. Thus he observed: "counter-revolutionaries must be eliminated whenever found, mistakes must be corrected whenever discovered."[36]

On the question of the cooperative transformation of agriculture, Mao said that although, it resolved the contradiction between the socialist industrialization and the individual peasant economy the contradictions such as those between the state and the cooperatives and those in and between the cooperatives themselves remained to be resolved.[37] In order to resolve these contradictions Mao felt the need of paying attention to the problem of production and distribution. For this purpose, to quote Mao: "We must properly handle the three-way relation between the state agricultural tax, the cooperative accumulation of fund and peasant's personal income and take constant care to make readjustment so as to resolve contradictions between them."[38]

The contradiction between the working class and the national bourgeoisie, i.e. industrialist and businessman, Mao argued, may also be treated as a contradiction among the people. Although, this contradiction appears to be antagonistic, he claimed, if properly handled, it can be transformed into a non-antagonistic one and be resolved by peaceful means. For this purpose, however, both the bourgeoisie and the working people need remoulding. Mao viewed that even after removal of "bourgeoisie level", ideological remoulding is necessary.[39]

The Contradiction within the rank of the people also found expression among the intellectuals. The intellectuals who worked for the old society, naturally found difficulty to fit in with the needs of the new society. The question that arose was how the people could make best use of the talent of the intellectuals for the task of building socialism and how the intellectuals would accommodate themselves in the newly emerged society. According to Mao this too was a contradiction among the people.[40] As a measure of resolution of this contradiction, Mao suggested that people should trust those intellectuals who wanted to serve the cause of socialism and should radically improve their relation with them. Similarly, the intellectuals must continue to remould themselves, gradually shed their bourgeoisie world outlook and acquire the proletarian communist outlook so that they can fully fit in with the needs of the new society and unite with the workers and the peasants.[41] Indeed, Mao wanted the intellectuals to involve in politics when he stated that "they must make progress ideologically and politically. Not to have a correct political orientation is like not having a soul."[42]

Although, almost 600 million people became an asset for China after revolution, it involved certain difficulties too in respect of progress and development of all the population. In spite of having tremendous social change, there were many difficult problems. As such, the progress and at the same time difficulties constituted a kind of contradiction. The guiding principle for its solution, Mao asserted, should be "Over all consideration and proper arrangement." Indeed, he emphasized that for the solution of problems concerning – food, natural calamities, employment, education, united front of all patriotic forces, one must proceed from the stand point of over all consideration which embraces the whole people and similarly must make proper arrangement after consultation with circle concerned.[44]

The slogan like "Let a hundred flowers blossom, Let a hundred schools of thought contend" and "Long term coexistence and mutual supervision" came to be put forward in the light of China's specific condition. In fact, it recognized the continued existence of various kinds of contradictions in socialist society and responded to the country's urgent need to speed up its economic and cultural development. Letting a hundred flowers blossom and a hundred schools of thought contend was the policy for promoting progress in the arts and science and flourishing socialist culture. Thus Mao observed:

> Questions of right and wrong in the art and science should be settled through free discussion in artistic and scientific circles and through practical works in these fields. A period of trial is often needed to determine whether something erroneous is rejected and particular truth accepted by mankind, new truth begin to struggle with errors. Such struggle will never end. This is the law of development of truth and naturally of Marxism.[45]

In view of this, Mao was of the firm opinion that Marxist should not be afraid of criticism from any quarter; they should win new position in the teeth of criticism. Therefore, carrying, out the policy of letting "hundred schools of thought contend and hundred flowers blossom", Mao believed, will not weaken but strengthen the leading position of Marxism in the ideological field. Mao, however, disapproved the idea of using crude methods in dealing with ideological question among the people. He asserted that the method of discussion, criticism, reasoning can only foster correct ideas and overcome mistakes. He however, insisted on the use of dialectical method instead of metaphysical method. What is needed, he felt is the scientific analysis and convincing argument. On criticism of oneself, Mao argued that criticism is of two kinds – that which is right and that which is wrong. One must learn from the former and demonstrately, refute the latter.[46] It is only those who fail to command convincing arguments 'hate' people and substitute repression for argumentation.[47] Mao's position is clear when he said that one cannot selectively apply the dialectical method to accommodate convenience. What is important, Mao thought, is to distinguish between a "poisonous weed and fragrant flower" and to use the correct method of eliminating poisonous weeds. For this purpose, it is necessary, he felt, to criticize, dogmatism and revisionism. He, however, believed, the revisionism is "more dangerous than dogmatism". Thus he maintained:

> Revisionism or right opportunism, is a bourgeoisie trend of thought that is even more dangerous than dogmatism. The revisionists pay lip-service to Marxism; they too attack dogmatism. But what they are really attacking is the quintessence of Marxism. They oppose or distort materialism and dialectics, try to weaken the peoples' democratic dictatorship and the

leading role of the communist party.[48]

The two slogans – let a hundred flowers blossom and let a hundred schools of thought contend – had however, no class character. As such, different classes, strata and social groups have their own views on what are fragrant flowers and what are poisonous weeds? In order to judge whether a person's words and deeds are right or wrong, i.e. distinguishing flowers from weeds. Mao provided the following six criteria:[49]

i. Words and deeds should unite people;
ii. What is done must be beneficial to society;
iii. Consolidate the people's dictatorship;
iv. Consolidate democratic centralism;
v. Strengthening leadership of the party; and
vi. Benefit international socialist unity

These criteria may be employed, Mao asserted, to determine people's works and deeds "whether they are fragrant flowers or poisonous weeds". The criteria were put forward to foster free discussion of questions among the people. "Within the rank of the people", Mao maintained "it is criminal to suppress freedom and free discussion in academic circle". He even went to the extent of saying that "let people demonstrate and strike as a way of exposing problems."[50] However, he admitted that these views are based on China's specific historical condition only. Similarly, the slogan – "Long term coexistence and mutual supervision was also a product of China's specific situation. In order to fit in with the needs of the new society, Mao wanted, all the democratic parties should pay attention to ideological moulding and strive for long terms coexistence with the communist party and mutual supervision.[51]

The disturbance created by small number of people in 1956 was also somehow related to the contradiction among the people. The causes of disturbances, as noted by Mao, were (1) failure of conceding some demands of the workers concerning their material benefit; (ii) lack of ideological and political education among the workers and students. Since, the contradictions among the people can be solved through the method of "Unity-Criticism-Unity", the disturbance should not be encouraged. In order to root out the causes of disturbances, Mao suggested certain measures such as: (i) overcoming bureaucracy; improving ideological and political education and properly dealing with all contradictions, (ii) using disturbance as a special means for improving working condition; educating the cadre and masses; and finding solution to those problems which were previously left unsolved.[52]

Mao further argued that although disturbance by the masses are bad, they enable people to learn lessons to overcome bureaucracy and to educate cadre and masses. In this sense, he claimed, bad things can be turned into good things. In given conditions a bad thing can lead to good result and a good thing to bad result. In pursuance of basic materialist dialectics, each of the two opposing aspects of a contradiction transforms itself into opposite as a result of struggle between them.[53] Without given conditions, however, neither of the two contradictory aspects can transform itself into its opposite.

Another contradiction among the people, as assumed by Mao as he put it: "Ours is a large socialist country but as economically backward and poor one this is a very big contradiction."[54] One way of resolving this contradiction was to make a sustained effort to practice strict economy in every field. Moreover it necessitated hard struggle pursuing the policy of building up the country with devotion and dedication.

Finally, while analysing the China's path of industrialization Mao mainly concerned with the growth of heavy industry, light industry and agriculture. Though the heavy industry is the core of China's economic construction, Mao, emphasized on the development of agriculture and light industry. Mao thus observed:

> As China is an agricultural country with over 80 per cent of its population in the rural areas, agriculture must develop along with industry, for only thus can industry secure raw materials and a market and, only thus it is possible to accumulate more funds for building a powerful heavy industry.[55]

Mao realized that without agriculture, there could be no light industry. At the same time, agriculture also provides heavy industry with an important market. This fact was also connected with the technical transformation and modernization of agriculture which called for more and more machinery, fertilizer and electric power project and transport facilities for farmers as well as fuel and building materials for rural consumers.[56] But, for materializing all these, Mao believed, sufficient experience of economic construction was yet to be gathered by the people. Therefore, Mao saw a contradiction, i.e. the contradiction between the objective laws of economic development of a socialist society and people's subjective cognition of them – which was to be resolved in the course of practice. This was also a contradiction among the people. In order words, it was a contradiction between those in whom the reflection of these objective laws is relatively accurate and those in whom the reflection is relatively inaccurate. This was as Mao called, a contradiction among the people.

IV

The dialectical method explains everything in nature and society in terms of a struggle of opposites, temporarily resolving into a higher form, further dividing and reuniting again into a still higher form in an unending process. Mao followed this method, but he did not trace its origin to modern times. The doctrine that everything has only one aspect has existed ever since ancient time and so has the doctrine that everything has two aspects. They are known as metaphysics and dialectics respectively. In the words of Mao:

> We Chinese often say – things that oppose each other also complement each other that is – things opposed to each other have identity. This saying is dialectical and contrary to metaphysics. Oppose each other refers to the mutual exclusion or the struggle of two contradictory aspects. Complement each other means that in given condition the two contradictory aspects unite and achieve identity.[57]

At any rate, Mao expressed allegiance to Marxism- Leninism and he used it as a weapon to a cherished end. Indeed, Mao revised and enriched an alien ideology in the light of indigenous experiences. Unlike his predecessors, Mao gave new meaning to the spiral development of history which he conceptualized as – (i) each component stage of development contributes to an expanding foundation stage, and (ii) the inherent potential for reversibility of a progressive stage. Mao's emphasis on the commanding role of the internal cause of change really gave new meaning to the need for minimum indigenous forces to develop rather than reliance on external forces. The external arena may be necessary, but it cannot provide sufficient conditions for "authentic change". As a matter of fact, Mao gave comprehensive meaning of the concept of "Contradiction" and refined it leading to certain logical conclusions so as to suit the condition of his time. The most striking of these is the notion of the permanence of contradiction. In the new democratic stage, the stage of transition, contradiction will be a mixed form– antagonistic and non-antagonistic. The former will not disappear until the last remnant of class society has been removed. The latter remains a permanent feature of human creativity, as society attempts to respond to the new challenges resulting from the interaction between the base and superstructure as well as the continuing tension between the productive forces and relation of production.[58] Antagonistic contradiction can only be resolved by the exercise of class war while non-antagonistic ones can be mediated by the process of debates, discussion and persuasion.

It logically follows that as long as classes exist, the struggle between them will also exist. But there may be some problem to distinguish (except the most obvious one) one form of contradiction from the other as they have the potential for transmitting one into another. Mao's guidance on this issue contains certain ambiguity but on balance his position is clear. He asserted, it is one thing to understand a general principle and another to properly apply "fragrant flowers from weeds" are themselves at the most general level.[59] On every concrete issue, however, Mao was far less ambiguous. The philosophic underpinning of this concreteness may be best understood against Mao's comment that contradiction means non-uniformity and that it is neither possible nor right to have uniformity of public opinion.[60]

Thus it appears that Mao, for the first time, put forward the scientific thesis that the contradiction between the proletariat and bourgeoisie, between the socialist road and the capitalist road will still exist for a long time after the basic completion of the socialist transformation of the ownership of the means of production. Similarly, his statement that in a "Socialist society, certain contradictions do exist between the leaders and the led" is unprecedented in communist literature. The new ideas, new theses of Mao about the correctly distinguishing and handling of the two types of contradictions in socialist society that are different in nature – those between the people and enemy, and those among the people – have greatly enriched the treasure house of Marxist-Leninist theory in the realm of philosophy, political economy and scientific socialism.

NOTES AND REFERENCES

1. Mao-Tse-Tung; 'On Contradiction", *Selected Works*; Nabajatak Prakashan [Calcutta], 1973, Vol.1, p.311 (Originally published by the People's Publishing House, Peking, 1960). Here in after referred to as *Selected Works*.
2. Ibid, p.312.
3. Ibid., p.314.
4. Ibid.
5. Ibid., pp. 316-18.
6. Frederick Engels; "Dialectics: Quantity to Quality", Anti-Duhring, Moscow, 1959,I p.166 cited in *Selected Works*, p.317.
7. V.I. Lenin, 'On the Question of Dialectics", *Collected Works*, Russ (ed.), 1958, Vol.XXXVIII, p.357, cited in *Selected Works*, p.317 (hereinafter referred to as *Collected Works*).
8. *Selected Works*, p.317.
9. Ibid., p.320.
10. Ibid.
11. Ibid., pp.321-22.
12. Ibid., p.331.
13. Ibid., p.333.
14. Ibid., p.332.
15. Ibid., p.337.
16. Ibid.

17. Ibid.,p.338.
18. Ibid.,p.339.
19. Ibid.
20. Ibid., p.341.
21. V.I. Lenin, *Collected Works*, p.358, cited in *Selected Works*, pp.341-42.
22. *Selected Works*, p.342.
23. V.I. Lenin, "What is to be done", *Collected Works*, Moscow, 1961.
24. *Selected Works*, p.343.
25. Ibid.
26. Ibid., p.344.
27. V.I. Lenin, "What is to be done ", *Collected Works*, Moscow, 1961, Vol.V, p.269.
28. J.V. Stalin, "The foundation of Leninism", *Problems of Leninism*, Moscow, 1954, p.31, cited in *Selected Works*, p.307.
29. Mao Tse-Tung, "On Practice", *Selected Works*, Foreign Language Press [Peking], 1977, Vol.V, p.304.
30. Mao Tse-Tung, "On the correct handling of contradictions among the people", *Selected Works*, Vol.V, p.392 (hereinafter on the *Correct Handling*).
31. Ibid., p.391.
32. Ibid., pp.384-421.
33. Ibid., p.385.
34. Ibid., p.393.
35. Ibid., Vol.I, p.322.
36. Ibid., Vol.V, p.397.
37. Ibid., p.400.
38. Ibid., p.401.
39. Ibid., p.403.
40. Ibid., p.404.
41. Ibid.
42. Ibid., p.405.
43. Ibid., p.406.
44. Ibid., p.407.
45. Ibid., p.408.
46. Ibid., p.411.
47. Ibid.
48. Ibid.
49. Ibid., p.412.
50. Ibid, p.374, cited in S.J. Noumoff, "Mao and Socialist Transition", *China Report*, Vol.XX, No.6, 1984, p.12.
51. *Selected Works*, Vol.V, p.413.
52. Ibid., p.415.
53. Ibid., p.417.
54. Ibid., p.419.
55. Ibid.
56. Ibid., p.420.

57. Ibid.,Vol.1, p.343.
58. Mao-Tse-Tung, "Speech at the Second Plenary Session of the Eight Central Committee of the Communist Party of China", *Selected Works*, Vol.V, p.338.
59. Mao Tse-Tung, "On Correct Handling", *Selected Works*, Vol.V, p.412.
60. Mao Tse-Tung, "In Refutation of Uniformity of Public Opinion", *Selected Works*,Vol.V, pp.172- 73.

4. Mao's Contributions to Marxian Epistemology

DHIREN BHAGAWATI

There are three pieces of writings of Mao, which are cited as his basic contributions towards Marxist philosophy. These are "On Practice" and "On Contradiction" which Mao delivered as speeches in 1937 and "On Dialectical Materialism" that Mao produced in 1940.[1] "On Practice" particularly emphasized Mao's ideas and thinking on the sources and methods of knowledge. A popular commentator observed that "much goodwill is needed to perceive any deep theoretical significance in these texts."[2] However, an objective analysis of it reveals certain novel ideas of Mao on epistemological questions. The present article aims at explaining how far Mao was in the framework of Marxian epistemology and how much he added of his own to it. It will also attempt to analyse how far his epistemological ideas were rather a justification of his theoretical position. Mao's article was occasioned by the contradictory positions taken in the party by two opposite groups – the dogmatists who advocated orthodox Marxist views and the empiricists who ignored the Marxist theory for the cause of revolution.[3] What was the real position of Mao?

There is no epistemological theory of Marx separate from his materialism. His epistemological ideas could be derived from his materialism. Marx believed that man developed his knowledge from his effort to master the forces of nature and the forces of production.Man produced for his subsistance and for development of the tools. Knowledge developed from the productivity of labour. Man's "purposive action with a view to the production of use-values, appropriation of natural substance to human requirements" was the substance from where knowledge grew. Man's creativity expressed through his labour working on nature resulted in knowledge. Man at first was involved in fulfilment of his primary needs. When production increased new needs were created and in the fulfilment of the acquired needs that science and knowledge developed. Knowledge was directly connected with labour and production process. That was the material basis of knowledge for Marx. If knowledge comprised of natural sciences, technology, human skill and invention, it was the result of labour power and was a part of production process. Two points are worth noting here – (i) Marx's materialism accepts productive process as its substance and (ii) knowledge not merely reflects it but it grows out of the productive process.

Engels emphasized a meaning of materialism which identified matter with a substance having certain qualities and characteristics. Engels brought the physical theory of natural sciences to materialism and held that thought was the product of human brain and brain was the product of nature and therefore nature was primary. Knowledge appeared to be cognition of matter by a process of mind. "Truth lay now in a process of cognition itself, in the long historical development of science, which mounts from lower to ever higher levels of knowledge . . ."[4] Close connection between development of nature of the material world and development of human knowledge is the summation of Engels' epistemology. To establish a relation between nature and man, Engels brought the idea of causality which explained how man could by his activity determine the motion of nature or could give the motion – a "predetermined direction and extent". This he called the alternation of nature by men" what was the basis of human thought and the "measure of human intelligence."[5] The common element in Marx and Engels was their emphasis on practice as the integral part of the process of knowledge. Marx called it transformation of reality and Engels called it application of experiment and industry to make nature serve human purpose.

Lenin accepted Engels' notion of materialism and added certain new dimensions to it. The notion of reflection as property of matter, consciousness as the higher stage of reflection and that objective reality existed outside and independent of human mind and it was given to man by his sensation were some of Lenin's distinct additions. Lenin's problem was twofold. First was his attempt at applying theory to practical situations which required certain adjustments and necessitated formulation of concepts of reflection and consciousness. Second was the development of scientific knowledge in physics which on the one hand accepted the relativity of knowledge and certain other ideas of Engels but on the other hand challenged the concept of matter as substance having specific characteristics and qualities. It was held that physics reduced matter to spirit or non-existence. The development in physics led the positivists to conclude that nothing existed except the perception. If matter disappeared or could not be comprehended, the existence of matter and God could not be denied or proved by science. This sort of skepticism and neutrality, Lenin felt, was pregnant with reactionary ideas and must be resisted. So Lenin held that ". . . the concept matter . . . epistemologically implies nothing but objective reality existing independently of the human mind and reflected by it."[6] In place of Marx's and Engels' monism, Lenin injected dualism to materialism and considered perception to be subjective because it was to be reflection of mind. As a result, knowledge based on perception could be extraneous to objective reality.

Within this broad framework of Marxist epistemology the ideas of Mao in his "On Practice" are to be assessed. Mao avowedly declared that once he accepted Marxism, he never wavered. Mao did not seem to be concerned with all the intricacies of the problems of materialism and shifts apparent in Engels and Lenin from the original position of Marx. Mao's materialism consisting of the fact that objective laws of external world could be identified both with Marx's productive process and Lenin's objective reality existing independent of human mind at different occasions. That problem apart, Mao's basic thrust in this article was the concept of practice and that was his major contribution to Marxist epistemology.

Mao began the article with an indirect reference to Feuerbach by way of suggestion how materialism before Marx did not consider social nature of man and did not base knowledge on practice. According to Mao, practice primarily involved man's activity in production and through it in class relations. Mao also included other aspects of social life like political life, scientific and artistic pursuits in practical life of society. Mao made two very important observations here. One, that the criterion of truth was social practice. Knowledge in every field of social life was to be verified through practice. Second, ideas of man must correspond to objective laws of external world. If man's ideas corresponded to objective laws of external world, they passed the test of practice. What was the exact relation between objective laws of external world and practice? Mao did not elaborate. It could be inferred from his ideas that Mao had in mind Lenin's objective reality which existed independent of mind. This would help him suggest that practice including knowledge of ideas and theory would have to correspond to it. Mao's notion of practice covered a very wide range of activity from perception to application or experimentation of theory.[7]

For Marx practice was the human sensuous activity. Man must prove his thinking in practice. Practice involved man's activity in changing his environment.[8] Engels narrowed the meaning of practice to experimentation and industry. Lenin while admitting that "the standpoint of life, of practice, should be first and fundamental in the theory of knowledge", observed that "the criterion of practice can never, in the nature of things, either confirm or refute any human idea completely".[9] By following a theory we could come closer to objective truth, the theory was confirmed to be true and the process of following the theory was called practice. The question of practice standing above theory did not arise here and Lenin did not want to make it so. Inspite of the fact that Lenin had to adjust the Marxist theory with practical situations, he always justified his position within the theoretical framework of Marxism of what he held to be its correct interpretation.

The wide connotation that Mao gave to the concept of practice put him in a convenient position to justify adjustment of theory with practical situation without resorting to Lenin's way of justification. Mao argued that theory should be developed on the practical experience of objective situation and again be applied to practical situation. In that sense theory and practice were interconnected. Marxian epistemology in its Leninist version suggested that theory should guide action, Mao appeared to reverse it. Perhaps not. In Mao's own words, "Marxism is a general truth which has universal application. We must accept. But this general truth must be combined with the concrete practice of each nation's revolution".[10] It is enriching ideas with practice. Mao was more explicit in the following passage.

> This means: take the ideas of the masses (scattered and unsystematic ideas) and concentrate them (through study turn them into concentrated and systematic ideas), then go to the masses and propagate and explain these ideas until the masses embrace them as their own, hold fast to them and translate them into action, and test the correctness of these ideas in such action. Then once again concentrate ideas from the masses and once again take them to the masses so that the ideas are preserved in and carried through. And so on, over and over again in an endless spiral, with the ideas becoming more correct, more vital and richer each time. Such is the Marxist Leninist theory of knowledge or methodology.[11]

The above paragraph expresses the gist of Mao's mass line where he advocated the active involvement and participation of the masses in the generation of ideas. Mao's emphasis on the role of subjective element in the cognition process goes much beyond Lenin's concept of reflection and consciousness. Masses are capable of initiating and developing progressive ideas; progressive ideas grow out of practical activity of the masses was the underlying assumption in Mao's epistemology. Such a faith cuts at the root of the commonplace observation of indifference, passivity, cultural and intellectual rigidity of the masses but it also refrains from exalting, like Sorel, its mythical spontaneity. If Lenin brought to Marxist theory the importance of human intervention in the process of historical changes through his theory of revolution, Mao further added to it the importance of genuine mass organization and participation in the revolutionary process. It is in contrast to dehumanization, mechanization and subordination of human element to technical laws of progress that is witnessed in the Marxist theory of the recent past.

Mao's another novel contribution to Marxist epistemology was his distinction in process of cognition between perception and conception. The process of cognition begins with perception which is mere observation of a thing, its external relations or aspects. It is mostly a physical act with little mental process of impression. As a result of continuous repetition of perception, conception, which Mao called a sudden change in brain, occurs. Conception is to grasp the essence, the internal relations of a thing, it is abstraction. One can proceed from conception to make logical conclusions through judgement and inference. Conceptual process of cognition is rational knowledge. Rational knowledge is the higher part of knowledge as it proceeds from the perceptual knowledge. Conceptual knowledge and perceptual knowledge are complementary. One can know a thing only by contact with it or living in its environment. To know theory and method of revolution one has to participate in revolution. What about knowledge of the past and from other situation which one cannot directly experience? Mao admitted of indirect experience. After perception or contact with the thing man has to reflect the essence of the thing and reconstruct the data of perception with his power of inference and judgement. Knowledge for Mao was much mere than mere perception, it meant making judgement which involved reason. Mao's analysis transcends the bounds of positivism because in Mao human reason ultimately decides on data of sense perception.

In the very Marxist tradition Mao held that the important part of knowledge was its application in transformation of reality. The knowledge one acquired was to be applied to the practice of revolutionary class struggle, revolutionary national struggle and scientific experiment. If knowledge was to correspond to objective laws of external world, how one knew whether one's knowledge so corresponded or not? From applying knowledge to social practice and observing if the desired objectives were achieved in practice. Testing of objectivity of theory depended on its verification by practice.

Mao attributed another meaning to objectivity in his "On Contradiction". There he suggested that one should look at a thing from all sides in its totality, if there were two sides of a thing, both the sides should be examined thoroughly.[12] It, of course, did not mean for Mao to give equal importance or no importance to all sides of a thing. Science could not be impartial as Mao already suggested that the dialectics was on the side of the proletariat. Like Marx, Mao's science is a dialectical relation between consciousness and necessity. From the contention that subjective knowledge is to correspond with the objective reality it follows that Marxism which belongs to subjective knowledge is not a mere set of fixed laws that applies automatically to a social situation, rather it is a possibility of revolutionary action that will have to be consciously developed through human effort, creativity and judgement. The possibility grows out of human practices.

Mao believed that progress of cognition from perception to conception and from conception to transformation of reality through revolutionary activity was not complete. Because in transformation of the objective process man could hardly realize in full what he had in mind. Man was limited by the existing scientific and technological conditions and also by the objective process itself whose development was not adequately manifest to a man. What was necessary here was correction of their subjective knowledge and theories in correspondence with the development of objective progress from one stage to another. New revolutionary tasks and new working programme were to be developed and that was to be done very rapidly along with rapid change of objective process. Knowledge must change alongwith the change of situation, new knowledge must be developed. Thinking must correspond to objective reality not lagging behind, not going ahead.

Certain conclusions can be drawn from the above discussion. Practice is an important part of knowledge in Marxian epistemology. But the idea has different connotations for Marxist thinkers. For Marx practice is basically social aspect of knowledge. Thought and action are interconnected. Truth about man can be understood only by looking at him in his social participation of material production. Engels accepts social component as an important part of knowledge and inducts materials drawn from the study of natural sciences to explain how knowledge develops in a historical way limited by scientific and technological conditions. Lenin infact brings practice to mean application of theory in social reality and includes revolutionary activity as part of knowledge. But Lenin does not give priority to practice over theory. He rather insists that theory should guide action. Mao considers practice as the criterion of truth and knowledge. Theory not only develops from practice but existing theory must be corrected in the light of practical experiences. Knowledge is subjective and is to correspond and must be made to correspond to objective process of reality.

In Mao's Marxian epistemology, Marx's philosophical materialism, Engels' substantial materialism and Lenin's "epistemological materialism"[13] are reduced to what can be termed as practical materialism. But Mao's greatness lies in his successful realization of the principles in practice, which he upheld in his 'On Practice'.

NOTES AND REFERENCES

1. Schram considered these three pieçes to be totality of Mao's philosophical expositions. See Stuart Schram, *Mao Tse-Tung*, Penguin, 1966, p.233. But Mao himself denied that he ever wrote any essay titled "On Dialectical Materialism". Mao also considered that his "On Practice" was a more important essay than "On Contradiction". See Edar Snow, *The Long Revolution*, Vintage Books, 1973, p.207.
2. Liszek Kolakowski, *Main Currents of Marxism*, Vol.3. Oxford, 1978, p.475.
3. Mao Tse-tung, "On Practice" (July, Penguin 1937), *Selected Works*, Vol.1,

p.295.

4. Frederick Engels, Ludwig Feuerbach and the End of Classical German Philosophy in Marx Engels. Lenin, *On Dialectical Materialism*, Progress, 1977, p.156.
5. Ibid., p.145.
6. V.I. Lenin, *Materialism and Empirio-Criticism in Marx Engles*. Lenin, *On Dialectial Materialism*, Progress, 1977, p.329.
7. Mao seems to encompass whole sphere of knowledge in practice as he said, "There can be no knowledge apart from practice" *Selected Works*, Vol.1, p.301.
8. Karl Marx, Theses on Feuerbach, in Marx, Engles Lenin, *On Dialectial Materialism*, Progress 1977, pp.29-30.,
9. Ibid., p.279.
10. See Stuart R. Sehram, The Marxist, in Dickwilson, ed, *Mao Tse-tung in the Scale of History*, Cambridge University Press, 1977.
11. Ibid., p.44.
12. Mao Tse-tung, "On Contradiction" (August, 1937). *Selected Works*, Vol.1, Peking, pp.323-24.
13. See S.A. Jordan, "The Dialectical Materialism of Lenin," in James V. Downton et al., eds., *Perspectives on Political Philosophy*, The Dryden Press Inc, 1973, pp.35-42.

5. Carrying the Revolution to Reconstruction Mao's Dilemma

SHANTI SWARUP

I

A researcher working on China and the evolution of Mao Zedong's strategy and ideas (I am deliberately avoiding the high sounding words "Political Thought" as Stuart Schram does, or the still more awe-inspiring term "Political Philosophy" as Manoranjan Mohanty does) is struck by a very interesting fact. There is far greater radicalism and revolutionary fervour during certain periods in his behaviour and writings, while during other periods, his writings and actions are marked by relative moderation. It is not appropriable to periodize this and characterize them as the writings of early and later Mao or younger and more mature Mao, for the samples of both types can be found in the writings of early and relatively maturer Mao. Thus in the early period we have such highly revolutionary writings as "Report on an Investigation into the Peasant Movement in Hunan" and "A Single Spark Can Start a Prairie Fire". At the same time, we also have his writings and policies on land question through New Democracy to 1947 which demonstrate considerable moderation towards the middle class, entrepreneurs well-to-do farmers and even some segments of the gentry. In his maturer years, if were have the highly aggressive and defiant revolutionary mood of the "On People's Democratic Dictatorship" and the period of the rectification and the anti-right movement and the cultural revolution. We also have the conciliatory attitude of the early 1950's culminating in the "Let a Hundred Flowers Blossom and A Hundred Schools of Thought Contend". In other words, there is a strong revolutionary enthusiasm in Mao's writings during 1927-32, a relative moderation during 1932-47, a shift back to revolutionary zeal during 1947-51, a return to moderation during 1951-57 and a highly charged revolutionary zealousness of the anti-right campaign, the

Rectification Movement, the Great Leap Forward and the Cultural Revolution.

How precisely to explain these changes in Mao's thinking? Are these changes to be explained in terms of some ideological shifts in Mao's ideas? Or is it that despite the apparent shifts, there is some basic underlying consistency? Or alternatively, can these shifts be best understood in terms of Mao's attempt to grapple with certain difficult dilemmas arising out of changing empirical reality?

II

One – and perhaps the easiest, if also an escapist – way to handle this problem would be to follow the early Kremlinologist-Pekinglogist perspective and to argue that the Communists everywhere are primarily interested in power and they resort to any means including ideological shifts in order to gain/stay in power. Such a view, however, besides being simplistic and empirically weak, misses the ideological overtones of a revolutionary movement and ignores the nationalist context and ethos within which the Chinese Communist movement developed. On the other hand, to argue in favour of an underlying consistency would demonstrately be tantamount to being unfaithful to truth . A third alternative would be to dismiss Mao as a self-contradictory thinker (as has been done in the case if some other thinkers such as Harold Laski) and therefore unworthy of notice as a thinker. This paper, however, rejects all these three perspectives and attempts to look at the evolution of Mao's ideas in the context of the dilemmas he faced, the alternatives he had and the choices he made and whether these choices were rationally justified.

III

The argument of this paper is that Mao was basically confronted by one serious problem with its attendant implications and most of his thinking was done in response to this problem for which he had not precedents to lean on or to learn from. Early in his revolutionary career, on the basis of his experience in Kiangs-Hunan border areas, Mao realized that it was possible to have small scale, piecemeal and slow revolution in China, but not a revolution throughout China in one clean sweep. The question naturally was how to reckon with this reality and deal with its implications. It was while dealing with this problem and reconciling its various implications that Mao developed his concept of revolution.

The western conception of revolution was a sudden change in the socio-economic structure and political order, accompanied by a short brief violent upheaval. In the Marxist thinking prior to the Bolshevik Revolution, the French Revolution and the storming of the Bastille were deemed to be the model ("ideal type" if that term finds greater favour with the social scientists) revolution. "Ten days that shook the world" more of less confirmed to this model. This may also have been the model of revolution which may have inspired Mao when he wrote the famous "Report on an Investigation of the Peasant Movement in Hunan". After all, in it he had asserted that "in a very short time", the peasantry would rise like a tornado or tempest, a force as extraordinarily swift and violent, that no power, however great, will be able to suppress it."

This conception of political revolution was fundamentally different from the manner in which the Chinese revolution developed. The Marxist, even Marxist-Leninist and generally the European conception of revolution was based on the assumption that any social system had a European sweep. The belief, despite evidence to the contrary, was that Europe could not have more than one social system for any length of time and that there was a tendency for the whole of Europe to have the same social system. If, therefore, a revolution did in fact break out, it would engulf the whole of Europe, the spectre of communism", his presumption was that it was haunting the whole of Europe. Even in the Leninist conceptualization, if the weakest link in the chain of capitalist system was to be broken, the revolution would not remain confined to the weakest link, but would rapidly burst into the European political centre. But even this conception necessarily involved the revolutionary control over the centre of political and economic power. Even initially, it involved control over the centre of political and economic power in the weakest link. It was unthinkable for Lenin that a revolution would break out in Russia and not touch Moscow and St. Petersburg.

Mao's conception of revolution was very different from this. That a revolution can occur in certain parts of China without its causing a ripple in Shanghai and Nanking seemed incomprehensible to the Marxists or the Marxist-Leninists. Originally, of course, Mao may also have thought that this was a very temporary phenomenon. He may have believed that he was merely extending "the weakest link in the chain" theory and that "a single (initial) spark (in the peripheries) . . . (wo-ld) start a prairie fire". In other words, the revolution would soon extend to the whole of China. He was, however, soon forced to admit that no such prairie fire was on the agenda and that a revolution would take sometime.

Mao was, therefore left with two options: (a) Either he should call off the revolution in the areas where it was occurring on the plea that what he was witnessing was not a real revolution, but an illusion or hallucination; or (b) to accept the reality of revolution and have slow piecemeal revolution confined to certain areas of China and then extend it to other areas. The choice was obvious for Mao. Since he could not deny the reality of revolution, he opted for the second course. The problem, however, was whether a revolution confined to small parts of China would last, or more appropriately, be permitted to survive. Or would the superior economic and military power of the central government defeat it, as indeed was to happen, when Mao was forced to pack up from the Hunan-Kiangsi border areas and trek on the Long March. But once again he succeeded in making revolution in other areas of China. This had been made possible, as this writer has argued elsewhere, by the fragmented nature of the Chinese political system prior to the establishment of the Peoples Republic of China.

IV

Such a conception of revolution has its own logic and implications of a serious nature. In a sudden country-wide (or Europe-wide) revolution, an old stable order collapses and is sought to be replaced by a new stable order. The post-revolutionary regime would naturally seek to restore order, assert its authority, to appear legitimate and to bring about stability in the system as a necessary condition for ordered progress and socio-economic development. This is not to suggest or imply that upheavals in society are not caused as a fall-out of tensions and controversies in society as was the case in revolutionary France or in the Soviet Union during Stalin-Trotsky or Stalin-Bukharin controversies. But cutting across factions, the regime seeks as far as possible to maintain order in society with a view to prevent any erosion of its authority.

In Mao's conception of revolution, socio-economic transformation and reconstruction, became imperative in the very act of making a revolution. Clearly reconstruction and orderly development could not wait till the completion of the revolution in the whole of China, or else the revolutionary regime would risk losing its support base. In other words, in a slow and piecemeal revolution, reconstruction becomes an important instrument of the consolidation of revolution and its extension by example.

Mao's revolutionary model had thus almost two apparently contradictory requirements – (a) to maintain or sustain revolutionary momentum through continuous mobilization; (b) not to disturb the society so much that those segments whose help is essential for socio-economic development are frightened and thus socio-economic development and economic growth are put in jeopardy or impeded, thus threatening the revolution itself.

V

It was to this twin need to sustain revolutionary momentum and simultaneously to maintain at least a semblance of order for socio-economic development and economic growth in the areas of successful revolution that Mao had to address himself most of the time. A good idea of his dilemma can be gauged from his writings and speeches during 1946 to 1948 when he finds the task of balancing these two requirements rather ticklish. Now the problem is that a revolution of the kind envisaged by Mao needs large scale mass mobilization and keeping vast numbers mobilized over long periods. At the same time, it requires cadres and organizers who generally come form the middle class. For the purpose of transformation and reconstruction, the regime needs engineers scientists, teachers and administrators who have to come from the middle class. It needs people with capital and entrepreneurial skill.

Here indeed was Mao's quandary. If the regime ignored the aspirations of the mobilized poor (peasants and others), it would face the wrath of the enraged tiger or elephant and would be trampled underfoot. If, on the other hand, it submitted totally to them, it would alienate the middle class. Mao could neither meet the hopes and urges of the masses, nor could he ride roughshod over the sensibilities of the middle class. He could not afford to sing lullabies to put the awakened giant back to slumber, for the revolution was not yet complete and the revolutionary momentum had to be kept up. Nor could he annoy the middle class to a point that it should cast its dice against the regime and support Chiang Kai-shek or even the imperialist forces.

How precisely to synthesize and deal with some time complimentary, some time contradictory, yet often conflicting demands of these two major social groups, whose support was necessary for the making of the revolutionary socio-economic reconstruction, revolutionary consolidation and the extension of revolution? This was the most serious problem which Mao faced. Thus during the period prior to the Long March in the Hunan-Kiangsi border areas, Mao sought to win over the rich peasants, the traders and other segments of the middle class. He continued with the same policy after the Long March. During the Sino-Japanese war, he further moderated his policy. During the revolutionary period when excesses inevitably take place, he quite often applied brakes on the excessive egalitarianism of some of his more zealous cadres, in order not to alienate the middle class. To gain their support, Mao also tried to convince the middle class that in China, the Communists alone had the capability of creating the conditions for (a) the fulfillment of their nationalist urges and (b) meeting the legitimate aspirations of the middle class. At the same time he could not but demonstrate in action to the poorer segments of the society (the peasants and the workers) on whom his revolution primarily depended and whose support was critical to his revolution) the positive utility of the revolution by giving them tangible gains, such as lower rents, lower rates of interest, somewhat higher and assured wages.

Reconciling these conflicting claims was no easy balancing act. But through most of the long revolutionary period and the period of the Sino-Japanese war, he managed it with remarkable deftness. The land reforms were moderate in nature to assuage middle class feelings (and seriously hurt only the landlord class) but aggressively implemented to maintain revolutionary momentum. There were, to be sure, occasionally some distortions from this carefully conceived synthesis, In May 1946, under the pressure from the revolutionary forces, the Central Committee of the Communist party of China issued a "Directive on the land question" whereby the policy was changed from reduction of rent to confiscation of the land of the landlords. But by and large the policy was carefully pursued and paid rich dividends, thus paving the way for gradual extension of the revolution.

V

Once the revolution had succeeded in the whole of China, the central question which Mao faced was: would a policy which had so eminently succeeded in consolidation of the revolution in limited areas and its extension to other areas and had brought the Communists to power, be applicable in the post-revoltuionary period?

The situation had, of course, undergone a radical alteration. The regime now had, of course, various options. It did not now need the compromises it had to make during the period of slow revolution. It could, if it wanted, have opted for order and completely called off the deepening of revolution. On the other hand, it could have thrown overboard its policy of moderation and pursued excessively radical policies. Flushed with victory, the regime could have opted for any policy and would probably not have faced any threat. But Mao decided, in the early years after the revolution, to continue with his time tested policy. After all the regime still needed the support of the mobilized masses for rapid development. At the same time, it still needed organizers and cadres to "educate" people about the regime policies. It also needed teachers, scientists, engineers for the task of rapid industrialization of China.

The policy seems to have had great success. The support which the regime got, particularly during the Korean War and the First Five Year Plan, cut across class lines and was far greater than anything which the regime had anticipated. It, therefore felt reassured about the loyalty of the middle class to the system.

Of course, the real reason for this may have been a new sense of pride (which the Chinese had not experienced for over a century) in the ability of China to stand up to the most powerful country of the world and not to be pushed around. There was in addition the rapid growth of the Chinese economy because of the moderate socio-economic reforms initiated or enacated by the Communists, but mainly due to the first few years of peace after almost forty years of turmoil in the form of wars, civil wars and revolution. In the international realm, the regime had good reason to be gratified by the wide acceptance it received among the Afro-Asian community. Not surprisingly the Communists felt relaxed and were emboldened to give further concessions to the middle class in the areas of intellectual freedom. Mao's "Let a Hundred Flowers Bloom and Let a Hundred Schools of Thought Contend" policy seems to have resulted from this confidence.

Some scholars have contended that Mao's 'hundred flower thesis was a clever move to bring middle class and other groups' reservations about the regime to the surface. This writer does not subscribe to such a conspiracy theory. There is no evidence to suggest that the regime was not genuinely satisfied with the loyalty of the middle class to the system. The regime was happy with the contribution of the middle class and its favourable attitude. Through the hundred flower policy it expected confirmation of its assessment and strengthening of its support base among the middle class.

The actual response of the middle class in the aftermath of Mao's Hundred Flower movement and the articulation of its submerged dissatisfaction with the regime seems to have shocked Mao out of his complacency and over-confidence, thus posing for him one of the most serious dilemmas of the post-revolutionary period. Without the support of the middle class, the task of reconstruction was well-nigh unthinkable. He needed scientists, engineers, teachers, organizers, propagandists, party and government bureaucracy and entrepreneurs. Of these scientists, engineers, managers were particularly important for the development of heavy industry on which Mao had set his heart and which constituted his top priority. At the same time, Mao's suspicion about the middle class came to the surface and remained fairly close to the surface. Mao now became increasingly apprehensive about the threat from the middle class to the egalitarian dimensions of the Chinese revolution. After all, the middle class occupied a strategic position within the system and could use that position for the subversion of the egalitarian dimension of his revolution. As early as 1957, he was critical of Teng Hsia-ping, with the support of Chou En-lai for encouraging bureaucratic attitude among the party functionaries. He saw in the attempt of Lin Shao-Chi to sideline him during 1956-58 and the systematic control by Teng Hsiao-ping of the party apparatus and their advocacy for incentives (as opposed to Mao's emphasis on egalitarianism) as a bid by the "capitalist roaders" to undermine his revolution ideologically by subversion within the party machine.

For Mao, this de-emphasis on the egalitarian aspect of the revolution was unacceptable. He threatened that if the party leadership attempted that, he would once again go to the country-side and make another Chinese revolution.

Mao's problem in other words, was how to cope with a situation in which he at once needed the middle class and seriously suspected the credentials of a considerable number of its members; in which he could neither afford to alienate it nor could he trust it as a class. To deal with this situation, Mao developed an ingenious strategy. He would maintain the alliance with the middle class, but maintain sufficient mass pressure and the momentum for social revolution, so that the middle class, or its erring members, would not be able to hijack the revolution and prevent the poor from enjoying the gains of the revolution for which they had fought and for which they had made so much sacrifice. Mao, after all, was no less a social revolutionary interested in an egalitarian order, than a nationalist. If he was prepared to apply brakes on his more enthusiastic radical cadres in the interest of nationalist goals, he was equally willing to keep up the tempo of mass participation and mass mobilization in the interest of an egalitarian order. He however, would not apply the technique of coercion or physical extermination. His was a two pronged strategy. In the first place he applied the technique of "reform" through indoctrination, euphemistically called *education*. The second part of the strategy was to keep up the pressure on the middle class through various mass movements (such as the "three-evils movement", "rectification movement", the "anti-rightist campaign", the "Great Leap Forward") to make that class to fall in line. The high-water mark of this technique was the Great Proletarian Cultural Revolution which in a sense was the encirclement of party and government bureaucracy by the masses. By maintaining this pressure Mao was able, during his lifetime, to prevent the middle class functionaries from cornering the gains of the revolution. It is true in this excessive enthusiasm for social revolutionary goals, some of the highly committed, able and competent functionaries such as Lin Shao-Chi were unfairly treated. But in the light of the post-Mao developments in China, it cannot be argued that Mao's fears were entirely misplaced.

The upshot of this argument is that if the gains of a social revolution or a revolution like struggle have to be saved, it is necessary to keep up the revolutionary momentum during the period of reconstruction. But it is not easy, for it requires a leader like Mao – or Gandhi – to do this.

6. New Democracy Its Role and Limits

BUDDHADEVA BHATTACHARYYA

The well-known paradox of marxian theory and revolutionary practice is that it theoretically predicts the possibility of revolutionary development only in developed capitalist countries like Great Britain but inspires the revolutionary activists to strike at the weakest link in the chain of world capitalist exploitation in underdeveloped (semi-feudal) capitalist countries like Russia or the countries of Eastern Europe or China, where the people are deprived of the blessings of capitalism but are bestowed with its curse. The actual world-capitalist development helped the old capitalist countries to exploit their peripheral areas, transfer resources, raise the living standard of their people and bourgeoisfy their workers and thus compelled the marxist revolutionaries to seek socialist transformation of the capitalist world order by launching social revolutions in less developed states that would at first complete the incomplete process of bourgeois-democratic transformation under their leadership and create the pre-conditions for socialist transformation – both in terms of human elements – their interrelations and technological development. Lenin had to telescope these two stages of social change, namely, the completion of bourgeois democratic revolution and the ushering of socialist transformation in what he called the socialist revolution. But in the opinion of Marx and Engels, the class that can usher in socialist revolution is only the working class and it will be able to usher in such revolution only when it 'forms the majority of all members of society'.[1] Lenin proposed to complete the bourgeois-democratic revolution under the political authority of the democratic dictatorship of the proletariat and peasantry in 1905 in his *Two Tactics*. Even after the February revolution he had to retain the peasantry as an ally of workers that includes its poor and semi-proletarian parts.[2]

As China was much more backward even in the thirties than the former

Soviet Russia in the pre-revolution period concentration of workers could only be found in the cities, treaty ports and coastal areas.[3] In Mao's estimate the number of modern industrial workers would not exceed 3,000,000; but this number would come to 12,000,000 if the workers in small-scale industry, handicrafts and shops were included. In spite of its smallness (as compared with the peasantry), its youth (as compared with the proletariat in the capitalist countries) and its low educational level (as compared with the bourgeoisie), the Chinese proletariat was nonetheless the basic motive force of the Chinese Revolution. And although 'it is the class with highest political consciousness and sense of organization, it cannot win the victory', as Mao asserts, 'by its own strength alone'. In order to win, it must, in Mao's opinion, 'unite, according to varying circumstances, with all classes and strata that can take part in the revolution and must organize a revolutionary united front'. But, as Mao emphasized 'among all classes in Chinese society, the peasantry is a firm ally of the working class', constituting, in Mao's estimate, 80 per cent of China's total population. Of this section of rural population, rich peasants who were anti-feudal and anti-imperialist and eager to accept socialism constituted 20 per cent and the poor peasants, who were in Mao's opinion 'the biggest motive force of the Chinese revolution, the natural and most reliable ally of the proletariat and the main contingent of China's revolutionary forces', constituted 70 per cent.[4]

This indicates how the political action to organize revolution in the context of the development of revolutionary situation in the underdeveloped countries, instead of developed capitalist countries, led to telescoping the stage of completing the bourgeois democratic revolution in the socialist revolution by Lenin and the mobilization of peasantry as an ally of proletariat workers in former Russia but as 'main contingent' of Chinese revolutionary forces in China. As Marx and Engels could not visualize fully such a course of historical development when they formulated their main theoretical plank, these revolutionary strategies, practices and experiences could have their theoretical backing. As their theoretical system was not self-contained but open-ended it might have revolutionary extension in the context of new revolutionary situation. The first such revolutionary extension of Marxism has undoubtedly been made by Lenin and the second by Mao Tse-tung. But Mao's extension has many distinguishing features, and one that distinguishes his practical-theoretical formulation from that of Lenin, to a considerable extent, is his new democratic revolution and the new democratic state as its political superstructure wherein, unlike Lenin, he did not telescope the stage of completing the unfinished bourgeois-democratic revolution in the socialist revolution.

Mao's formulation about two-stages of revolution is not something totally novel. First of all, different stages of social development as formulated by Marx and Engels may prompt many a marxist to think in such terms. But actual social condition in Tsarist Russia and the enunciation of revolutionary stratagies for its revolutionary transformation by Lenin at different times might have prompted Mao to develop such a theory in the context of Chinese condition. Around 1905-6 Lenin thought about the requirement of two revolutionary stages in Tsarist Russia. The development of Lenin's thought on the stages of revolution may be traced succinctly:

> Russia is a peasant country, one of the most backward of European countries. Socialism cannot triumph there directly and immediately.[5]

Distinguishing between two types of struggles, i.e. one for bourgeois-democratic and another for socialist, he observed:

> A class-conscious worker calls himself a social-democrat for the reason that he understands the relation between the two struggles. He knows that there is no other road to socialism save the road through democracy, through political liberty. He , therefore, strives to achieve democratism completely and consistently in order to attack the ultimate goal–socialism.[6]

Lenin denied the possibility of transformation of one type of revolution into other in the following lines:

> Such a victory (of bourgeois-democratic revolution – added) will not yet by any means transform our bourgeois into a socialist revolution: the democratic revolution will not immediately overstep the bounds of bourgeois social and economic relationship . . .[7]

While distinguishing between major stages of development in spite of the fact that feudal social elements are interwoven with those of the capitalists in actual social life he did not deny the possibility of elements of one revolution intertwining with another in the following:

> Of course, in actual historical circumstances the elements of the past become interwoven with those of the future. . . . But this does not in the least prevent us from logically and historically distinguishing between the major stages of development. . . . However, can it be denied that in the course of history individual, particular elements of the two revolutions become interwoven.[8]

Lenin then moved to the idea of continuing the political process of one revolution in an uninterrupted manner till the victory of another revolution, as the following lines indicate:

> From the democratic revolution we shall at once . . . begin to pass to the socialist revolution. We stand for uninterrupted revolution.[9]

He then discarded the attempt of Kautsky to distance and compartmentalize these two stages of revolution:

> To attempt to raise an artificial Chinese Wall between the first and the second, to separate them by anything else than the degree of preparedness of the proletariat and the degree of its unity with the poor peasants, means to distort Marxism dreadfully, to vulgarize it. . .[10]

And only after the October Revolution Lenin asserted:

> We solved the problems of the bourgeois-democratic revolution in passing, as a "by-product" of our main and genuinely proletarian-revolutionary, socialist activities. The Soviet system is one of the most vivid proofs, or manifestations, of how the one revolution develops into the other.[11]

So it is on the basis of such observations that Lenin made after the October revolution and the actual socio-political practice that one could say that the tasks of unfinished bourgeois-democratic revolution could be completed as the first part of socialist reconstruction and thus talk of telescoping one into the other. So one cannot assume before hand the certainty of this process as a general one, as Lenin even could not.

Having gained prolonged revolutionary experience since the twenties in the peculiar Chinese context Mao observed in 1940:

> In the course of its history, the Chinese Revolution must go through two stages, first, the democratic revolution, and second, the socialist revolution, and by their very nature they are two different revolutionary processes.

Having two following steps:

> The first step is to change the colonial, semi-colonial and semi-feudal form of society into an independent democratic society. The second is to carry the revolution forward and build a socialist society.

But this 'independent democratic society' will be different from the old bourgeois-democratic one because:

> It is no longer a revolution of the old type led by the bourgeoisie with the aim of establishing a capitalist society and a state under bourgeois dictator-

ship. It belongs to the new type of revolution led by the proletariat with the aim, in the first stage, of establishing a new-democratic society and a state under joint dictatorship of all the revolutionary classes. Thus this revolution actually serves the purpose of clearing a still wider path for the development of socialism.[12]

Mao's observation about the character of the first revolution might be said to have its basis in Lenin's following analysis although Lenin did not call it new-democratic:

> The victory of the bourgeois revolution is impossible in our country *as the victory of the bourgeoisie.* This sounds paradoxical, but it is a fact. The preponderance of the peasant population, its terrible oppression by the semi-feudal big landowning system, the strength and class-consciousness of the proletariat already organized in a socialist party – all these circumstances impart to our bourgeois revolution a *specific* character. For a "coalition of the proletariat and the peasantry" winning *victory* in a bourgeois revolution, happens to be nothing else than the revolutionary-democratic dictatorship of the proletariat and the peasantry.[13]

As regards the classes which should be taken as allies of the proletariat against the Tsarist autocracy in the democratic struggle Lenin maintained the following:

> The democratic struggle is waged by the workers together with a sanction of the bourgeoisie, especially the petty bourgeoisie . . . The struggle against the bureaucrat and the landlord can and must be waged together with all the peasants, even the well-to-do and the middle peasants.[14]

The basic forces of China's new democratic revolution, in Mao's view, will be 'the proletariat, the peasantry, the intelligentsia and other sections of the petty bourgeoisie'. In addition to these forces 'national bourgeoisie retains a certain revolutionary quality at a certain period and to a certain degree' in spite of the fact that 'it is unwilling to break with imperialism completely and moreover, it is closely associated with the exploitation of the rural areas through land rent'.[15] Although Mao's new democratic state will be led by the proletariat it would have other classes as components of the state structure as he asserted:

> the proletariat, the peasantry, the intelligentsia and other sections of the petty bourgeoisie undoubtedly constitute the basic forces determining China's fate. These classes . . . will necessarily become the basic components of the state and government structure in the democratic republic of

> China, with the proletariat as the leading force. The Chinese democratic republic must be a democratic republic under the joint dictatorship of all anti-imperialist and anti-feudal people led by the proletariat. . .[16]

Lenin emphasized the role of proletariat as the 'chief combatant' even during democratic revolution[17] and asserted that

> it can become victorious fighter for democracy only if the peasant masses join the revolutionary struggle.

and warned that

> If the proletariat is not strong enough for this the bourgeoisie will be at the head of the democratic revolution. . .[18]

As such, even after winning victory in bourgeois-democratic revolution Lenin allowed, as has been quoted earlier, no other class except the proletariat and the peasantry any representation in the structure of the state and government as he clearly stated:

> For a "coalition of the proletariat and the peasantry", winning victory in a bourgeois revolution happens to be nothing else than the revolutionary-democratic dictatorship of the proletariat and peasantry.[19]

What is more important is that such 'revolutionary democratic dictatorship of the proletariat and the peasantry', that excludes other petty bourgeois or bourgeois elements, is essential if the proletariat wants to move ahead towards socialist revolution because the representation of the petty bourgeois, bourgeois (in the case of China it is national bourgeois) elements in the structure of the state and government (as envisaged by Mao in his new democratic state and government) may obstruct the socialist revolutionary process from within the state structure. And such a political superstructure cannot be said to be a dictatorship of the proletariat required as a transitional political system for the socialist transformation of post-revolutionary society. It is because of this that Lenin emphasized the requirement of the 'socialist dictatorship of the proletariat' to usher in socialist revolution[20] and that is the form of the state in such period. In his opinion, the revolutionary classes capable of ushering in such revolution also differ from that of democratic revolution. While the democratic revolution 'is waged by the workers together with a section of bourgeoisie, especially petty bourgeoisie', 'the socialist struggle is waged by the workers against the whole bourgeoisie' and 'it is only together with the rural proletariat that the struggle against . . . the well-to-do peasants too, can be properly waged'.[21]

But unlike Lenin, Mao did not want to have a state-form different from that of the multi-class new democratic one to carry out the socialist revolution as the following lines indicate:

> The first step or state in our revolution is . . . the establishment of a new-democratic society (under the new democratic state) under the joint dictatorship of all the revolutionary classes of China headed by the Chinese proletariat. The revolution will then be carried forward to the second stage, in which a socialist society will be established in China.[22]

Although Mao emphasized that

> Except for the Communist party (representing the proletariat), no political party (bourgeoisie or petty bourgeois) is equal to the task of leading China's two great revolutions, the democratic and the socialist revolutions, to complete fulfillment.[23]

he was not agreeable to exclude non-proletarian classes as collaborating forces in the struggle for socialism after new democratic revolution as the reply to his own question would indicate:

> What will the socialist factors be?. . . leadership by the proletariat and the Communist Party which the peasantry and, intelligentsia and the petty bourgeoisie already accept or are likely to accept and the state sector of the economy owned by the (four class) democratic republic . . .[24]

Thus the classes led by the Communist Party and the proletariat and the classes represented in the new democratic republic were retained as collaborating classes in the struggle for socialism. A more explicit reference to the four classes was made by Mao in 1945.[25]

Mao did not deny, rather he admitted long before the victory of the new democratic revolution, that

> A certain degree of capitalist development will be an inevitable result of the victory of the democratic revolution in economically backward China.[26]

And even after the revolution Mao recognized the requirement of bourgeoisie and their specialists for industrial and commercial expansion. It was in this context that Cohen has made the following observation:

> It was as though he (Mao) was starting a NEP policy in 1949.[27]

But indicating its difference from the Russian experiment Cohen has pointed out

> Lenin discovered, however, that he had to fall back on the administrative and technical (and even commercial) talents of some members of the Russian bourgeoisie. But they were never given formal rights in the Soviet Republic's "dictatorship of the proletariat".[28]

It is the requirement of reflecting the economic base of 'NEP' type 'new democratic' society in its political superstructure which might be said to have prompted Mao to retain the non-proletarian classes and their political parties in the socio-economic base and its political superstructure till their elimination in the gradual and continuous process of socialist transformation.

As such , First Plenary Session of the Chinese People's Political Consultative Conference on 29 September 1949 declared:

> The Chinese People's Democratic dictatorship is the state power of the people's democratic united front composed of the Chinese working class, petty bourgeoisie, national bourgeoisie and other patriotic democratic elements, based on the alliance of the workers and peasants, and led by the working class.[29]

Although the non-communist political parties had ceased to be competitors of power in Mohanty's view, still "both in the National People's Congress as well as in the State Council there were many non-communist members and the CPC Central Committee continued to have a United Front Department at least till the Cultural Revolution."[30]

Thus having retained the apparently powerless, root-loose, foot-loose non-proletarian, capitalist and pro-capitalist class forces in the State and governmental structure, China, in Mohanty's assessment, embarked upon the socialist construction in the year 1956 because:

> Only when the major programmes of socio-economic change are fulfilled a revolution can be said to have been completed. From this perspective, the year 1956 could be described as the end of the new-democratic phase, for by then new democratic economic measures were fully implemented. Agriculture was cooperativized and socialist transformation started.[31]

But probably the prospect of gradual and peaceful transformation of socio-economic base in a non-antagonistic manner leading to the elimination of root-loose and foot-lose capitalist and pro-capitalist forces became bleak by 1956 and these root-loose, foot-loose capitalist and pro-capitalist class-forces found their political support among the CPC theoreticians and leaders who opposed Mao and Maoists as Mohanty has indicated:

> Now we know that the CPC leadership was divided by 1956 over the pace and nature of the socialist transformation. According to the Maoists, the Lin Shao-chi group and their philosopher spokesman Yang Hsien-chen advocated the continuing of the new democratic economy so that the joint sector, including the capitalists could continue to function efficiently. (In their opinion) the socialist superstructure should 'serve the entire economic base' including the capitalist economy, and 'also serve the bourgeoisie'.[32]
>
> But
>
> Against this Mao argued for a speedy change over to socialist form of ownership both in agriculture and industry.
>
> While
>
> Yang Hsien-chen had argued that when the productive foray were highly developed, conditions would be favourable to the creation of socialist form of organization.[33]

Probably the present leaders of PRC are following this policy of developing productive forces through marketization, privatization and westernization. This will develop the productive forces along with the capitalist class forces demanding the superstructure to subserve them.

Thus it is painful to see that when the first protagonist of New Democracy was bargaining hard for ending it as an outlived political superstructure in 1964, probably non-proletarian class forces retained by it were trying to retain the new democratic superstructure through so many advocates:

This is what Mao had to say:

> To consolidate New Democracy and to go on consolidating it for ever, is to engage in capitalism. New Democracy is a bourgeois democratic revolution under the leadership of the proletariat. It touches only the landlords and the comprador bourgeoisie, it does not touch the national bourgeoisie at all. To divide up the land and to give it to the peasants is to transform the property of feudal landlords into the individual property of the peasants, and this still remains within the limits of the bourgeoisie revolution.[34]

This, once again, indicates absolute importance, priority and relatively greater effectivity of the political superstructure in the socialist transformation and cleansing non-socialist elements from socialist superstructure prior to the ushering in socialist transformation and negates the productionist views of the late leader of the Second International epitomized by Stalin.

REFERENCES

1. Karl Marx and Frederick Engels, *The German Ideology*, Progress Publishers, Moscow, 1968.
2. See V.I. Lenin, 'The Proletarian Revolution and the Renegade Kautsky," in *Collected Works* (hereafter LCW), Progress Publishers, Moscow, 1965, Vol.28.
3. Michael Lowy, *The Politics of Combined and Uneven Development: The Theory of Permanent Revolution*, Verso, London, 1981.
4. *Selected Works of Mao Tse-tung*, Foreign Languages Press, Peking, 1976, Vol.2, pp.323-5.
5. *LCW*, 1964, vol.23, p.371.
6. *LCW*, 1962, vol.8, pp.384-5.
7. *LCW*, 1962, vol.9, p.57.
8. Ibid., p.85.
9. Ibid., pp.236-7.
10. *LCW*, vol.28, p.300.
11. *LCW*, 1966, vol.33, p.54
12. *Selected Works of Mao Tse-tung*, vol.2, pp.341-2, 344.
13. *LCW*, 1963, vol.15, pp.56-7.
14. *LCW*, vol.9, p.443.
15. *Selected Works of Mao Tse-tung*, vol.2, pp.348-50.
16. Ibid., p.350.
17. *LCW*, vol.8, pp.384-5.
18. *LCW*, vol.9, p.60.
19. *LCW*, vol.15, p.57.
20. *LCW*, vol.9, pp.83-6.
21. *LCW*, vol.8, pp.384-5.
22. *Selected Works of Mao Tse-tung*, vol.2, p.347.
23. Ibid., p.331.
24. Ibid., p.330.
25. Arthur A. Cohen, *The Communism of Mao Tse-tung*, The University of Chicago Press, Chicago, 1966, p.80.
26. *Selected Works of Mao Tse-tung*, Vol.2, p.329.
27. Cohen, op.cit.,p.75.
28. Ibid., p.74.
29. Quoted in Manoranjan Mohanty, *The Political Philosophy of Mao Tse-tung*,

Macmillan, New Delhi, 1978, pp.37-8.

30. Ibid., p.39.
31. Ibid., p.40.
32. Ibid., p.40.
33. Ibid., p.41.
34. Cited in Philip Corrigan, Harvie Ramoxy and Derek Sayer, *Socialist Construction and Marxist Theory: Bolshevism and Its Critique*, Monthly Review Press, New York and London, 1978, p.101.

7. Marxism, Mao Zedong and the Concept of Peasant Communism Towards an Asiatic Model

ASHISH K. ROY

Marxism is essentially a European current of political thinking. It constitutes a response to the problems of social revolution in the advanced capitalist systems of the West. Until Lenin's ascendancy as the main architect of the Bolshevik revolution in Russia, there was no serious attempt among Marxists, including Marx himself, to set out a strategy for revolutionary struggle in the non-European agrarian societies.

As a product of European civilization, Marx himself was subjective in analysing his contemporary socio-economic milieu. And when he turned to inquire into the economic and political dynamics of the non-European social systems, his analysis suffered from opacity.

It appears that Marx, like his contemporaries, believed in the superiority of Western civilization and could not concede to non-European countries the role of conscious actors in history to be master of their own destinies. Marx's attitude towards the Asiatic patterns of civilization is nowhere typically more Western than when he speaks of India. As regards the character of Asian civilization in general, Marx said that it was not only qualitatively different from that of Europe but decisively inferior to it. He held the view that Asian economic and social systems were invariably marked by a peculiarly crude 'Asiatic mode of production'. The two basic features of this Asiatic mode of production, according to Marx, are: (1) a rather simplistic economic structure erected on the foundation of a cluster of small village communities insulated from one another and tied to a crude agrarian system; and (2) at the top of the economic structure is the 'despotic' state which appropriated the major portion of the surplus produced by the village communities, and which took charge of the public works, especially for irrigation indispensable to the functioning of such an economy.[1]

Taking the institution of private property of European society as a basic criterion of an advanced social system, Marx concluded that its absence in Asiatic societies led to what he called 'oriental despotism'. Writing in 1853, Marx insisted that Asiatic civilization with its peculiar mode of production was at a very rudimentary stage of human civilization, that of primitive communism; and that the mass of Asian humanity was hopelessly beyond redemption without Western intervention. This was Marx's conclusion about Asia in general and of India in particular.[2]

In his two articles entitled 'The British Rule in India' and 'The Future Results of British Rule in India' written on 10 June and 22 July 1853 respectively for the New York Daily Tribune and also in a letter to Engels on 14 June 1853, Marx elaborated his pet themes of 'Asiatic mode of production' and 'Oriental despotism'. Describing the Indian society as 'an ancient form of civilization', Marx said: ". . . We must not forget that these idyllic village communities, inoffensive though they may appear, had always been the solid foundation of Oriental Despotism, that they restrained the human mind within the smallest possible compass, making it the unresisting tool of superstition, enslaving it beneath traditional rules . . ."

Marx further held that an 'Asiatic system' like India's would never be able to come out of the 'semi-barbarian' and 'semi-civilized' stagnation unless the country was sufficiently 'Europeanized'. According to him, 'the break-up of these primitive stereotype forms was the condition sine qua non of Europeanization'; and it was the introduction and penetration of British rule that brought about a social revolution in India. Marx held that this social revolution had a dual role: destruction of the primitive Asiatic society, and introduction of Western science and cultural values.[3]

It is interesting to note in this context that both Marx and his associate Engels were of the identical view regarding the Asiatic nature of Czarist Russia. For example, Engels wrote in an article in 1875: "Such complete isolation of the various villages from one another is . . . the natural basis of Oriental Despotism, and from India to Russia, wherever it has existed, this social form has always produced despotism . . . The despotism of the Czar . . . is a necessary and logical product of Russian social conditions."[4]

Both Marx and Engels held that if Russia, rather the whole of Asia, were to be supported and guided by Western industrial proletariat, the process of their march towards a socialist economic system from the stage of primitive communism would be cut short and they would be able to skip the protracted stages in the evolution towards the capitalist system. But what about the *dramatis personae* of this revolution in Asia? Which sector of the population would receive support from the Western proletariat? The answer from Engels was rather confused and uncertain. He held that the revolution in Russia would be initiated by 'the upper classes in the capital – perhaps by the government itself'. Then he stated in a half-hearted manner that the peasants might have to complete it.

Now, what is the implication of this answer? Looking back over a century it would not be naive to suggest that both Marx and Engels assigned, though somewhat tentatively, a leading role to peasants in the coming revolutionary struggle in the absence of a well-organized industrial proletariat. As Helence Carrere d'Encausse and Stuart R. Schram have rightly suggested: "This train is extremely important, not only because of its implications for Russia, but because the same logic was extended by certain of Marx's disciples and in particular by Lenin to other Asian societies, and served as a starting-point for theories of a 'non-capitalist path of development' in the backward countries."[5]

It seems quite evident from the writings of Marx and Engels that, apart from making this casual reference to the role of the peasantry in the event of a revolution in Russia, they did not attach much significance to this question. The works of Marx and Engels contain only piecemeal analyses of the problems of non-European societies. They were mostly pre-occupied with the growing contradictions in the European capitalist system, in the theorization of which most of their wisdom and energy were consumed. Also, of course, colonial expansion in their time had not reached the proportions it did towards the close of the nineteenth century.

If Marx had made some references to the non-European world, these were never too rigid, which suggest that his views on Asia were adaptable. This task was left to Lenin who, in his celebrated work *Imperialism: The Highest Stage of Capitalism*, first systematically developed the thesis that the East had a vital role to play in the scheme of the world communist revolution. He looked upon the phenomenon of national liberation struggle against imperialism as an integral part of the most important struggle of the proletariat to liberate itself since the national struggle could not be successful without the final liquidation of the colonial system.

Among his contemporaries, Lenin was the first Marxist theoretician to break out of the oyester of Eurocentrism and to express the view that the East could play a significant role in the international communist movement. His first definite assertion on the importance of national liberation movements in the colonies came in 1916: "National wars waged by colonies and semi-colonies in the imperialist era are not only probable but inevitable. Some 1,000 million people, or more than half of the world's population, live in the colonies and semi-colonies (China, Turkey, Persia). Here, national liberation movements are either already very powerful or are growing and maturing. Every war is the continuation of politics by other means. The continuation of the policy of national liberation by the colonies will inevitably lead them to wage national wars against imperialism. . ."[6]

It may be pointed out that, although Lenin had been developing his ideas about the colonial countries of the East since the Japanese victory over Czarist Russia in 1905, his views did not receive formal recognition and acceptance until July 1920, when the Second Comintern Congress held its marathon session. This delay may be explained by the fact that the Bolsheviks were preoccupied with the problems of a revolution in their own country – the double threat of intervention and civil war. Also, it was due to the exclusive importance attached by Marxists to the revolutionary potential of the urban working class, that revolution in Europe, especially in Germany, still remained a fixed idea with them. The inevitable conclusion of European Marxists was that in view of the immaturity of the Asian proletariat the best that could be expected at that stage was a 'bourgeois democratic' liberation movement.

It was with a deep sense of frustration at the failure of communist revolution in Europe (which had been believed to be round the corner) that the Marxists of the world met at the Second Congress in Moscow. The main debate regarding the tactics and strategy of world communist movement took place between M.N. Roy, charged with the spirit of extreme Asiocentrism, and Lenin with an outlook of modified Eurocentrism.[9] The main points in Roy's thesis were, first, that the Soviet leaders had been putting too much emphasis on a bourgeois democratic revolution in Asia and that in the process they had been underestimating the role of the Asian proletariat in revolution in Asia. In so far as India was concerned, Roy declared that the nationalist movement which had been launched under the banner of the Congress in the 1880s 'found no response among the popular masses'. The masses of India, according to Roy, "are not fired with a national spirit. They are exclusively interested in problems of an economic and social nature. The situation of the population of India is difficult in the extreme. Since the establishment of British capitalism in India, the 80 per cent of the population which lives by agrarian work has lost its property and has been transformed into hired labour. . . . Compared with the rural proletariat, the industrial proletariat in India is small in number. . . . The trade union movement is spreading rapidly among these workers. . . . These elements exist in India for creating a powerful communist party. But as far as the broad popular masses are concerned, the revolutionary movement in India has nothing in common with the national liberation movement."

The second major point which Roy asserted very forcefully was that the key to world revolution lay in Asia: ". . . the fate of the revolutionary movement in Europe depends entirely on the course of the revolution in the East. Without the victory of the revolution in Eastern countries the communist movement in the West would come to nothing. World capitalism draws its main resources and income from the colonies, principally from those in Asia. If it comes to the worst, the European capitalists can give the workers the full surplus value from their revolutionary aspirations. And these same capitalists will continue to exploit

Asia, with the help of the proletariat. Such an outcome would suit the capitalists very well. This being so, it is essential that we divert our energies into developing and elevating the revolutionary movement in the East, and accept as our fundamental thesis that the fate of world communism depends on the victory of communism in the East. . . ."[7]

Contesting Roy's extreme view point, Lenin observed: "Roy goes too far when he asserts that the fate of the West depends exclusively on the degree of development and the strength of the revolutionary movement in the Eastern countries. In spite of the fact that the proletariat in India numbers five million and there are 37 million landless peasants, the Indian communists have not yet succeeded in creating a communist party in their country. This fact alone shows that Comrade Roy's views are to a large extent unfounded." The Congress adopted Lenin's thesis with a few concessions to Roy. The mutual dependence of the social revolution in Europe and the national revolution in Asia was recognized but no mention was made as to which was primary. On the strategic level it was resolved that in the colonial countries the communists would collaborate not with the 'bourgeois-democratic' but only with 'national revolutionary' movements.

One fundamental feature of the Comintern line in 1920 on revolution in the colonies was that it brought to the fore the importance of the role of the peasantry.

It was at the Second Congress of the International that Lenin very aptly depicted the future of peasant communism in the national revolutionary movements of Asian countries by stressing the special role of 'peasant Soviets'. He was the first Marxist theoretician to initiate the idea that the peasantry would constitute the chief force of communist revolution in Asia.

It is rather interesting to note in this context that in the course of a protracted debate with M.N. Roy over the question as to how the communists could bring about a successful revolution in the East, Lenin put forth his original thesis on the organization and structure of peasant Soviets. Roy argued that in view of the fact that a powerful, although numerically limited, industrial proletariat with a high degree of Marxist ideological orientation had already emerged in the under-developed countries, especially in India, the Soviets which would be established would definitely be 'if not purely proletarian, at least workers' and peasants' Soviets". He was laying stress on a decisive political role for the industrial proletariat.

Lenin, on the other hand, had quite a different idea about the Soviet organizations. While working for the Bolshevik revolution in his own country Lenin had to reorient the Marxist prescriptions to suit the requirements of revolution in Czarist Russia which was still in the pre-capitalist stage. When Russia finally emerged as the first socialist country from out of 'oriental despotism' characterized by a primitive 'Asiatic mode of production' this was, for the first time, proved beyond doubt. In fact, it was the successful completion of socialist revolution in his own country that made Lenin assert that the capitalist stage of development of the national economy would not be inevitable for the underdeveloped countries engaged in national liberation movements. He justified the outbreak of revolution in Russia, rather than in an industrially developed country by applying his theory of 'the weakest link'. He argued that because of the uneven development of a large country like Russia with underdeveloped industries and communications, it ws possible to set off revolution in areas where bourgeois control was the weakest. On the role of the peasant Soviets he said:

> The practical work carried on by the Russian communists in the colonies which formerly belonged to tsarism . . . confronted us with the question of how to apply communist tactics and policy amidst pre-capitalist conditions; for the most important characteristic feature of these countries is that pre-capitalist relations will predominate in them, and therefore, a purely proletarian movement is out of the question in them. . . . Our work has revealed to us that in those countries we have to overcome colossal difficulties, but the practical results of our work revealed to us that, notwithstanding these difficulties, it is possible to arouse among the masses a striving for an independent political thought and an independent political activity, even where there is almost no proletariat. This work was more difficult for us than for the comrades in West European countries, because the proletariat in Russia is overwhelmed with state work. It is quite understandable that peasants who are in a state of semi-feudal dependence can fully appreciate the idea of Soviet Organization and put it into practice. It is also clear that the oppressed masses, who are not only exploited by merchant capital but also by feudal rulers, and by the state on a feudal basis, can wield this weapon, this form of organization, even in conditions under which they live. The idea of Soviet Organization is a simple one and can be applied, not only to proletarian but also to peasant feudal and semi-feudal relations . . . .[8]

Although Lenin recognized the revolutionary potential of peasant soviets, he had reservations, like all Marxist compatriots of his days, about the peasants' capacity for independent revolutionary action. While he was instructing the communists in the underdeveloped countries that they must 'adapt' not only the Soviet institutions but also the Soviet communist party (its composition, its special tasks, etc.) to the level of the peasant countries of the colonial East,[9] so as to facilitate the entry of a great number of peasant cadre into the communist party which would be led by the proletariat, he at the same time almost ruled out any suggestion that such a party would be formed exclusively of the peasantry.

In 1920 Lenin could not harbour the thought that the rural proletariat in backward societies could bring about a successful revolution on their own. His conclusion, on the contrary, was that 'with the aid of the proletariat of the most advanced countries, the backward countries may pass to the Soviet system and, after passing through a definite stage of development, to communism, without passing through the capitalist stage of development.'

Lenin did his job well at the Second Congress of the Communist International. As rapporteur on the national and colonial question, he carefully balanced his views as against the extreme Asiocentric standpoint resolutely defended by M.N. Roy, who was to play a 'role' in China later.[10] In fact, Lenin was the first Marxist theoretician to discover the elements of adaptability and flexibility lying dormant in Marxism itself. His ideas regarding peasant Soviets constituted the first unorthodox assertions about the adaptable properties of Marxism by an orthodox Marxist. Lenin had already done the spade-work in a direction which ultimately led to Mao Zedong's peasant communism as its logical conclusion. In fact, Mao began where Lenin had left. The Maoist tactics of revolution is consequently an extension of the Leninist theory. And if Mao Zedong was original as regards the Chinese pattern of communist revolution, he was so only as far as tactical innovations during application and adaptation of the Marxist-Leninist doctrines to Chinese conditions were concerned. It is by adopting the Chinese traditional pattern of peasant revolts and by developing a strategy and tactics around it in order to realize the Marxist-Leninist objectives that he made an important, if not absolutely original, contribution to Marxist thought.

Peasant Power and Communist Revolution in China

In what follows an effort would be made to bring into relief the stages in the evolution of the Marxist strategy and tactics of armed agrarian revolution in China, which was later projected by Chinese Communist Party as the only valid model for revolution in the Third World.

Mao Zedong's formal conversion to Marxism almost synchronized with the founding of the Chinese Communist Party. The inception of the CCP dates from the time the Communist International decided in its Second Congress in 1920 to maintain the closest contact with the revolutionary forces in the politically and economically oppressed nations which had been working for the overthrow of imperialism; when the Committee on Nationality and Colonial Problems was created under the direction of Lenin himself as the guiding agency for investigation of movements of liberation by the oppressed nationalities; and when Grigori Voitinsky was sent to China by the Comintern for the purpose. The Chinese Communist party was formally inaugurated on 1 July 1921 when its First National Congress was held in Shanghai. It was around this time that Mao was drawn towards Marxism, and 'by the summer of 1920', declared Mao, 'I had become, in theory and to some extent in action, a Marxist, and from this time on I consider myself a Marxist'.[11]

It is, however, rather interesting to note that, although born in a peasant family, Mao as a student had developed a feeling of disdain towards the rural life. He said as such in a speech of 1942.[12] During this formative stage Mao had mainly worked first among the students and then in the labour unions. After the First Congress of the CCP in July 1921 Mao started working at Changsha as secretary of the Chinese Communist Party for Hunan province, his urgent tasks being induction of students and workers in the socialist youth corps and the establishment of a party cell among the coal miners at Anyuan in West Kiangsi. Actually, the labour movement in China began in right earnest after the First Congress of CCP, and the miners' strike at Anyuan and the strike on the Canton-Hankow railroad in September-October 1922 were important land-marks in the history of the labour movement in Hunan. On the threat of arrest, however, Mao had to leave Hunan for Shanghai in 1923. At this stage Mao had not developed any interest either in the agrarian problems of China or in the revolutionary potential of the Chinese peasantry.

It was in June 1925 that Mao Zedong switched his political interest to China's countryside and to the peasant aspect of the Chinese revolutionary movement. But again as a warrant of arrest was issued against him he fled to Canton. This, however, proved to be a blessing in disguise for Mao as he was put in charge of the Kuomintang Peasant Movement Training Institute.[13] In this capacity he continued to acquire considerable knowledge and direct experience of the peasant movement. Mao's new conviction about the importance of the peasant question was strengthened by the events which followed the incident of 30 May 1925 in which the Kwangtung peasants demonstrated their hostility to the indignities inflicted on the Chinese people by the foreigners.[14] 'Formerly I had not fully realized the degree of class struggle among the peasantry', Mao confided to Edgar snow, 'but after the May 30 incident . . . and during the great wave of political activity which followed it, the Hunanese peasantry became very militant. I left my home, when I had been resting, and began a rural organizational campaign.'[15] Mao, however, did not move away from the ortho-dox Comintern position. In his first important essay on the revolutionary peasant movement in China entitled 'Analysis of Classes in Chinese Society', written in March 1926, Mao observed: 'The industrial proletariat is the leading force in our revolution. All sections of the semi-proletariat and the petty bourgeoisie are our closest friends.'[16]

It may be remembered that in the middle of 1926 Mao Zedong shifted his area of operation from the newly created Peasant Department of the Chinese Communist Party.[17] But shortly after the occupation of Hunan in July 1926 by Chiang Kai-shek during the Northern Expedition, Mao went back to his native province Hunan and started working among the peasants. In fact, the period of nine moths from August 1926 to May 1927 that Mao spent among the Hunanese peasants actually shaped the destiny of Chinese Communist Party. He presented his 'Report of an investigation into the Peasant Movement in Hunan'[18] which can be taken as the symbolic starting -point of Mao's evolution toward genuinely original position regarding the revolutionary way applicable in China'.[19]

Highlighting the outstanding success of the peasant revolution Mao wrote ". . . the broad peasant masses have risen to fulfill their historic mission; the democratic forces in the rural areas have risen to overthrow the rural feudal power . . . What Dr. Sun Yatsen aimed at the forty years he devoted to the national revolution but failed to accomplish, the peasants have accomplished in a few months. This is a marvelous fact which has never been achieved in the last forty or even in thousands of years."

Enumerating the 'Fourteen Great Achievements'[20] by the revolutionary peasants in five hsien (Changsha, Li Ling' Hsiangar, Hung Shan and Hsianghsing) Mao stated: "The main force in the country-side which has always put up the bitterest fight is the force of the poor peasant. Throughout both in the period of under-ground organization, the poor peasants have fought militancy all along. The poor peasants, being the most revolutionary group, have gained the leadership of the peasant associations . . . Leadership by the poor peasants is absolutely necessary . . . . To deny their role is to deny the revolution."[21]

Further, quite contrary to the Comintern in line on the question of revolution in China that 'in the given situation in China the proletariat is the only class able to pursue a radical agrarian policy',[22] Mao strongly put forward his thesis that the mass of poor peasants constituted 'the vanguard of revolution' in China. While submitting his 'Report' to the Central Committee of the CCP, he urged the members for the adoption of this new line regarding the revolutionary potentiality of the peasant movement in China. But this was rejected by the Central Committee led by the Party's General Secretary Ch'en Tu-hsiu who persisted in 'following a Right-opportunist petty-bourgeois policy'. Mao told Edgar Snow: "I was very dissatisfied with the party movement. I think today that if the peasant movement had been more thoroughly organized and armed for a class struggle against the landlords, the soviets would have had an earlier and far more powerful development throughout the whole country.[23]

It may be pointed out that from 1927 onwards Mao became more and more confident about the practicability of peasant revolution in China. Although in the initial stages he had admitted the necessity of proletarian leadership over the peasant movement in China, this was more in the nature of an ideological-tactical concession to the tenets of Marxism-Leninism and the political line of the CCP, and an emphasis on the revolutionary potentiality of the rural proletariat, rather than a characterization of the revolution as it actually developed in China under his leadership. "It was this peasant base and essentially agrarian character of the Maoist revolution that impelled Mao to innovate the transitional ideology of the 'new democratic revolution', in which the emphasis was on the broad alliance of the masses rather than on the leadership of the proletariat, and to name the government which came to power in 1949 as the 'people's democratic dictatorship' rather than dictatorship of the proletariat. . . Mao has argued that the successful self-identification of the Communist Party with the peasant masses and the failure of the Kuomintang in this respect was the principal cause of the success of the Communist revolution in China."[24]

Writing in 1951, only two years after the completion of the communist revolution in China under the leadership of Mao Zedong, B. Shwartz wrote in his book *Chinese Communism and the Rise of Mao*[25] that by presenting his Hunan Report to the CCP Central Committee Mao had introduced 'a unique trend within the Chinese communist movement' because the attention of the Chinese communists was for the first time directed to the countryside 'as the key centre of revolutionary action.' And the strategy that was adopted by Mao since 1927 essentially 'involves the imposition of a political party, organized in accordance with Leninist principles and animated by faith in the tenets of Marxism-Leninism, on to a purely peasant mass basis'.[26] It is interesting that the essence of the Maoist strategy, viz. reliance on the peasant masses, the establishment of rural bases and the building up of a peasant army remained the same.

It may, however, be pointed out that during the period between 1927 and 1937 when the civil war had been raging throughout China, Mao gradually shifted from complete reliance on poor peasants, as he expressed in his Hunan Report, to the idea that 'political power grows out of the barrel of a gun'.[27] From his experience during the ten gruelling years of civil war, Mao concluded that for the victory of communist revolution in China the support of the peasant masses was indispensable. But for the final seizure of state power and for its consolidation, an independent military force under the exclusive control of the party was an historical necessity. With this Mao solved the 'strategic problems of China's revolutionary war'. Commenting on Mao's contribution to the development of the Marxist-Leninist military theory, Jerome Ch'en writes:

> While admitting the logical sequence from reliance on the poor peasants to that on a peasant military force, we must come to the inevitable conclusion that the essence of Maoism (Mao Tse-tung ssu-hsiang) lies in the man's theories on strategy which, instead of being "a union of . . . Marxism-Leninism and the (mere) reality of China", is in fact that of Marxism-Leninism and the Chinese traditional pattern of peasant revolts. The Chinese were used to protracted revolutions which normally lasted years before success or failure came, the revolutions of the peasants spreading out from one or several base areas, such as the Red Eye-brows from AD 18 to 27 (9 years),

the Wakang Army form 611 to 618 (7 or 8 years), the Manichalars from 1353 to 1367 (14 years), Li Tzu-ch'eng's rebellion from 1630 to 1645 (15 years), Chang Hsien-chung's rebellion from 1630-1646 (16 years) and the Taip'ing rebellion from 1850 to 1864 (14 years). All these revolts fell into pattern similar to the Communist revolution led by Mao Zedong from 1927 to 1949. By using Marxism-Leninism, relying on the peasants and applying his political and military genius, Mao has not only forged "a firm Marxist (or Maoist) military line" but also created a pattern of revolution new even to the most alert brains of the world of politics.[28]

Fairbank also has suggested that Mao Zedong's application of the communist theory to rural China's concrete realities implied that the peasantry would be the class on which revolution was founded and that 'this became the basis of "Maoism" which was the final sinification of communism in China'.[29]

In fact, the claim for 'sinification of Marxism' was for the first time put forward by Mao himself as early as 1938, even more than a decade before the success of the CCP in China itself, in his report to the sixth plenum of the Central Committee of the Chinese Communist Party. He declared *inter alia*: Today's China is an outgrowth of historic China. We are Marxist historicists; we must not mutilate history. . . A Communist is a Marxist internationalist, but Marixsm must take on a national form before it can be applied. There is no such thing as abstract Marxism, but only concrete Marxism. What we call concrete Marxism is Marxism that has taken a national form, that, Marxism applied to the concrete struggle in the concrete conditions prevailing in China . . . If a Chinese Communist, who is part of the great Chinese people, bound to his people by his very flesh and blood, talks of Marxism apart form Chinese peculiarities, this Marxism is merely an empty abstraction. Consequently, the signification of Marxism – that is to say, making certain that in all of its manifestations it is imbued with Chinese peculiarities, using it according to these peculiarities – becomes a problem that must be understood and solved by the whole party without delay . . . . We must put an end to writing eight-legged essays on foreign models . . . . We must discard our dogmatism and replace it by a new and vital Chinese style and Chinese manner, pleasing to the eye and to the ear of the Chinese common people.'[30]

Stuart Schram has, however, suggested that although Mao had first called for the 'sinification of Marxism' in his report of October 1938, at that time he had not suggested that he himself had already accomplished this fact. But by 1942 such a claim was already implicit in the way the rectification campaign was conducted in January 1942. However, Mao himself ordered all cadres and especially the army to study thoroughly 'The Resolution of the Ninth Congress of the Fourth Army' which he had written in December 1929.[31] And this process took final shape in 1945 when, at the Seventh Congress of the Chinese Communist Party, the dual claim of 'uniquencess and universality' of Mao Zedong's thought was vigorously asserted by Liu Shao-chi'i. He declared:

> The General Programme of the Party constitution stipulates that the thought of Mao Zedong shall guide all the work of our party. The constitution itself provides that it is the duty of every party member to endeavour to understand the fundamentals of Marxism-Leninism and the thought of MaoZedong. This is the most important historical characteristic of our amendment of the constitution at this time . . . . For over a century, the Chinese nation and people . . . have accumulated immeasurably rich experience in the course of their bloody struggle for their own emancipation. Their political struggles and the experience thus gained inevitably culminated in the creation of great theories of their own, thus showing that the Chinese nation is not only a nation capable of fighting, but also a nation which has a modern scientific revolutionary theory . . . This theory is none other than the thought of Mao Zedong . . . The thought of Mao Zedong is the thought that unites Marxist-Leninist theory with the practice of the Chinese revolution.

Claiming 'universality' for the Maoist revolutionary theory, Liu said:

> The thought of Mao Zedong is a further development of Marxism in the colonial, semi-colonial and semi-feudal countries of the present epoch. . . . What Comrade Mao Zedong has done as a disciple of Marx, Engels, Lenin and Stalin is precisely to unite Marxist theory with the practice of the Chinese revolution, thus giving rise to Chinese communism – the thought of Mao Zedong. And Mao Zedong's thought, too, has guided and is guiding the Chinese people to achieve complete emancipation; it will, moreover, make great and useful contributions to the cause of the emancipation of the peoples of all countries, and of the peoples of the East in particular. The thought of Mao Zedong from his world view to his style of work, is sinified Marxism (Chung-kuo-hua ti Ma-k'o-szu-chu-i) in the process of development and perfection . . . . These theories and policies are thoroughly Marxist, and at the same time thoroughly Chinese. They are the highest expression of the wisdom of the Chinese nation and its highest theoretical achievement.[32]

From 1949 onwards it became a persistent effort of Beijing ideologues to propagate the relevance of Maoist thought and action to the Afro-Asian and Latin-American revolutions in a dual perspective: first, that it would serve as a definite model for the national liberation struggles in the Third World and second, that as a global revolutionary strategy it could ensure and expedite the defeat of imperialism.

At a meeting of the World Federation of Trade Unions held in Beijing in November 1949, shortly after the victory of the communist revolution in China, Liu Zhao-ch'i declared emphatically in his opening speech that the 'Chinese way' was applicable throughout Asia. He proclaimed: 'The way taken by the Chinese people in defeating imperialism and its lackeys and in founding the People's Republic of China is the way that should be taken by the peoples of many colonial and semi-colonial countries (in Asia and Australia) in their fight for national independence and people's democracy.'[33]

In December 1950 a booklet was published in China which strongly emphasized the key role of the People's Republic of China in revolutions in the East and the universal validity of the Chinese example.[34] This document, moreover, attributed greater weight to the Chinese example as compared to Soviet experience and teachings.

Finally, at the height of the Sino-Soviet ideological schism came the most vigorous assertion of the Maoist strategy of 'people's war' by Lin Biao on 2 September 1965 in a lengthy thesis entitled 'Long Live the Victory of the People's War', which according to him, upheld the Maoist model of revolution for the Third World.[35]

Lin Biao observed that the October Revolution began with armed uprisings in the cities and then spread to the country-side, while the Chinese Revolution won nation-wide victory through the encirclement of the cities from the rural areas and the final capture of the cities. Commending Mao Zedong's theory of the people's war as the 'common asset of the revolutionary people of the whole world', he declared that it had 'characteristics of our epoch' and that it 'has been proved by the long practice of the Chinese revolution to be in accord with the objective laws of such wars and to be invincible. It has not only been valid for China, it is a great contribution to the revolutionary struggles of the oppressed nations and peoples throughout the world.' Lin Biao also asserted:

> It must be emphasized that Comrade Mao Zedong's theory of the establishment of rural revolutionary base areas and the encirclement of the cities from the country-side is of outstanding and universal practical significance for the present revolutionary struggles of the oppressed nations and people in Asia, Africa and Latin America against imperialism and its running dogs . . . The basic political and economic conditions in many of these countries have many similarities to those that prevailed in China. As in China, the peasants constitute the main force of the national democratic revolution against the imperialists and their running dogs. In committing aggression against these countries, the imperialists usually begin by seizing the big cities and the main lines of communication, but these are unable to bring the vast country-side completely under their control. The country-side and the country-side alone, can provide the revolutionary basis from which the

> revolutionaries can go forward to final victory. Precisely for this reason, Comrade Mao Zedong's theory of establishing revolutionary base areas in the rural districts and encircling the cities from the country-side is attracting more and more attention among the people in these regions.[36]

Lin's strategy aimed at linking all the people's war in the Third World into a global front against the United States, reinforcing each other and merging into a 'torrential world-wide tide'. His thesis concludes with a frontal attack on the Soviet 'revisionist' ideological positions highlighting the general line of 'three peacefuls' – peaceful coexistence, peaceful competition and peaceful transition.[37] As it emerges from the foregoing analysis, Lin Biao's thesis marked the culmination of the Chinese attack on Soviet 'revisionism', and in so far as the Third World was concerned, the attack was to be carried out through an escalation of national liberation movements relying on the 'thought' of Mao Zedong. In fact, the publication of the Lin Biao thesis should be viewed as the beginning of the series of attempts made by the Chinese throughout the 1960s to project a Maoist revolutionary line (as against the 'peaceful transition' line of the CPSU) to the Third World countries, wherever they saw an 'excellent revolutionary situation'. In 1967 India was picked up by the CCP as the 'testing ground' for the 'myth' of peaceful transition to socialism because of Beijing's prevailing hostile relations with India arising out of the border dispute and because of India's position in the Sino-Soviet ideological rift.[38]

NOTES

1. For details see George Lichthein, 'Marx and the Asiatic Mode of Production', *St. Anthony's Paper* No.14, Chatto and Windus, London 1963, pp.86-112.
2. Notwithstanding the fact that Marx had information about the landed property system in ancient China, he insisted that China was a classical example of the Asiatic system and was not prepared to characterize her as a 'peculiar Asiatic form of feudalism', as claimed by Chinese communists subsequently.
3. For details see Helene Carrere d'Encausse and Stuart R. Schram, *Marxism in Asia*, Allen Lane, The Penguin Press, London, 1969, pp.115-19.
4. Ibid., p.10.
5. Ibid., p.11.
6. Lenin, *Polmoye Sobraniye Sochinenii*, Vol.XXX, pp.1-9 (italics in original). For the English rendering, see Encause and Schram, op. cit., pp.144-45.
7. Another person involved in the debate was an Italian Marxist Serrati, Because of his extreme Euro-centric view and his contemptuous treatment of the national liberation movements in Asia, his thesis was unanimously rejected by the Congress.

8. For a summary of the theses of Lenin and Roy, see Allen Whiting, Soviet Policies in China: 1917-1924 New York, Columbia University Press, 1954, pp.54-55.
9. Lenin, *Selected Works*, Lawrence and Wishart, London, 1938, Vol.X, pp. 239-44.
10. Originally, these portions of Lenin's statement at Second Comintern Congress had not been included. They were, however, inserted into the fifth Russian edition of his works, *Polnoye Sobraniye Sochinenii*, Vol.41, p.457, For the relevant excerpts see Encausse and Schram, op. cit., p.30.
11. For details see Robert C. North and Xenia Budin, *M.N. Roy's Mission to China*, University of California, Berkeley, 1963.
12. Edgar Snow, *Red Star Over China*, Victor Gollanz Ltd., London 1968, p.155.
13. Mao Zedong, 'Literature and Art in the Service of the People'. For relevant information see the English translation of Mao's speech in Stuart R. Schram, *The Political Thought of Mao Zedong*, Pelican Books Ltd., London, 1969, p.362.
14. In 1924, during his stay in Shanghai, Mao had worked with Hu Han-min in the KMT's Shanghai bureau. For this he was accused of 'class collaborationism' by his party comrades..He, however, fell ill at that time because of overwork and retired to Hunan for rest. During his convalescence he made a thorough study of the peasant problems and started organizing peasant associations.
15. For details see Schram, *Mao Zedong*, Simon and Schuster, New York, 1966, pp.72-73.
16. Snow, op. cit., p.157.
17. Mao Zedong, *Selected Works*, Beijing, 1960. Vol.1, p.20. Mao's view is identical with that of the Executive Committee of the Comintern evolved in its sixth plenum held in March 1926.
18. Mao, however, simultaneously served up to October 1926 as Principal of the Sixth Session of Peasant Movement Training Institute, which was instrumental in training a number of men and women to take part in the peasant uprisings which were to come a few years later. The victory of the revolutionary democratic tendency . . ., depends on the degree to which the 400 million Chenese peasants take part in the decisive revolutionary struggle together with the Chinese workers and under their leadership. For details see Jan Degras, *The Communist International: 1923-1947, Documents*, London, 1960, Vo.II, p.279.
19. This Report is an exclusive account of the peasant movement in Hunan from July 1926 to February 1927.
20. Stuart R. Schram, *The Political Thought of Mao Zedong*, p.51.
21. For details of the 'Deeds' see *Mao Zedong*, op. cit. Vol.I., pp. 34-56.
22. Ibid.
23. For the text of the resolution passed by the seventh plenum of the Executive Committee of the Comintern see Degras, op.cit., Vol.II, p.343.
24. Edger Snow, op. cit., p.161.
25. See J. Bandyopadhyay, *Mao Zedong and Gandhi: Perspectives on Social*

Transformation, Allied Publishers, Calcutta 1973, pp.45-46.

26. Harvard, 1951.
27. Ibid., p.189.
28. Mao's views were presented on this line at the sixth Plenum of the CCP Central Committee in November 1938.
29. Jerome Ch'en, *Mao and the Chinese Revolution*, Oxford University Press, London, 1965, pp.224-25. For details of the pattern of peasant revolts in China see Barrington Moore, *Social Origins of Dictatorship and Democracy*, Beacon Press, Boston, 1967, Chapter IV.
30. J.K. Fairbank, *The United States and China*, Cambridge, Mass., 1968, p.240.
31. For the full text of this document see Scharam, *The Political Thought of Mao Zedong*, pp.171-74.
32. For details see Schram, *Mao Zedong*, pp. 215-16. 'Thus began', writes Schram 'the shift from the adaptation of Marxism to the language, mentality and conditions of the Chinese people (Mao's original definition of sinification) to the replacement of all other forms of Marxism (including that of Marx himself) by the infallible thought of the leader. See, *The Political Thought of Mao Zedong*, p.72.
33. Liu Shao-ch'i, On the Party, Peking Foreign Language Press, 1950. For the English translation of the original Chinese text see Encausse and Schram, *Marxism and Asia*, pp. 259-61.
34. For the English translation of Liu Shao-ch'i's speech, see Encausse and Schram, *Marxism and Asia*, pp.269-73.
35. Meng Hsieng-Chang, *Tung-fang min-tsu Chieh-fang chang-cheng ti hsin hsing-shin*, Commercial Press, Shanghai, 2nd edn., January 1967.
36. Lin Biao, "Long Live the Victory of the People's War", *Beijing Review*, 3 September 1965.
37. Italics added. In fact, while waging people's war in his own country, Mao Zedong was quite conscious of the international significance of this kind of war and of his own strategic thought. See, *Mao Zedong Selected Works*, Vol.II, p.196.
38. For details see N.S. Khrushchev, Report of the Central Committee of the Communist Party of the Soviet Union to the XX Party Congress, 14 February 1956, Moscow, 1956, pp.42-46.
39. For details see Asish Kumar Roy, *The Spring Thunder and After,* Minerva Associates, Calcutta, 1975, Chapter I.

8. Rural Development in Socialist Construction in Mao's China an analysis of Mao Zedong's thought and its contemporary relevance

SAMIRENDRA N. RAY

I

The purpose of this paper is not to present any 'factual information' or a 'running commentary', to use Stuart Schram's words (Schram, 1974), about the history of China during Mao Zedong's stewardship, or, more particularly, about China's economic policies and programmes during the period of socialist construction, or even an exhaustive scholarly compilation of all of Mao's speeches and writings representing his thoughts, ideas and programmes of action; but to provide a brief perspective of his thinking about the most pressing economic, and along with it, the attendant social and political problems, which might contribute to a better understanding of, and insight into one of history's most remarkable examples of social transformation through democratic revolution and socialist construction. Emphasis has been laid on giving a fresh look at some of his most outstanding ideas in so far as these related to the actual policies and programmes for such a gigantic enterprise, so that a better idea of the man and his mission could be obtained, especially when the leadership in the post-1978 and contemporary China is busy downplaying his role and contributions as well as achievements in fulfilling the dreams of socialist revolution.

Mao attempted to adapt the theory and practice of Marxist revolution to China where the peasantry, rather than the proletariat, was the main locus of social discontent. In seeking to make his thought accessible to the people, he is supposed to have made substantive theoretical contributions to modern Marxism. Mao's voluminous writings were acknowledged even by Khruschev to contain 'new contributions' to Marxist thought. He had been the central personality in China's revolution and post-revolution socialist construction; not just a party boss, but genuinely a teacher, a statesman, strategist and tactician, philosopher, national hero and a great liberator in history (Snow, 1970). Under him, the Communist Party of China evolved its own interpretations of Marxist theory, its strategy and tactics, its own idiom and 'line' to fit Chinese conditions. His theory of the Chinese revolution has been regarded as a new development of Marxism-Leninism in the revolutions of colonial and semi-colonial countries. The Chinese revolution itself, developing out of the great 4 May Movement of 1919 and culminating in the proclamation of the People's Republic of China in Beijing on 1 October 1949, represents one of the greatest upheavals in the history not just of Asia, but of the whole world. With rapid and spectacular economic achievements, unified and renewed by Mao's invigorating thought and leadership since that historic day, China underwent transformations unprecedented in human history. The advent of Mao led, in fact, to the most gigantic agrarian and rural reform history has ever known.

Controversy about Mao and his thoughts and programmes of action has persisted to this day. While he has been assailed by his own countrymen and detractors as an unprincipled opportunist in his occasional concessions to the national bourgeoisie in 1938, 1945 and early 1950s, as well as a 'capitulationist', and his theoretical formulations branded as a perversion of Marxism, there are others who have been impressed by his uncompromising emphasis on class struggle, proletarian values, and his implacable carrying of the revolution till the end. Among his positive contributions may be mentioned: a) the concept of 'mass line', which ultimately involved an element of democratic participation from below, b) his idea that human change must accompany and support economic and technical progress, c) his trenchant and all-out attack on bureaucracy, and d) his conviction, born out of real life experience, that the centre of gravity in Chinese society was to be found in the country-side, and that the peasantry must play an active role in building a new socialist China. Mao had correctly understood the obvious but neglected facts which brought him to power, namely, 1) that the vast majority of the Chinese people were poor and illiterate; 2) that China's greatest reservoir of creative energy lay in this majority; 3) that political leadership would go to the person or persons who would succeed in winning its confidence and effectively organizing it; and 4) that in this massive labour power lay all the 'capital' necessary to industrialize China and make it a wealthy and mighty nation (Snow, 1970). To Mao, people, and the people alone, are the creative force in world history.

Mao claimed that Marxism-Leninism does not provide for all alternatives for a communist society, and that Marxism-Leninism 'has in no way put an end to the discovery of truth'. The struggle between that which is true and that which is false, detrimental and useless to a socialist society perhaps constitutes the core of Mao's thinking and strategy. He realized that a correct paradigm for a socialist society has not been discovered yet, and that the task of communists was through analysis and expansion of man's cognitive abilities and skills, to search for better ways of solving society's problems. Drawing on the rich heritage of ancient Chinese culture, Mao did not claim to know, for example, what the ultimate truth and the ultimate good are. He believed that one should be constantly involved in searching for it, and that through proper utilization of one's intellectual processes, one would be able to recognize the truth when one sees it. In Mao's opinion, introspection, one's self-evaluation, and the desire to purge oneself from errors, will expedite the search for a good model of a just society. Contradictions, as Mao said, are everywhere in the world, the very stuff of life and reality, and 'without contradictions, there would be no world'.

II

With the achievement of independence and political freedom by a large number of nations in Asia, Africa and Latin America in the wake of decolonization after the Second World War, the question of economic freedom and the task of development assumed a new sense of urgency. The correct path of development, socialist or capitalist, came to occupy the centre-stage of intellectual debate as well as ideological conflict between the two superpowers. It is indeed significant that the emergence of the People's Republic of China largely coincided with this new scenario in world politics. While some of these newly independent nations chose the capitalist path of development so avidly advocated and sponsored by the USA through its modernization paradigm and foreign aid programme, others opted for the socialist path of the then Soviet Union. However, in most of these developing nations, the policy makers and planners had been emphasizing the need to transform rural areas where the overwhelming majority of their people lived. This emphasis on rural development had been due to several factors like political mobilization of the peasantry and their pressures on the national elite, concern of their governments about growing disparities between urban and rural areas, and the desire to seek greater political legitimacy. The need to eliminate poverty and rural unemployment and modernize agriculture became the cornerstone of public policy in these countries. Programmes and projects were introduced in these countries to increase agricultural productivity, raise incomes and living standards, especially of the rural people, provide employment opportunities, facilitate participation of the local rural people in local decision making, and increase access of the rural poor to government facilities and programmes. Broadly speaking, these policies of rural development adopted by the developing countries in Asia were based on any one or a combination of three strategies: technocratic (productivity-oriented), reformist (solidarity-oriented) and radical (equity-oriented). It is significant that the last of these strategies, radical or equity-oriented, was mostly followed by the countries following the socialist path of development. Countries adopting the modernization paradigm of development advocated by the structural-functionalist scholars chose the first two strategies or a combination of the two (G. Shabbir Cheema, 1985).

What happened in these countries was that rather than seeking to achieve comprehensive agricultural and rural development which could provide a sound foundation for industrialization, public policies in these countries were geared to rapid economic growth in a capsule form through urban and industrial development with accent on growth rather than distributive justice. Even where agriculture was sought to be modernized on the basis of the technocratic strategy, the emphasis on growth and the neglect of distributive justice and equity could not lead them to the desired stage of development. The 'trickle down' did not materialize, and the fallacies of the modernization paradigm were exposed by the scholars in these countries, especially in Latin America, in no uncertain manner. This gave impetus to fresh thinking on a reconceptualized development, particularly rural development, which was now considered as more than mere agricultural development, something comprehensive, integrated, total and holistic, with tremendous emphasis on equity and distributive justice, self-reliance, decentralization and participation, community management and socio-cultural development, with a view to not just fulfilling the basic and minimum needs but to improving the quality of life. The story of Mao's China during these crucial decades of the fifties and the sixties and the early seventies, in its determined and steadfast effort to find the most appropriate path to achieve socialist construction for an allround development of society, economy, polity and culture in the transition to communism, offers a very interesting canvas for comparison and contrast with other developing nations. While China learnt much from its own mistakes and failures, the lessons of the Chinese experience have been and still are of great significance and importance to those countries who are still searching for the most appropriate goals, strategies and tactics for development. For the Asian countries in particular, India included, the remarkable achievements of China in respect of social transformation, some glaring failures notwithstanding, have been a beacon light for emulation. Such comparison seems to be particularly relevant in the light of the changes in public policy, strategy and tactics coming in the 1980s in these two countries with the world's two biggest populations and demographic problems. The winds of liberalization, globalization and privatization and open door policies blowing in these two countries, and the consequences and effects so far comprehended, provide an excellent basis for assessing the earlier efforts: pre-1978 in China and pre-1991 in India.

III

At the founding of the People's Republic of China in 1949, Mao proclaimed: 'The Chinese people have stood up'. It was indeed a glorious moment not only for the people of China, but signalled and symbolized a new hope and opportunity for colonized and exploited people all over the world for national liberation. Winning state power was, however, only the first phase of the revolution. It had to be followed by direct and all-out attacks on the historical roots of poverty and by building the nation on the basis of social justice and economic development. The latter, in Mao's view, is a spiral process in which successive increments in material and human resources combine and reinforce one another to produce a continual forward movement. One may distinguish between several periods of China's economic development and several phases and steps in the national policy during Mao's period. While the first period from 1949 to 1952 was utilized for recovery and rehabilitation, the subsequent years, from 1952 to 1962, coinciding with the first two Five Year Plans, augmented by the Great Leap Forward in 1958-59, marked very great achievements in industrial production even at the cost of agriculture, possibly on the then Soviet advice. The first phase saw land reforms in a big way introduced for eliminating dependency relationship in rural areas. Influenced by Soviet development strategy, policy priorities included the establishment of political controls, rebuilding infrastructure, ensuring the efficiency of investments and establishment of heavy industries. To forestall capitalist tendencies among rich peasants, mutual aid teams and agricultural cooperatives were formed. The establishment of People's Communes in 1959 reflected a shift in policy and the abandoning of the Soviet model. The failure of the Great Leap Forward led to a period of 'readjustment' in 1962-65. A further shift in policy occurred during the years of the 'Cultural Revolution' in 1966-76, coinciding with the Third and the Fourth Five Year Plans. Since the end of the Cultural Revolution, a new set of economic development policies was initiated, and the post-1978 Reforms virtually ended the line adopted by Mao so far and heralded an entirely different development path that has continued to this day and even strengthened itself, in the process generating debate and controversy about their efficacy and effectiveness and their compatibility with doctrinaire or pragmatic socialism or Mao's declared goals of socialist construction during his lifetime.

The demographic and the agrarian questions, especially the land question, were most daunting in the beginning. Mao realized long ago that in a country that was underdeveloped economically, a large population was a help rather than a hindrance to increasing development (Hongqi, No.9, 1958). Mao declared that 'China had not only one mouth, but two arms'. At the same time, however, he admitted that it was an arduous task to provide an adequate standard of living for hundreds of millions of Chinese, and 'to transform our country which is behind economically into a prosperous one'. In a country comprising 960 m hectares, only 100 m of which were cultivated by some 500 m people (the average holding being 1.5 hectare), the agrarian problem, with the additional disadvantage of an unfavourable natural background, must obviously remain in the forefront of all political questions and agenda (Jean Pierre Brule, 1971). The law of agrarian reform of 2 June 1950, was promulgated bringing to an end a system that had existed for thousands of years. Mao said:

> Our agrarian revolution has followed and will continue to follow this process: the land-owning class who possess the land are changed into a landless class, and the landless peasants become small landowners by being given the confiscated land: the private property of the peasants, in turn, will be transformed into community property with socialist agriculture. This has already happened in the Soviet Union, and will finally take place all over the world.

Further,

> the reform of the land system is the main content of China's new democratic revolution. The general line in the land reform is to rely on the poor peasants, unite with the middle peasants, abolish the system of feudal exploitation step by step and in a discriminating way and develop agricultural production.Only the poor peasants can and must be the basic force to be relied upon in the land reform. . . The main and immediate task of the land reform is to satisfy the demands of the masses of the poor peasants and farm labourers . . . The aim of land reform is to abolish the system of feudal exploitation, that is, to eliminate the feudal landlords as a class, not as individuals . . . The system of feudal exploitation should be abolished step by step, that is, in a tactical way (Selected Works, IV, 235-236).

During the period 1949-58, when the Soviet models dominated virtually everything they did, the Chinese built heavy industries as fast as they could, neglected consumer-goods industries, and regarded agriculture mainly as a source of savings for heavy industrialization. With widening gaps between advancing industrial sectors and a socially and economically stagnant agriculture, the Chinese became dissatisfied. The Yenan period, as an experiment in the liberated society of the future, taught them that development must be *comprehensive* (emphasis mine), must bring all sectors up and not just some chosen few, and must, above all, be in the interests of the poor peasants as they themselves see them and not just seen by planning theorists.

The internal policy and economic planning of the People's Republic of China began to deviate markedly from Soviet models with the proclamation in 1958 of the Great Leap Forward, a new system of economic development based on the organization of the peasant population into rural communes and the use of labour-intensive as opposed to capital-intensive methods of production. One of the major turning points was the 'hundred flowers' movement of 1956, designed to liberalize China's political life and shake up the bureaucracy. Mao welcomed public criticism of his regime's shortcomings ("Let a hundred flowers bloom"). This movement had occurred in the context of a debate within the CPC about China's future economic development. While a moderate section of leadership in the Party held to the view that the pattern established by the First Five Year Plan was essentially correct, and with moderate modifications stressing greater material incentives and technical assistance for the peasantry, could effectively stimulate agricultural production to reach satisfactory levels, Mao advocated the more radical vision for a thorough break with the Soviet model of cautious planning and technocratic management. The result was the Great Leap Forward – a great leap into both prosperity and communism, and it was hoped that in a few years, China would jump into the forefront of industrial nations while at the same time completing the building of socialism to enter the more egalitarian communist stage of social development.

In just seven years, China had traversed the difficult path to socialist ownership of the means of production in the dual form of cooperatively owned farms and state-owned industries. The economic gains of this period testified to the vitality of the new socialist system. The institutional foundations had been laid for a future in which poverty would be eliminated, common prosperity would prevail, and the full promise of communist society would finally be realized (Selden, 1979).

The Great Leap Forward was indeed a turning point, advancing and clarifying goals that would henceforth be central to China's socialist development, in particular, the task of moving systematically to eliminate the 'Three Great Differences', namely, the inequalities dividing the city and the countryside, workers and peasants, and mental and manual labour. The establishment of the People's Communes with all-round management of agricultural forestry, animal husbandry, sideline occupations and fishery, where industry, agriculture, exchange, culture and education, and military affairs merge into one, was now the fundamental policy to guide the peasants to accelerate socialist construction, complete the building of socialism, even ahead of time, and carry out the gradual transition to communism (Peoples's Communes in China, 1958). The communes were expected to institute a system of centralized leadership with management organs at various levels, in order to operate a responsible system of production. By 1958 November, China's 74,000 advanced agricultural cooperatives, embracing 99 percent of the peasantry, had been engulfed by 26,000 (later consolidated into 24,000) communes, and the commune administration took over direct management of trade and commerce, small industries, bookkeeping, banking, marketing and supply, education, communal dining halls and kitchens, housing, medical care, and the training and command of the militia as well as public works. The communes represented a collectivist system radically different from the Soviet pattern.

Unlike the Soviet Union, the People's Communes represented the ultimate level of the state. Ideologically speaking, they were a denial of the then Soviet Union's monopoly in the transition to communism, at the same time negating the Soviet thesis that the communist principle could not be applied to rural situations. Mao's communes were extraordinary at the social level, since, as the basic unit of socialist society, they brought together workers, peasants, shopkeepers, soldiers and students, creating a full and clear image of an egalitarian society. They were daring new multi-level rural local government structures at the commune, brigade and team levels for facilitating the mobilization of rural labour for productive purposes, providing the instrumentality for transmission of policy directives, agricultural technology and social services from the central and provincial governments to rural areas, leading to the development of local political leadership capabilities, providing the minimum basic needs to the rural poor, and enabling the government to implement its egalitarian policies for socialist transformation. Thus, the Communes were much more than collective farms which pool labour and share gains. With their various levels, they were a framework in which people functioned politically to voice their interests, economically to produce and consume, and socially to form a community beyond that of family and neighbours (Milton, 1974).

All these do not mean that the Communes worked with unalloyed success. Several weaknesses were inherent in their design and working, like the reduction of incentives which negatively affected agricultural productivity, too much of administrative and political intervention in production planning and management, lack of management skills on the part of the cadres and central guidelines leading to the imposition of a uniform pattern (Shabbir Cheema, 1985). Even if the idea of communes was logical in theory, things went wrong very soon. In their modified form after the disasters of the Great Leap Forward, especially in consequences of the concession, known as 'little freedoms' granted in December 1960 in the aftermath of the natural calamities, the disasters could be overcome. On hindsight, it seems that the hasty and euphoric decisions regarding the Communes were basically Mao's failure of strategy and tactics. But one has to remember that it was Mao himself who had said in 1975: 'fight no battle that is not well prepared , no battle whose outcome is uncertain', and that a great deal of spadework was necessary for consolidation of cooperatives, let alone technical transformation of agriculture on a national scale. Famine, depression, withdrawal of Soviet advisors and technical assistance, as well as faulty implementation led to China's economic misfortunes during this time. However, the Communes, although gravely weakened, did not disintegrate. Villages throughout China continued the search for forms appropriate to local conditions and the level of productive forces, hoping to reinvigorate the collectives and stimulate economic growth. From 1961 onwards, the imbalance was corrected when agriculture was acknowledged as the 'foundation' of the economy, with industry as the 'leading factor". In June 1961, the CPC Central Committee foresaw two or three years of consolidation, and years of concentration on 'strengthening the agricultural front'. By late 1960, the Party had thus clearly reversed itself on the 'continuous leap forward' policy in favour of an undulatory development of the economy. During this period, the Chinese also made self-reliance their guiding policy in economic development. Speaking at the Central Committee of the CPC in 1962, Mao said:

> In the field of heavy industry especially, we copied almost everything from the Soviet Union with very little creativeness on our part. It was absolutely necessary to do so at that time and yet it was also a weakness – a lack of creativeness and of ability to stand on our own feet. Certainly this could not become a long-term policy. Beginning from 1958, we established the policy of relying mainly on our own efforts, while seeking foreign aid for support. At the Second Session of the Party's Eighth National Congress, in 1958, we adopted the general line of 'going all out, aiming high, and achieving greater, faster, better and more economical result in building society.

In a fairly objective assessment of the Chinese experience in agricultural and rural development during this period, it has been very appropriately observed that 'the collectivization of Chinese agriculture may not have contributed to that growth of agricultural production greatly. But it had provided solutions to most of the rural problems. Most rural resources were fully utilized; starvation became an experience of the past; even population growth appeared to have come under control; and modernization was slowly in the making – all as the result of an extraordinary revolutionary movement' (Humberto Garza Elizondo, 1992, p.245).

IV

The 'Great Proletarian Cultural Revolution' which began in 1966, was a period of turmoil that deeply affected China's politics, economy, culture and society. Apparently believing that the revolutionary of the CPC had succumbed to bureaucratization, Mao launched this movement to reassert the primacy of Marxist-Leninist doctrine against 'revisionist' tendencies imputed to leading elements within the Party. Mao believed that he and China had been betrayed by some of the highest ranking members of the CPC, especially Deng Xiaoping and Liu Shaoqi, and that the whole Party and country were in need of a reinfusion of revolutionary spirit. It was an engineered mass movement to isolate and remove those leaders who were believed to be leading China down the 'capitalist road'. Mao forged an alliance of radical party ideologues, loyal military commanders, and tens of millions of student Red Guards to carry out his crusade against revisionism.

Even foreign critics admit that viewed from a developmental perspective, the Cultural Revolution marked a new drive to eliminate inequalities and spur decentralized, self-reliant economic growth, while training a new generation of youth committed to continuing the revolution. Over the course of ten years, it shored up the tenuous cooperative foundations of the collective economy; achieved breakthroughs in rural industrialization and mechanization, thus providing the firm technical foundations that had been lacking in the development projects of the Great Leap era; and made strides towards adequate low-cost cooperative medical care and the extension of education throughout the country-side. And it was partly as a result of such gains that this period showed significant if uneven economic growth (Selden, 1979, 31-32). Building on the visions and practical lessons of the Great Leap Forward, it sought to devise workable means to narrow the difference between city and country-side, worker and peasant, mental and manual labour, and above all, to extend the power of working people over the workplace and society as a whole. At the same time, however, it helped in the creation of a Mao cult and the ritualization of politics and culture, the formation of warring cliques whose differences degenerated into violence and paralyzed the political process, and gutted higher education, research and culture resulting in dearth of scientists, intellectuals and artists (Ibid., 32). The country was plunged into near-anarchy, and the economy was virtually disrupted, the greatest casualty being policy thinking. Lin Biao and the Gang of Four carried things to excesses in their zeal to overplay the so-called sharp struggle between 'two classes, two roads and two lines'. They stigmatized the commodity and currency economy, sabotaged the system of distribution according to work, and spread various 'leftist' theories, implemented ultra-Leftist agricultural policies, and propagated the movement to 'learn from Dazhai' coined by Mao himself in 1964. Politics was in command and ideology in the lead (Luo Hanxian, 1985, 89-98). The mid-1970s witnessed a cataclysmic confrontation between defenders of the legacies of the Cultural Revolution and more conservative leaders including Zhou Enlai and the rehabilitated Deng Xiaoping, who urged that the nation's priorities be shifted from class struggle politics to economic modernization.

Following the death of Mao Zedong in 1976, a sea change took place in Chinese political economy. The Third Plenary Session of the Eleventh Central Committee, held at the end of 1978, dominated by Deng Xiaoping and other survivors of the Liu Shaoqui faction, marked a switch of policies and a beginning of 'reform', a shift from working class power and politics to bourgeois power and politics, from the socialist road to the capitalist road. It marked the dismantling of both the socialist economic base and the socialist superstructure that the Chinese people, during Mao Zedong's lifetime, and under his vigorous leadership, had built with such effort for about three decades (William Hinton, 1991). Within an astonishingly short period, the whole edifice of Maoist political economy was demolished (Nolan, 1991, 218), and the sweeping reform in agricultural policy, as implemented in 1979-1980, progressively nullified the commune system and replaced it with the 'responsibility' family contract system under which individual family units contract to work on a certain amount of land and in return promise to pay a certain amount of grain and cash. There is a view that even though there were enormous changes which occurred in rural institutions, one can identify certain continuities too with the pre-1978 scenario (Nolan, 1991, 218-19). It is also believed by some that even though extraordinary progress in China's rural economy after 1978 has taken place in respect of farm output, farm productivity, the nonfarm sector, living standards and the decline of poverty, the rural reforms have also producted serious problems, like faltering agricultural growth rates, structure of the rural economy, village class relations, spatial inequality, welfare and human capital, accumulation and physical capital, population growth and obsession with money making ('take the lead in getting rich') (Nolan, 1991, 218-254), as well as high rates of inflation, deteriorating living standards, and official corruption. The 1989 Beijing protests, culminating in the Tiananmen Square massacre of student demonstrators, reflected the accumulation of a number of pressures that had been building up in China during the late 1980s. Despite sustained efforts on the part of the present leadership to disown Mao and remove his memory from public life, the question of Mao's contributions, achievements and relevance continues to be a matter of debate, and the last word may not have been utterred on the claims of the post-1978 reformists about the failure of Mao's policies and programmes of action relating to rural modernization.

Let this be mentioned at this stage, before concluding this exercise, that it has been based mainly on published, translated and generally available literature on the man and his mission and accomplishments on a subject that has generated tremendous interest and debate during the last three decades or more. Even though many unknown facts have come to light in recent years about the personal life and the darker sides of this genius of a leader, these have not been taken into consideration in the absence of a clear establishment of their authenticity and acceptability and even their relevance to the understanding of Mao. Recent Western assessments reveal a newer appreciation of his ideas and role. The present paper is merely a very modest effort towards this appreciation. Many of the problems facing our country bear strong resemblance to those of China in the fifties, and India could have been richer with ideas and actions of a leader of that vision and mission.

REFERENCES

Breman, Jan and Studipto Mundle (eds.), *Rural Transformation in Asia* (OUP, New Delhi, 1991)

Bruler, Jean-Pierre, *China Comes of Age* (Penguin, London, 1971)

Cheema, G. Shabbir, (ed.), *Rural Development in Asia* (Sterling, New Delhi, 1985)

Elizondo, Humberto Garza, "Revolution and Agrarian Reform in China and Mexico" in Manoranjan Mohanty (ed.), *Chinese Revolution: Comparative Perspectives on Transformation of Non-Western Societies* (Ajanta, New Delhi, 1992), ch.11, pp.235-260.

Gittings, John, *China Changes Face: The Road from Revolution, 1949-1989* (OUP, New Delhi, 1989)

Hanxian, Luo, *Economic Changes in Rural China* (China Studies Series) (New World Press, Beijing, 1985).

Hinton, William, "The Chinese Revolution", *Monthly Review*, Vol.47, No.6, Nov.1991.

Hongqi, No.9, 1958.

Milton, David, et al. (eds.), *People's China: Social Experimentation, Politics, Entry on to World* (Penguin, London 1974)

Mohanty, Manoranjan, (ed.), *Chinese Revolution: Comparative Perspectives on Transformation of Non-Western Societies* (Ajanta, New Delhi, 1992).

Mao Zedong, *Selected Works*, Vols.I-IV.

Monthly Review, Vol.31, No.1, May 1979; Vol.42, No.6, Nov.1990; Vol.43, No.6, 1991.

Nolan, Peter, "Petty Commodity Production in a Socialist Economy: Chinese Rural Development in Post-Mao Period", in Breman and Mundle (eds.), op.cit. pp.218-254.

People's Communes in China, 1958 (Beijing).

Schram, Stuart, (ed.), *Mao Tsetung Unrehearsed: Talks and Letters, 1956-1971* (Penguin, London, 1974).

Selden, Mark, "China's Uninterrupted Revolution", *Monthly Review*, Vol.31, No.5, October, 1979, pp.24-36.

Snow, Edgar, *Red China Today: The Other Side of the River* (Penguin, London, 1970).

9. Mao's Practice A Sociology of Knowledge Interpretation

MAQITUL HUSSAIN

The objective of this paper is to bring out a sociology of knowledge interpretation of Mao's essay "On Practice: On the relation between knowledge and practice, between knowing and doing" (1937)[1] on the basis of Mead's analytical framework known as the symbolic inter-actionist approach in sociology presented in his book *Mind, Self and Society*.[2] While making such analysis I intend to make an humble attempt at limited relevant diffusions and integration of Mao and Mead which might lead us to construct a sociology of knowledge model. In western sociological literature sociology of knowledge (SOK)[3] has already been accepted as a theoretical approach to analyse society for more than half a century. Without getting into the details of the SOK, suffice it to state with Berger: "The sociology of knowledge, therefore, must concern itself with the social construction of reality. In other words, an adequate understanding of the "reality sui generis of society requires an inquiry into the manner in which this reality is constructed." This inquiry, we maintain, is the task of the sociology of knowledge.[4]

It is found in Mao's logistics of knowledge an inherent potentiality to develop into a sociology of knowledge framework. Similarly in Mead a sociology of knowledge approach is very much evident though he did not state explicitly about the same. "Mead's work abounds in suggestive leads for the sociology of knowledge."[5] Mead is usually known for his pragmatism vis-a-vis his analysis of human existence in society. But we are putting stress on his sociology of knowledge part.[6] Let us briefly summarize Mao's and Mead's analyses of knowledge in society.

The moot points in Mao's theory of knowledge are the following:[7]

1. Knowledge begins with experience.

2. Perceptual knowledge needs to be developed to the rational stage.
3. Rational knowledge depends upon perceptual knowledge, perceptual knowledge remains to be developed into rational knowledge.
4. Rational knowledge must manifest itself in the revolutionary practice.
5. "Practice" has priority over "theory".
6. The cycle of practice-knowledge-practice and again knowledge is endless.
7. There is an unity of theory and practice-knowing and doing. The moot points in Mead's sociology of knowledge are the following:[8]

   1. Human 'mind' starts functioning with experience in and through the 'significant others' (parents, guardians, friends).
   2. 'Mind' moves from the 'play stage' to the 'game stage' of development by learning to take 'the role of other'.
   3. A 'minded' individual develops into a 'self' when an individual learns to view oneself as an object-self consciousness.
   4. 'Self' has two parts – 'I' and 'Me'. 'I' is the "response of the organisms to the attitude of the others".[9] 'Me' is "the organized set of attitudes of others which one assumes."[10]
   5. "The nature self"[11] develops the moment an individual self accepts internalizing the "generalized other" (the attitude of the whole community).

In both Mao and Mead three specific stages of knowledge or cognitive development may be delineated:

	MAO	MEAD
Stage III	Revolutionary practice	Mature self
Stage II	Conception	Self
Stage I	Perception	Mind

Both the thinkers start with the same basic epistemological premise that knowledge is a posteriori and consequently irrespective of societal structure ('class' or 'classless') individual knowledge or consciousness depends on society or societal interaction. "In a classless society every person, as a member of society, joins in common effort with the other members, enters into definite relations of production with them and engages in production to meet man's material needs. In all class societies, the members of the different social classes also enter, in different ways, into definite relations of production and engage in production to meet their material needs. This is the primary source from which human knowledge develops."[12] Mao's such contention is echoed in Mead's theory as well: "Consciousness, usually defined in vague, ambiguous and static terms, is now conceived behaviouristically as on going, purposive life process and interaction . . . . Mind or consciousness is rather an instrument in the service of the organism's better adjustment to its environment. It is volitional as well as sensory. It seems to have likes and dislikes, it attentively selects and rejects its content."[13] Similarities abound with reference to origin, formation, and development of knowledge between Mao and Mead but I have quoted only a few passages to drive this point home. Mao said: "As social practice continues, things that give rise to man's sense perceptions and impressions in the course of his practice are repeated many times, then a sudden change (leap) takes place in the brain in the process of cognition and concepts are formed."[14] Similarly Mead said: "Thinking is simply the reasoning of the individual, the carrying on at a conversation between what I have termed the 'I' and the 'Me'."[15]

It is obvious that Mead's pragmatism nurtured in the early part of this century did prompt him to reject prevalent ideas of idealistic philosophy and introspectionist psychology. Consequently, truth claim of any situation depends on societal structure vis-a-vis who or what defines a situation. To clarify "the definition of a situation" Mead's concept of "meaning" may be equated with Mao's concept of "Leap". "Meaning is thus not to be conceived, fundamentally, as a state of consciousness or a set of organized relations existing or subsisting mentally outside the field of experience into which they enter, on the contrary, it should be conceived objectively, as having its existence within this field itself."[16] If we dare infuse Mead's concept of 'Role taking' of others by an individual in the process of socialization of that individual then the movement of knowledge from 'percept' to 'concept' and 'concept' to 'higher' or 'finer' concepts (Revolutionary practice' in Mao and 'Mature self' in Mead) could be interpreted not only as a 'sudden change (leap) in the brian but also a societal interaction process in the formation of individual 'self'. When Mao said, "The expression . . . 'knit the brows and a stratagem comes to mind', or in everyday language, 'let me think it over, refers to man's use of concepts in the brian to form judgements and inferences".[17] In Mead's social psychology thinking, judgements and inferences are developed and refined in and through the interaction between "I" and "Me" – two societal processes or phenomena in 'self'. Mao's very phrase 'every day language' is echoed in recent understanding of 'Ethnomethodology'[18] in sociological literature. Integration of Mead's social psychology with Mao's theory of knowledge may provide us with a sociological, rather sociology of knowledge, framework to analyse society. Berger, a sociology of knowledge analyst, modified Mead's ideas and suggested that Mead did not develop an analysis of 'social structure' in his writings. But his 'micro' analysis of the genesis of self vis-a-vis society could be integrated with any social structure which provides a 'generalized other' for the individual self.[19] This plasticity of Mead's theory allows us to integrate Mead with Mao's theory to arrive at a heuristic model. We are borrowing several terms from Berger to make such an integration viable.

Berger[20] gives us four aspects of sociology of knowledge: (a) Organization of knowledge; (b) Style of knowledge; (c) Horizon of knowledge; (d) Symbolism of knowledge. Any kind of consciousness is "plausible" only in a specific social situation and in between 'consciousness' and 'social situation' a 'plausibility structure' should exist in which certain 'carriers' (positive or negative) would (either allow to transmit or prevent from such transmission) play the role of a 'cognitive go between' in between consciousness and social structure. Berger's SOK framework may place Mao and Mead in the following manner:

Elements of SOK	Mao	Mead
Horizon of knowledge (i.e. limits of knowledge)	Micro-macro vice-versa	Micro-macro vice-versa
Symbolism of knowledge (i.e. culture content of knowledge)	Social structure	Social structure
Organization of knowledge	As reflected in institutions	As reflected in institutions
Style of knowledge (i.e. how of knowledge)	Movement of knowledge	Movement of knowledge

From this above integration the following model may be proposed

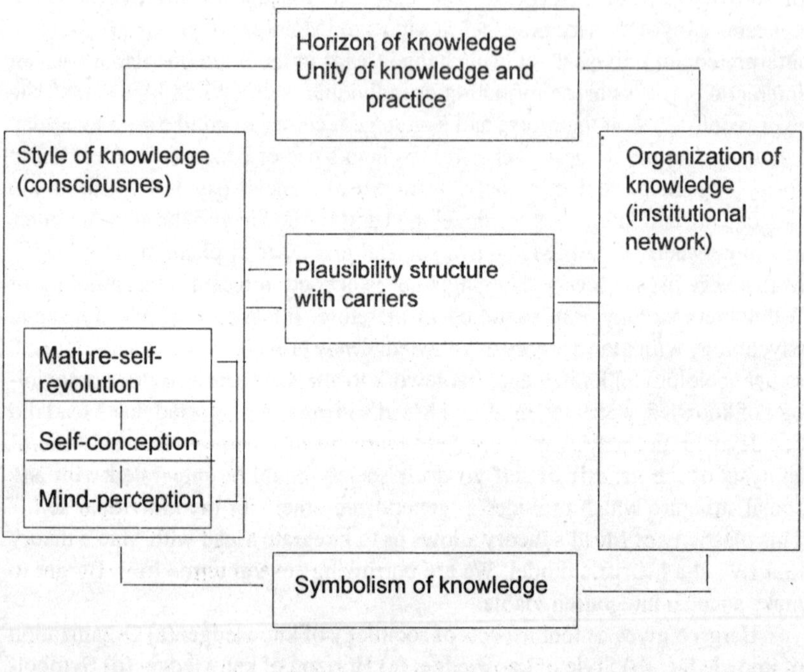

Except the issue of the culture content of knowledge both Mead and Mao could easily sit together in the same practical or intellectual compartment. I propose to go one step further to say that due to the plasticity in Mead's case (culture content of knowledge) our SOK framework should not have problem in analysing society. Common sense 'What' of knowledge centres around the truth claim of a specific societal situation or institution based on the cognitive style of knowledge. Both Mead and Mao agree that "movement of change in the world of objective reality is never ending and so is man's cognition of truth through practice".[21] Mao's statement is echoed in Mead's statement that ". . . so far as our experience is concerned, the world is always different. Each morning we open our eyes upon a different universe. Our intelligence is occupied with, continued with adjustment to these differences . . . novelty reaches out in both directions from each present experience".[22] As the search for truth is never ending so is our search for an approach, a framework for sociological analyses.

This SOK framework as presented is only heuristic in nature and this short paper is no more than a working one. We conclude with the hope that "The sociologist in the long run must be able to do better than to attribute the emergence and solution of problems to the mere existence of certain talented individuals. The existence of and the complex inter-relationship between the problems of a given time and place must be viewed and understood against the background of the structure of the society in which they occur, although this may not always give us an understanding of every details".[23]

Mannheim's observations should be taken as a pointer to the fact that certain social reality like a movement (as an example) may be interpreted and analysed through a sociology of knowledge framework. In this context Horowitz's observation with special reference to the anti-war movement in the American society vis-a-vis Mao's importance may be taken into consideration. "I think it is much more important to familiarize ourselves at the moment with Mao Tse-tung than Henry David Thoreau."[24] Taking the cue from Horwitz's analyses of 1960s anti war/youth movement in the US we dare say that to understand any social movement with particular reference to so called 'extremist movement' in any society our proposed model may be applied. Of course, a hermeneutical study[25] of the specific movement vis-a-vis the society in question is a sine qua non for the application of this model. Further hermeneutical reading of Mao and Mead should be proposed to refine our contentions.

NOTES

1. Mao Tse-tung (1937), "On Practice: On the relation between knowledge and practice, between knowing and doing", *Selected Works*, Vol.I, Peking,

pp.295-308.

2. G.H. Mead (1934), *Mind, Self and Society*, University of Chicago.
3. R.K. Merton (1957), *Social Theory and Social Structure* (ref. two chapters on Sociology of knowledge), Free Press, New York.
4. P. Berger and J. Luckmann (1967), *The Social Construction of Reality: A Treatise in the Sociology of Knowledge*, pp.15-16.
5. L. Coser (1977), *Masters of Sociological Thought,* Harcourt, New York, p.339.
6. P. Berger and J. Luckmann (2967) op.cit, pp.194-95.
7. Mao-Tse-tung, op. cit.
8. G.H. Mead, op.cit.
9. IBID, p.175.
10. IBID, p.175.
11. L. Coser, op.cit., p.337.
12. Mao-Tse-tung, op.cit., p.295-96.
13. Paul Pfuetz (1954), *The Social Self, Bookman*, London, pp.40-41.
14. Mao-Tse-tung, op.cit., p.298.
15. G.H. Mead, op.cit., p. 335.
16. Ibid., p.78.
17. Mao-Tse-tung, op.cit., 298.
18. Ethnomethodology of E. Goffman and Phenomenology of A. Schutz may be referred in this context.
19. P. Berger may be referred to observe the use of Mead's approach in European Sociology. P. Berger and J. Luckmann, op. cit., pp. 194-95.
20. P. Berger et. al (1973), *The Homeless Mind*, Basic Books, New York.
21. Mao Tse-tung, op. cit., p.307.
22. G.H. Mead (1936), *Movements of Thought in the Nineteenth Century*, University of Chicago, pp.290-91.
23. Karl Mannheim (1936), *Ideology and Utopia*, Harcourt, N.Y., p.97.
24. I.L Horowitz (1970), *The Struggle is the Message: The Organization and Ideology of the Anti-war Movement.* Interested reader may refer to pp. 121-142 for a verbatim report of the Hearing held by the National Commission on the Causes and Prevention of Violence in executive session on 23 October 1968. Horowitz was a consultant to the task force on anti-war movement. The Glendessary Press, Berkeley, p.138.
25. H.G. Gadamer (1980), *Dialogue and Dialectic: Eight Hermeneutical Studies on Plato*, Translated by P.C. Smith, Yale University Press. H.G. Gadmer (1975), *Truth and Method*, Translated by G. Barden and J. Cumming, Seabury, N.Y. A. Sica (1981) "Hermeneutics and Social Theory", *Current Perspectives in Social Theory: A Research Annual*, Vol.2, pp.39-54. R. Rorty (1982), *Consequences of Pragmatism*, University of Minnesota Press.

10. Mao: China, The World and India

MIRA SINHA BHATTACHARJEA

INTRODUCTION

Premier Zhou Enlai, who dominated this sector of Chinese polity for close on half a century of time, has been widely credited with the crafting of what is called China's 'foreign policy'. However, the basic presumption of this paper is that for Mao Zedong, foreign policy was an integral part of a holistic strategy for what he called making revolution. Consequently during the Maoist era, 'foreign policy' was not distinguished from 'domestic policy', and the compulsions of state and national interests in 'foreign policy' were no less amenable to ideas and value change than were those in the arena of 'domestic policy'.

It is the burden of this exploration that the ideas and perceptions, the methods of analysis, the identification of objectives and the strategies for their realization that dominated the making and implementation of 'foreign policy' (or, what the Chinese call 'diplomatic work') were those of Mao. They were derived, as will be discussed below, from the understanding that Mao came to acquire of the *objective world* of China and of its domestic and external oppression. This understanding provided Mao with the answers he had been seeking to the three linked questions of *what* was meant by making revolution, *who* would make revolution, and *how* it was to be made. From the answers relating to making revolution in China, Mao was to draw large generalizations about the *what*, *who* and *how* of making revolution worldwide. Even more, the possibilities as well as the fate of the Chinese revolution were for Mao linked inseparably from those of the revolutionary forces in the world as a national part of a global whole. In Mao's holistic approach, the revolutionary prospects of the global whole exercised hegemony which, in varied and critical ways, determined the prospects for revolution within China and all other countries.

Consequently, no other leader in the post-war world has taken the interaction between states, the analysis of the global balance of power or the education of the masses and the training of diplomatic cadres with the same seriousness as did Mao. The corpus of Mao's writings is interspersed with periodic analyses of the present situation that Mao undertook in order to identify the state of the world revolution and the tasks and goals of the CCP in both its domestic and diplomatic work. A constant purpose of such analysis was to assess the alignment and distribution of global power. Each such assessment reaffirmed the Maoist conclusion that the global and national balance was heavily weighted in favour of the reactionary or imperialist forces. Mao was therefore constantly aware of the weakness or of what I have called the minority status of revolutionary forces within China and in the world.[1] He therefore made developments in the outer world, the *critical* determinant of the strategy and tactics, the methods and objectives of making revolution even within China.

Yet Mao did not abandon the possibility of or abdicate the domestic and national responsibility and initiative for 'making revolution'. What he did was to inspire a revolutionary optimism, born of a distinctive perception and a unique mode of analysis, and to innovate the strategy of the united front as a means of transforming present weakness into future strength. Such transformation was, for Mao, a process not an event. The present therefore acquired great significance. It was the womb and the guarantor of the desired future, as was the insightful identification of objective universal trends. Thus, as the situation in the outer world changed so did the Maoist style of leadership, his broad strategy and methods of work. The core of Mao's holistic approach, namely, anti-imperialism and the paired objective of making revolution, nevertheless, remained constant, as did his strategy of the united front. What changed was his personification of 'imperialism' identified as a particular state and determined by an alteration in its power and policy. Thus imperialism was first personified in Japan, then the US and in his last years, as the Soviet Union.

The above is by way of explaining the title of and the exploration behind this essay. It takes Mao and his perception of the objective world, and his delineation of strategy for making revolution as the founts of China's interstate behaviour and its 'diplomatic work'. Consequently it also takes as credible the Maoist concern with establishing new norms of state behaviour, namely, the Panchsheel, as well as the attempt to introduce these in the behaviour of the Chinese state.

The essay will analyse *eight* interventions made by Mao in response to developments in the outer world, that brought about a change of Maoist strategy and method. Three of these interventions took place prior to the founding of the PRC and five between 1949 and 1976. It will also, in keeping with the title, examine China's bilateral relations with India to argue that Nehru and India were given a pivotal rôle in the united front strategy throughout the Maoist era. Consequently, all bilateral Sino-Indian issues were demoted in significance and were not permitted, to upset the united front against US imperialism. The 1962 war, from this analytical perspective had large strategic and political purposes for Mao, precisely because of India's pivotal role in the united front. The confrontation with India, it will be argued, was intended to forestall a Soviet inspired fundamental change in the agenda of world policies from anti-imperialism to anti nuclear war, and the consequent realignment of world power would in Mao's perspective, be greatly detrimental both to the Chinese state and to 'making revolution'.

Though the intervention of 1962 was from Mao's perspective, largely successful, it was not however, decisive. It set Mao on the awesome task of substituting, in the world's eye, the USSR – the world's first socialist state – for the US as the contemporary personification of imperialism. To prepare China, the CCP and its leadership for battling the dangers posed by Soviet revisionism to 'making revolution', Mao launched the Cultural Revolution within China. In the mid 1970's he then offered a new paradigm of international policies, contained in the Three Worlds Thesis to explain the distribution of global power after the defection of the Soviet Union to imperialism, as well as the dynamics and trends in the contemporary world. Mao was too old and too feeble perhaps to lead China out of the chaos of the Cultural Revolution and to ensure that future leaders would follow his strategy for making revolution. His last intervention failed and brought to an end the Mao era of 'making revolution' together with its unique way of perceiving the interlocking relationships between China, the world and India.

Mao's Quest: Making Revolution

The central political question in China particularly after the May 4 Movement (1919) that had been sparked off by the infamous 21 Demands made by Japan was how to counter imperialism, save the nation from 'subjugation' and from any further erosion of its national sovereignty. 'Anti-imperialism' and 'anti-militarism' were thereafter enshrined in Sun Yatsen's Three Peoples Principles, in the constitution of the newly reorganized KMT, and in the first manifestos of the young Chinese Communist Party (CCP).[2] Nevertheless Mao Zedong, who helped found this party was still, as he later told Edgar Snow, confused and unclear about what "road" China was to take, even though he was he said "definitely, anti-militarist and anti-imperialist."[3] This uncertainty was evidently not dispelled even after he had accepted Marxism and joined the Communist Party committed to these goals. With hindsight the reasons for Mao's continuing uncertainty are not too difficult to identify.

For one, the 'anti-imperialism' that was written into the first and second manifestos of the CCP (1922) was in the context of China's times a mewling bloodless abstraction, which was given rather short shift.[4] In vulgar imitation of Soviet Russia the manifesto referred to anti-imperialism more as an ideological slogan than as a dominant and oppressive national reality. Czarist Russia, it may be recalled, was not a victim or object of imperialist aggression: It was itself imperialist. For the Bolsheviks, therefore 'anti-imperialism' was directed only somewhat vaguely against 'world imperialists' and more urgently against *Czarist* imperialist policies: At home in relation to non-Russian nationalities, and abroad to Czarist expansionism particularly in China. 'Anti-imperialism' as included in the CCP manifesto blindly followed this formulation. It conveyed little of the gravity of the imperialist onslaught that China had suffered since the Opium Wars. It resonated even less, with the contemporary and growing menace of enlarging Japanese aggression.

Moreover, for the Comintern and for all Marxists including the young CCP nationalism was suspect. It was regarded as the 'handmaiden' of the bourgeoisie, the dynamic only of the bourgeois democratic revolution. The leadership of the Chinese revolution which was democratic and national was consequently gratuitously entrusted to the KMT by the CCP. Thus, while it supported the 'bourgeois' revolution led by the KMT, the CCP in keeping with Comintern orthodoxy awaited the right historical moment when as the vanguard of the proletariat it would be called upon to conduct China's proletarian revolution. For almost 15 years thereafter, that is for as long as it held to this understanding of imperialism and of its own historical role the CCP was unable to register success or to discover that its awaited historical opportunity had or was about to arrive.[5] The CCP, needless to say, had no solutions or answers to the central political question in China for the simple reason that it did not pose the central question as a national not a class, question. Mao's confusion therefore persisted. Some decades later he was to describe his dilemma thus:

> When I joined the Communist Party, I knew that we must *make revolution*, but against what? And how were we to go about it? Of course we had to make revolution against imperialism and the old society. I did not quite understand what *sort of a thing imperialism was* still less did I understand how we could make revolution against it. None of the stuff I had learned in thirteen years was any good for making revolution. I used only the instrument-language.[6]

In those intervening years the revolution and the CCP failed in its repeated attempts at fomenting urban insurrections and suffered a major defeat at the hands of the KMT in 1927.[7]

Discovering the Kay

It was about that time that Mao began a long journey of investigation away from party and Comintern orthodoxy to seek answers to *what* 'making revolution' was all about, *who* would 'make revolution', and *how* it was to be made. In order to do so he moved from the realm of the 'idea' to that of China's objective situation that is to its contemporary social and political realities. This was to result in a unique Maoist understanding of the concrete substance of domestic and external aggression and of the strong linkages between them. His investigation into domestic oppression resulted in his discovery of peasant unrest and revolutionary ferment in Hunan in response to the multiple oppression of the peasantry. From the specific investigations he conducted in Hunan in 1927 Mao generalized an entire Chinese country-side awash with revolutionary potential. He concluded that without the peasantry and more specifically without the poor peasant there would be no revolution of the oppressed. As for external aggression Mao found evidence of it writ large across China. It pointed to Japanese imperialism as the aggressor at a time when the western imperialists seemed to be in retreat. It was through these twin 'discoveries' that Mao came, as he put it, "to understand the objective world of China". Working thereafter from inside out, from Chinese reality to the Marxist idea from CCP practice to CCP theory, Mao summarized the revolutionary experience of those 15 years, and gradually arrived at the "correct line", that is, at the strategy and tactics for 'making revolution'. The conclusions he drew from his discoveries of the *what*, *who* and *how* of 'making revolution' came to form the basis of his strategy of revolution and what has been called his sinification of Marxism.

In brief, Mao concluded that Japanese aggression posed the principal danger as well as a new threat to China in that Japan, unlike the western imperialists, was determined to control the *whole* of China and to transform it into a *colony* like India. Anti-imperialism for the CCP unlike for the CPSU could not therefore remain an abstract slogan: It codified the hegemonic reality of China. He therefore argued that this new danger had fundamentally transformed class relations within China, making resistance to Japanese *imperialism* a *national* not a *class* issue. The CCP's past experience of unsuccessful urban insurrection and his discovery of the revolutionary potential of the peasantry, led Mao to transfer the locale of the revolution from the cities to the country-side. But, in those early years, still with the objective of setting up *Soviets*.

The theoretical question that Mao faced thereafter was how to link together the two dominant features of China's 'objective world'. An oppressed therefore revolutionary peasantry, and a nationwide anti-Japanese struggle, and how to do so without denying the ideology he had espoused, that is while pursuing the goal of 'making revolution'. By relying on his perception of China's 'objective world' and by rejecting Soviet/Comintern/CCP orthodoxy, Mao was to stumble upon and so discover the 'key' to 'making revolution.

Maoist Strategy

The essential features of Mao's strategy are well known. They are: the controlled guidance of peasant revolution to direct it not only against 'feudal elements' and 'militarists' as the direct oppressors of the peasantry, but also against them as *natural allies* of Japanese imperialism; the call for a nation-wide struggle against Japanese aggression: the innovative strategy of the united front from above; the legitimation of Chiang Kai-shek and the KMT as leaders of the united front in the national war of resistance; the separate but simultaneous training and honing of the CCP and the Red Army in Yunan for later seizure of power from the KMT: and finally the establishment of an intimate; inseparable and critical linkage between the outside world (including imperialists) and the Chinese struggle and the call for building a parallel international united front against Japan (or fascism).

It was also at this time that Mao undertook a reconstruction of the concept of China as a "single multinational state" and of the Chinese nation as"a union of all nationalities" including the Han. No longer was the party to promise statehood and self determination to the various nationalities of China as it had done in the Ruijin Constitution of 1931. Instead Mao began to posit a larger unity, that of the people, which included all, regardless of ethnicity or social class, who supported the struggle against Japan. Mao's reconstructed China was presented as a country with a "rich revolutionary tradition", but which was "semicolonial and semifeudal" and for whom "*imperialism* was the most ruthless enemy."[8] Japanese imperialism was thus cast as the most important contemporary reality, a non-national external factor that threatened the entire Chinese people and the Chinese state. Accordingly, the principal goal of the Chinese Revolution was redefined as resistance to Japan and not the struggle against militarists and anti-democratic forces within China. Accordingly, the high ideological CCP objective of conducting a pure or orthodox proletarian revolution led by the working class to usher in socialism was also scaled down. The task of the CCP was also thereafter to resist Japan and complete the national and democratic revolution that had so far been entrusted to the KMT. Thus from about the mid 30's the CCP under Mao was no longer content to await conditions for a proletariat led revolution: It was to use the struggle against Japan to *create the conditions* for this eventuality to come about. In Mao's new strategy this called for direct CCP participation in the national struggle and the later leadership of the national democratic revolution, and its transmutation into a movement of national liberation. From about that time the enlarged meaning given to the term 'national liberation' and the revolutionary role assigned to it by Mao and the CCP were to differ from Soviet usage and practice. These differences were to persist and to be reflected in CCP strategy and policy, even after the PRC came into being.

The Inner and Outer Worlds of China

An essential feature of Maoist analysis from then on was the intimate, inseparable and critical relationship he posited between the *outer* world and the *inner* world of China. The boundaries of the Chinese nation as he had delineated them in 1939 enclosed the domestic of *inner* of China as they did for all other states. And together with the right to sovereignty they separated the inner from the outer of China in seemingly traditional ways. Influenced by Marxism, however, Mao superimposed on this conventional divide a structure of systemic unity between elements belonging to the traditional domestic and elements belonging to the traditional external. Thus, not Japan but Japanese *imperialism* was linked to domestic counter-revolutionary forces in an inseparable *class* pairing. This conjoining blurred the line separating the conventional domestic and external of China, as it did for all other states. It also altered their meaning and concept. For example, form the conventional perspective, all of Japan was the external enemy of all within China's domestic world. At the same time, however, Japanese imperialism had breached the traditional domestic to find a support base within China. This consisted of more than the traitors or collaborators that every war or revolution has known. They were in Maoist analysis social groups and classes, the seedlings of domestic imperialism within China – the comprador classes or elements. Together with Japanese *imperialism* they constituted for Mao a new non-conventional '*outer*' of China. As counterpoint the revolutionary '*inner*' comprised the revolutionary anti-imperialist forces within China that, in like manner, had systemic links with similar forces within the conventional domestic of Japan and of other imperialist countries. The balance of forces and the balance of power that existed in both the traditional and non-conventional meanings of the inner/outer world concept became thereafter the most *critical detriment* of the Maoist strategy for making revolution both at home and abroad.

Mao's holistic approach and mode of analysis acknowledged with stark realism that the revolutionary forces were in the minority in the world, as were the CCP and the revolutionary forces within China. Mao's awareness of being in the minority in both global and national terms appears to have dominated all his thinking and analysis thereafter. To counter this disadvantage Mao argued that weakness could be transformed into yet undiscovered advantages or strengths. Mao thus innovated the appropriate strategy and tactics for bringing about this dialectical transformation in the political and organizational form of the united fronts. Both the domestic and international united fronts had the same 'principal enemy' – Japan or imperialism or fascism. Thus, in the anti-Japanese war, revolutionary optimism meant perceiving the alliance opportunities, and the spaces for political action provided by China's *semi-colonial* status, in the outer world by carefully differentiating between the competing interests of the various imperialist powers and by aggregating the support of all countries and groups opposed to Japan or fascism and within the inner world of China by aggregating the strength of disparate social groups in joint resistance to Japanese aggression and by introducing hitherto peripheral group or people into the calculus of forces. In short, within the outer world, the Maoist strategy attempted to enlarge the space between Japan and all possible constituents of the international united front. In the inner world of China, he attempted to narrow the political space between the disparate, often mutually hostile, elements that were to be brought into the domestic united front. The 'single spark' thesis explained the possibility of victory in the Chinese anti-Japanese war together with support that would be provided by the international united front. Later, during the civil war, when both united fronts had broken down, Maoist calculations included intangibles like the inherent weakness of the KMT and the support of the people to anticipate the collapse of the KMT and the victory of the CCP.

The above is intended to convey the manner in which Maoist analysis was conducted, and to emphasize that for Mao, development in the outer world that altered the global balance of power and forces, were critical determinants of his strategy and policy. Consequently, international relations and foreign policy developments were followed and analysed with great seriousness by Mao himself and within the decision making, educational and information systems of Yanan. After the founding of the PRC, Maoist understanding of developments in the outer world, continued to influence the periodic identification of CCP objectives and the alteration of strategies for their realization. The Maoist approach, mode of analysis and strategy were replicated almost in its entirety in the PRC's dealings with the outer world, that is in its diplomatic work. It is in this sense, that a seamless continuum was created between China's inner and outer worlds. Thus, no sooner was the domestic united front brought about after the Xian incident, than the CCP established the International Propaganda Bureau (IPB) at Wuhan with Zhou Enlai in charge.[9] The task of the IPB was to create the parallel *international* united front envisaged by Mao of friends and sympathizers of the anti-Japanese resistance war. Simultaneously, the IPB was urged to devise an *alternate* CCP diplomacy to that of the KMT in consonance with the overarching cause of 'making revolution'. The personnel who worked with Zhou Enlai, the principles of analysis, of policy and diplomacy, that were then designed, as well as the modalities of implementation were, in their essentials, continued even after the formation of the PRC. It is in this sense that the PRC's 'foreign policy' pre-dates the PRC by some twelve years. It required only expansion, detail and adjustment after the People's Republic came into being.

From 1937, the united front strategy thus became the preferred strategy of the CCP for making revolution for the entire period in which revolutionary forces occupied a minority status in the global balance of power and forces. Its successful working however, as discussed above, relied on an insightful assessment of this balance in both the inner and outer world. This task Mao took upon himself. Thereafter, he was to intervene at critical junctures of time, to redefine or alter priorities and policies towards the outer world and to redefine the goals of the domestic revolution. Each such intervention was followed or accompanied by a shift in domestic policy. Each reflected Mao's awareness of CCP and socialism's minority status and the critical role of events in the outer world in changing the delicate balance of power and forces Three interventions made by Mao between 1945 and 1949 that resulted in an alteration of CCP strategy and policies, need to be analysed carefully. The first was in 1945; the second in 1946, and the third in 1949.

1945: Chiang as 'Enemy'; US as 'Imperialism'

It is part of the mythology of CCP revolutionary history that the Chinese national war of resistance, brought about the defeat of Japan in the inner world of China. This defeat was by any reckoning one of history's critical junctures. It resolved also the central political question that had faced China since the May 4 Movement. In brief the danger of China becoming a Japanese colony had been averted. Even more, China's role as a frontline state in the global anti-fascist war had finally brought about the end of the unequal treaty system and so ended China's century of humiliation. It is one of the ironies of history that China in its time of greatest weakness gained recognition as a great power. It was made a founding member of the United Nations, a permanent veto-wielding member of the Security Council. For many within China the defeat of Japan meant also a decisive victory of the national democratic revolution and the fulfillment of its broad objectives. A democratic government capable of ending the disunity that had bedeviled China since the fall of the Manchus, seemed in sight. Many could also have argued that the era of imperialism and the struggle for a reunited China had ended.

It was at this stage that Mao chose to intervene in a manner that was to have far reaching strategic consequences for the Chinese state and its polity This intervention took the form of declaring Chiang and the KMT to be the enemies of the *people*, and China's erstwhile ally the US, to be a reactionary imperialist power that supported the KMT against the CCP and the people.[10] There is some evidence to indicate that this view was not shared by many of the CCP's partners in the anti-Japanese united front, and even within the war weary CCP itself. Mao's intervention nevertheless influenced CCP strategy and was responsible for destroying both the united fronts that had been so assiduously built since 1937.

For Mao, however, this intervention provided the catalyst that transformed the anti-Japanese national struggle into a national liberation movement which, in turn, promised a transition to China's other destiny of socialism. It led inevitably to the KMT-CCP war and the seizure of power by the CCP. Like most of Mao's other interventions it was high risk policy. Mao's assessment defied all on-the surface estimates of the balance of power. His calculations relied heavily on his understanding of the inner class nature of the KMT and the US which rendered them incapable of decisive action and victory. It relied also on tapping the spirit of the times, the latent unarticulated desires of the people, and on visible demonstration of how the disciplined CCP and its soldiers were different. The intervention and the consequent assumption of power by the CCP qua socialist party, in turn, inspired a realignment of world forces more favourable to the world's revolutionary forces.

1946: Envisaging an Intermediate Zone

In an interview to Anna Louise Strong (not made public till 1958), Mao posited a three way division of the world that interposed a vast intermediate zone lying between the Soviet Union and the United States.[11] It reflected Mao's analytical method and arranged the world forces in three vertical bands. It therefore differed with Stalin's two bloc 'we' vs 'they' division of the world's forces, the rigidity of which left no political space for 'friends' in Soviet global strategy by discounting the dynamic of nationalism. Mao's intervention on the other hand enlarged and created political space between the newly independent countries and imperialism. In short Mao gave recognition to nationalism as the contemporary global dynamic of political changes, emphasized its anti-imperialist, pro-democracy character and created the possibilities for the implementation of his broad united front strategy. In the outer world, this enabled China to make common though limited cause with all anti-colonial national liberation struggles, as well as with newly independent states anxious to protect sovereignty. By doing so the ground was prepared for a global international united front so essential for Mao's strategy of making revolution. In the same interview, Mao also attempted to dispel fear of the nuclear weapon whose terror had been demonstrated in Nagasaki and Hiroshima. He revived revolutionary optimism by describing it, in strategic terms, as a 'paper tiger' that could be defied by a resolute peoples struggle. By undertaking and winning the civil war, the CCP was to demonstrate that this could indeed be done.

1949: Reaffirming Commitment to Socialism

Months before the PRC was formed, in an essay entitled 'On Peoples

Democratic Dictatorship' Mao reaffirmed the CCP's commitment to socialism and its membership of the socialist camp. By then, as will be recalled, the fragile wartime alliance between the US and the USSR had already broken down to be replaced by the Cold War. Once again Mao responded to critical change in the international arena in a manner consonant with his commitment to socialism. As earlier, this was accompanied by a change of pace and strategy at home. In anticipation of CCP victory in the civil war and its assumption of leadership of the nation and the Revolution, the CCP commitment to *New Democracy* innovated in 1940,[12] was upheld but in the significantly new form of a peoples democratic dictatorship. After victory, the CCP organization of state power would be such as to ensure that the CCP would effectively have the power and authority to undertake the gradual transition to socialism. The political agenda of its national and revolutionary strategy however was to uphold the promises of New Democratic politics and carry through the agrarian and social revolutions. The style and policies by which this was to be done, were to prepare the real political possibility of the evolution of New Democracy, over time, into socialism.[13] At the same time, the political agenda of New Democracy helped to create the prospects for constituting a new democratic and international united front for objectives consonant with the ideals of democracy, national sovereignty and peace.

From then on, because of the seizure of power by CCP, a marked symmetry was introduced between the stage and goals of the Chinese revolution, and those of other anti-colonial national liberation movements of international revolutionary forces and those of newly dependent states like India, all putative constituents of the international united front. In many ways, Maoist China assumed the role of an exemplar for other societies on how to carry national and liberation struggles beyond the anti-colonial goal of national independence towards socialism. But, as long as all these continued to be anti-colonial and anti-imperialism even though not led by communist parties, they were regarded by Mao as being revolutionary in nature. The international united front that CCP China encouraged after 1949 therefore had a single reference point at its core –anti-imperialism. But, and this is important, the leadership and example of appropriate united front politics for progressive nationalists was left to others to provide. For instance, from 1954, it was left to Nehru and Nehru's India, just as it had been left to Chiang and the KMT during the national war of resistance to Japan.

The cumulative effect of these three decisions was profound. The first brought the CCP to power and heightened the ideological divide in international politics. It unified China under a strong and purposeful government for the first time in a 100 years. The second, though not known at the time, challenged the ideological leadership of Stalin and contained the seeds of the Sino-Soviet schism of the 1960's. Also, as mentioned above it gave socialist legitimacy to nationalism and helped create the political space for assertive action by the weak new states. It introduced the numbers game into international politics and brought peripheral groups into the calculus of power. By doing so, it established the context for the pursuance of the united front strategy. The third transformed the traditional US-China relationship into one of confrontation and in doing so placed anti-US imperialism at the heart of the international political agenda.[14] By doing so it altered the alignment of world power, strengthened both the revolutionary and anti-colonial nationalist forces in the world and shifted the focus of cold war rivalry to the east.

All three decisions, as should be apparent created a natural and special role for Nehru and India in the Maoist scheme of things. The legitimation and recognition of the force of nationalism appealed to Nehru who had long sympathized with China's fate. Nehru was moreover eager to witness the emergence of India and China as well as the colonized world into proud independence where they would no longer be 'the playthings of the west'. It was also part of the Nehrurian vision of the future that these countries, having suffered aggression and colonization, would strive jointly to introduce a new moral pattern of interstate behaviour. The intermediate zone of Mao's conception could, from Nehru's perspective help to confirm his rival concept of a nonaligned grouping of countries following a third path in world politics. In the Nehrurian vision as it unfolded, China occupied the same pivotal role as was assigned to India in Maoist strategy.

After 1949: The PRC, The World and India

From 1949 until his death in 1976, except for a brief period after 1957 Mao extended this holistic approach and analytical method to the international arena to arrive at broadly the same strategy and tactics of the united front that he had adopted both during the anti-Japanese war and the later civil war. During this period, Mao intervened on at least five occasions to ensure the continuance of his strategy of making revolution. Each intervention came in response to developments in the outer world but impacted on domestic policy. Each intervention acknowledged that the balance of forces globally and nationally continued to be unfavourable. Nevertheless, the course of making revolution could be pursued with cautious optimism if appropriate strategy was devised to take advantage of favourable trends. Thus, with each intervention Mao attempted to create conditions for the constitution of a new united front by redefining its central idea, namely, anti-imperialism. At the time of his last intervention this redefinition, that cast the world's first socialist state as the number one imperialism more dangerous even than the United States was so startlingly unorthodox as to find few sympathizers. Whether his attempt in the mid 1970's to create a new international (and domestic) united front, against Soviet imperialism, would have succeeded or not, will remain one of history's unanswered questions. Mao was too ill and too old' to provide the continuing leadership to do so. His death in 1976 opened the domestic flood gates for an almost complete denial of his holistic approach, his mode of analysis and his broad strategy for 'making revolution' by the new leadership.

Mao's Five Interventions

1950: Establishing the US as Imperialism

China's decision to enter the Korean War and to confront the powerful Unites States despite weakness and the tasks of reconstructing a wartorn economy and society is attributed to Mao.[15] It derived form his analysis of US policy towards revolution and China following US action in Korea and the June decision to recognize Chiang, protect Taiwan and isolate China, Mao concluded that the US had reached a *strategic* decision to oppose the Chinese Revolution and overthrow the CCP government. He envisaged a US threat and possible attack against China from vulnerable points along China's periphery: Taiwan, Korea, Indochina and even from far away Tibet. In response to this perceived multiple threat, China, almost simultaneously, took the following actions: It despatched volunteers and advisers to North Vietnam: sent 'Volunteers' to North Korea: claimed sovereign right to Taiwan and charged the US with the occupation of its territory of Taiwan. The cumulative effect of those actions was to confirm ideological and strategic confrontation with the US and to cast the US as the principal threat to China, nationalism and socialism.

These actions and responses, however, weakened the immediate possibility of building a new international united front. China's willingness to wage war and use force to achieve its national goals, had dismayed many of its would be supporters. China, had moreover, antagonized India deeply by its action in Tibet which made China for the first time in history a strong neighbour and a potential threat to India's territorial integrity and security. Full Sino-Indian normalization was consequently delayed as was the process of constituting an international united front with India as China's most significant partner. The 1950 decision was a high risk strategy that confirmed China's minority status in the international community; its diplomatic isolation; as well as its greater dependence on a reluctant Soviet ally. It also risked triggering off a third world war and China's defeat.

1951 Limiting the Damage; Preplanning the Ground for a United Front

One year later, Mao intervened personally to set in process a policy of damage limitation targeted at India and the colonized world. It was designed to contain and limit the fall out of the Tibetan events on Nehru and India to revive the possibility of future political cooperation between the two countries.

In a most unusual and highly symbolic gesture. Mao attended the national day celebrations at the Indian Embassy in Beijng in 1951. His speech called for unity with India in 'working for peace'.[16] This gesture gave public sanction and legitimacy to Beijing's desire for a special relationship with India in the common cause of 'working for peace'.

As part of its policy of damage limitation, China proceeded to handle sensitive issues in the bilateral relationship in a manner that would not be immediately provocative to India. For example, Beijing did not protest independent India's exercise of erstwhile British rights in Tibet. Nor did it end them unilaterally as it had done in the case of the rights that had been exercised by the imperialist powers in China. Taken together the Mao gesture as well as the sensitive handling of delicate bilateral issues helped to assuage Indian fears of China. Indeed it was shrewd Maoist understanding of Nehru's personality and politics and of his dominant role in the making of third world public opinion and Indian national policy, that enabled the policy to succeed. Its success, in turn revived the possibility of united action for shared purpose by Mao's China and Nehru's India in the international arena. As Maoist strategy unfolded, India was cast once more in a pivotal role: as the champion on nationalism and anti-colonialism and as the natural leader of the newly independent countries. This was a variant of the role that had been assigned to Nehru as leader of the Indian national movement by the IPB in the international united front of 1937. The success of the policy of damage limitation (that encompassed also the armistice in Korea and the Geneva spirit), led swiftly to the Zhou visit to India in 1954: to the India-China agreement on Tibet; and to the Panchsheela as new universal norms of state behaviour. The momentum was maintained with Nehru's 'Roman triumph' visit to China later that same year. Within a few months, it led to Bandung and the emergence of an Asian-African grouping that included a CCP China willing to leave future initiative and leadership to India and Nehru.

Bandung demonstrated how successfully the PRC had overcome the grave risks that attended Mao's 1950 decision to enter the Korean war. In fact, it did more. It brought into being the intermediate zone that Mao had envisaged in 1946 as an essential requirement for the pursuance of the united front strategy. Friendship and common cause with India and the newly independent countries of Asia, moreover, helped to project a PRC identity distinct from that of the Soviet Union despite ideological fraternity and treaty partnership.The PRC's new image was that of an Asian country struggling to develop and modernize its economy and society and safeguard its sovereignty as were all the newly independent countries, particularly India.

1957: Combatting Revisionism to Tilt the Revolutionary Balance

Mao's third intervention in this year, came in response again to two developments in China's outer world, this time within the Soviet Union. One was Khrushchev's alteration of revolutionary strategy pronounced in 1956. The other was the Soviet advance in space and missile technology which he saw as narrowing, if not bridging, the *strategic* gap that existed between the USSR and the US.

The first event initiated a Chinese sponsored discussion within the socialist community on the dangers of 'revisionism'. The second prompted him to declare in Moscow, that the balance of power and forces was so delicately poised that it could be made to tilt in favour of global revolutionary forces to end their minority status. The East Wind, he said now prevails over the West Wind. In short, Mao was arguing the possibility of a strategic shift from the defensive to a seizure of the initiative. For Mao the two events were interrelated. The strategic shift demanded a recognition that 'revisionism' which he saw to be inherent in Khrushchev's 1956 strategy of peaceful coexistence was enfeebling, and would be unable to seize the historical opportunity.

The Maoist intervention of 1957 was not episodic. It continued over many years in which the central issue of debate was revisionism. Its episodic failure of 1957 resulted in grave ideological and political cleavage between China and the Soviet Union, and dominated Maoist thinking and strategy thereafter.[17] As earlier, Mao initiated new policies within China that divided the CCP leadership and led inexorably to the Cultural Revolution and to the ensuing power struggle. It was accompanied in China's diplomatic work by the temporary abandonment of the united front strategy. In its place, China supported socialist forces everywhere. It tested the outside limits of US and USSR strategic and ideological responses to this initiative during the Quemoy crisis of 1958. India's friendship and Nehru's commitment to progressive policies were similarly under test over the India-China boundary issue.

1962: Not Territorial Concerns but Strategic Considerations

The border war with India of that year developed ostensibly out of rival nationalisms and conflicting territorial claims. But, if analysed in the context described above, it was a major strategic decision designed to alter the Khrushchevian/Nehruvian agenda of world politics.

This new agenda took detente and prevention of nuclear war instead of opposition to imperialism, as the central concern of international politics. Its acceptance by the countries of the third world – Mao's intermediate zone –

would alter the balance of world forces in favour of a revisionist Soviet Union and, therefore, in the Maoist view, of imperialism. In this still transitional phase, India's role acquired signal importance precisely because of its leadership of the third world and the pivotal role it had been given in Mao's united front strategy.

The new agenda was seductively attractive for many in the nonaligned world and particularly for Nehru who had long espoused these concerns. Thus a strong almost ideological commonality came into being between Khrushchev's USSR and Nehru's India. It was to be reflected in Nehru's welcome of superpower detente and of the test ban treaty. Thus form 1959 there was growing convergence in Indian and Soviet strategic perceptions of China – which opposed both – and its role in the world. Soviet reluctance to support its fraternal neighbour in its territorial dispute with India was a manifestation of this convergence. The realignment of forces that it would bring into being would not in Maoist analysis, be favourable to China and to making revolution.

China's hardline policies and its 'testing' of the responses to its initiatives by the leaders, as it were of all three zones of Mao's framework, i.e. of the Soviet Union the US and India was thus an attempt to deny legitimacy and centrality to the new Soviet agenda. By simultaneously fanning tensions between them Mao was attempting to create political space and greater manoeuvreability for Chinese diplomatic, state, and revolutionary action.[18] The failure of the Zhou visit to India of 1960, shadowed the prospects of arriving at a peaceful settlement with India. For the next two years however, China continued to adopt a dual track policy: It pressed for negotiations or for an agreement to respect the line of actual control and non-disturbance of the status quo. Simultaneously it strengthened and advanced its position on the ground as India was also doing.

The Chinese decision to use force in 1962 was once again a calculated high risk policy Like the decision to enter the Korean War, it revealed China's minority status and possible isolation in world affairs. As in 1950, it also destroyed all possibility of Indian participation in any future united front in partnership with China; 1962 furthermore compounded China's security concerns for it had in effect created three live fronts. The decision to use force was, it must be presumed, not taken lightly. Its importance for Mao's strategy of 'making revolution' as also for the Chinese state, may be gauged from the fact that it was taken at a time of severe economic and leadership crisis in China. China's military and diplomatic success despite these highly adverse factors can be attributed, once again to a shrewd understanding of Nehru's personality and India's lack of military preparedness, and to a remarkable capacity for innovation.

China's military strategy of conducting a controlled war, limited in time and depth across the length of the entire border, tookNehru, India, and perhaps the world by surprise. It resulted in a humiliating defeat for India: and the exposure of its inability to provide for national defence even against a third world country. Diplomatically it revealed that India did not command the support of third world countries.

This intervention was accompanied once again by a policy of damage limitation. This time unlike in 1951 its success relied on demonstrating China's ability to take independent decisions and actions (unlike, by comparison, India): as well as on the display and acquisition of sufficient capability for national defence. It also aimed, in essence, at establishing China as an independent power centre. The military success of 1962 was followed swiftly by the first atomic test in 1964 and by the more intangible assertion of national will by the Chinese in their millions, to defend their country. Like the resort to force in 1962, these were presented to the world as defensive measures forced on the Chinese state.

The war itself had been preceded by a diplomatic initiative that resulted in the conclusion of a series of border agreements with neighbouring countries most of them also India's neighbours. These agreements suggested that China's bark was worse than its bite, that China's *real* territorial demands were reasonable and limited. It was followed by a statement of China's territorial policy and negotiating strategy vis-a-vis India which remained unchanged despite its military victory. By not enlarging the war, and by refraining from occupying Indian and disputed territory into which it had advanced in the eastern sector, China gave credibility to its intention of limiting the political damage and keeping the door open for a return to the negotiating table. The Maoist policy of damage limitation was as earlier, targeted primarily at India to prevent 1962 from making China the national and strategic enemy of India. Eight years later in 1970 as in 1951, Mao was to personally and publicly articulate China's desire to end the past and forge a new constructive relationship with India. This time however, this gesture was made as China moved towards normalizing its relations with the US and as Mao prepared to identify the Soviet Union as the principal imperialist power. Once again Mao cast India as an important though no longer the pivotal player in a putative united front, directed more against Soviet imperialism. At that time in Maoist calculations *the* pivotal player in a realignment of world power to counter the Soviet Union was the United States.

From 1962 for the rest of the Maoist era, the policy of damage limitation in relation to India was in effect a holding operation. Its underpinning was an undisturbed line of control along the India-China boundary, an unchanged policy position on the territorial issue, and skilful management of its new status as a nuclear weapons power. China relied on the passage of time for the Indian wounds of 1962 to heal, for greater exposure of the Soviet Union's expansionist and interventionist tendencies as well as for the resurgence of an Indian search for an independent and sovereign role in world affairs. This policy began to pay dividends a long fourteen years after the disastrous war of 1962. In 1976, the year of Mao's death (and after India's first nuclear 'implosion') the two countries raised their diplomatic representation to ambassadorial level. The Indian ambassador the first to be withdrawn was thus the first to resume his mission.

The process of opposing 'revisionism' and the new international agenda proposed by the Soviet Union that was initiated by Mao in 1957 was thus advanced further in 1962. It was to culminate in his next major intervention in 1964, accompanied by a profound change in domestic politics, namely, the Cultural Revolution. The objective of which was to weed out 'revisionists' from the leadership of the CCP and keep China on the path of making revolution; provide an alternative to Soviet revolutionary strategy for revolutionary forces everywhere.

1964: Spelling out the Maoist Alternative

The Maoist intervention of 1964 came once again in response to development in the socialist world. It followed what he was to call the systemization of revisionism at the 22nd Party Congress of the CPSU into a general strategy for all socialist countries and parties. In proposing an alternate strategy for the international communist movement and not just for China, Mao challenged not only Soviet strategy for opposing imperialism but also its leadership of the socialist world.

This is too complex an era to encompass in a brief paragraph. Suffice it to say that this was as momentous a decision as was the decision of 1946 to embark on civil war with a KMT supported and equipped by a nuclear United States and that of 1962 to take on confrontation with India. In both instances, the odds were stacked against Mao and China. If 1962 destroyed the international united front, 1964 split the socialist bloc and communist parties everywhere. In doing so, it marked the end of a pattern of international politics that had existed since 1945. Consequently, it initiated a process of realignment and readjustment of world forces that was to influence the collapse of the Soviet Union and socialism and to plunge global (and nationalist) revolutionary forces into disarray.

The Mao challenge was accompanied within China by the destruction of the organized party and the desperate attempt to reconstruct the ideology, organization and leadership of the CCP on Maoist lines. From this analytical perspective, the Cultural Revolution was unleashed to simultaneously train and hone party cadres as well as an entire people, in ideological politics; to train successors in the Maoist art of 'making revolution'; to finally destroy the 'burial puppets' of imperialism and revisionism within China; and to so gain at last *majority* support for CCP strategy and programmes for making revolution, within the party and the people.

In the mid 70's, Maoist China began to resume interaction with the international community after the Cultural Revolution years of Maoist concern with politics in the inner world. By then China was no longer an international outcast: The PRC had finally occupied the China seat in the UN, received US President

Nixon in Beijing; and exchanged diplomatic recognition with those countries that had refused to do so in 1949-50. It was recognized widely as an independent centre of power and, despite the chaos of the Cultural Revolution, as the fount of revolutionary politics.

Accordingly, Mao prepared to revert to his holistic approach, analytical method and strategy of making revolution to the PRC's interaction with the outer world. As was his style, Mao offered a fresh assessment of the global balance of power and forces and of the dominant or universal trends in world politics. Having firmly placed the Soviet Union in the imperialist camp, it is not surprising that he found the balance to be grossly disadvantageous to the revolutionary cause, and to the Chinese state. In his perception however the world of states could still be divided three ways but not, as earlier, into three broad horizontal zones of countries distinguished by their ideological proclivities. Mao's new paradigm was triangular seemingly similar to the hierarchical ranking of states in terms of power that was traditional. It differed, however, in that it clubbed countries together to create new unities, of three worlds, distinguished by the degree of combined economic and political power each commanded. Significantly Japan was not placed in the first world as an economic superpower. But, largely because it lacked independent military capability, it was placed in the second world of developed countries.

At the apex of Mao's paradigm were the two superpowers, constituting the first world. The second world was that of the middle ranking developed countries that now approximated the intermediate zone of Mao's conception. The developing countries together formed the third world. The Maoist paradigm rested on the assumption that the era of anti-colonialism had ended with the emergence into nationhood of the colonized territories. The dominant trend as he identified it was the search for economic and technological development by all *states* whether capitalist or socialist. The universal dynamic however was still identified as being nationalism.[19] Thus, in Mao's perception, the international arena continued to be marked by inter-state struggle that could be moulded into an inter-world struggle which, in turn, created fresh possibilities of erecting a united front against imperialism, now aspected as hegemonism. The possibility flowed from two fault lines that Mao perceived within the international system. One created by the resistance of second and third world states to the exercise of hegemony by either or both of the superpowers. The other by the spontaneous and natural rivalry that he saw as existing between the two superpowers and their friends and allies. Both fault lines also created large fields of possible unity among states on the other side of the line. Thus a united front against 'hegemony' directed against one or both superpowers, at any given time, became plausible. The differentiation between the three worlds based as it was on economic and political power, reduced the third world to playing the role of the poor peasant, oppressed by the rich, the developed and the powerful. Consequently, the countries of the third world and India in particular continued to have a revolutionary but no longer a pivotal role to play in bringing about an alteration in the world balance. That role was now assigned to countries of the second world and particularly to Japan. China on its part stood alone and apart *with* the third world but not of it. A lone socialist country ploughing a lonely furrow as exemplar. The world as perceived by Mao in the mid 70's was a far more complex world than that of two decades earlier. It was spontaneously less revolutionary, more likely to succumb to the sugar coated bullets of the superpowers and to the goals and fears of conventional nation states.

Consequently, when Mao's three worlds thesis was boldly pronounced at the UNGA in 1974, it was accompanied by a long list of what the Chinese state – as exemplar of a revolutionary state – would or would not do in its international behaviour. Ironically, this pronouncement was made by Deng Xiaoping, recalled for this purpose from political exile when illness struck down both Mao and Zhou Enlai. Four years later, after Mao's death in 1976 and a succession of power struggles during which he again fell from power, Deng Xiaoping emerged as China's strong man and leader. As he consolidated his power Deng, once the second most important target of Mao's Cultural Revolution, put forward a long term strategy of modernization. He advocated integration with the world economy and the opening of China to foreign investment. Five years after Mao's death, the Cultural Revolution was severely condemned for having obstructed and delayed China's economic and technological development and for the cleavages it had introduced into both its inner and outer worlds. Soon thereafter, the three worlds thesis was given an unceremonious burial together with the approach and the method of analysis for making revolution unique to Mao. In the outer as in the inner world of China the Mao era had ended. With it had ended the era of anti-imperialism of the united front strategy and of purposive amity with India.

NOTES

1. See *Selected Works of Mao Tse-tung*, Vol.I (Peking: Foreign Languages Press, 1967), p.162.
2. See Comrad Brandt, Benjamin I. Sehwartz and John K. Fairbank., *A Documentary History of Chinese Communism* (Cambridge, Massachussets: Harvard University Press, 1959), pp.54-63.
3. Edgar Snow, *Red Star Over China* (London: Victor Gollancz Ltd.,1942), p.146.
4. See Brandt, Schwartz and Fairbank op.cit., pp.54-65.
5. See *Central Committee of the Chinese Communist Party: A Proposal Conceming the General Line of the Intemational Communist Movement* (June, 1963), (Peking: Foreign Languages Press, 1963), pp.1-61.

6. "Talk on Questions of Philosophy" with Kang Sheng and Chen Boda, 18 August 1964, in Stuart Schram (ed.), *Mao Tse-tung Unrehearsed* (Harmondsworth: Penguin Books, 1969), p.230.
7. "The Chinese Communist Party and China's Revolutionary War", *Selected Works*, Vol.I, op.cit., p.192.
8. "The Chinese Revolution and the Chinese Communist Party December 1939", *Selected Works of Mao Tse-tung*, Vol.II (Peking: Foreign Languages Press 1965), pp.305-331.
9. Ronald C. Keith, *The Diplomacy of Zhou Enlai* (London: Macmillan, 1989), pp.22-23.
10. See "The Situation and Our Policy After the Victory in the War of Resistance against Japan August 13. 1945", *Selected Works*, Vol.IV, (Peking: Foreign Languages Press, 1969), pp.20-21.
11. "Talk with the American Correspondent Anna Louise Strong August 19-16". Ibid., pp.99-100.
12. "On New Democracy", *Selected Works*, Vol.II, op.cit., pp.339-382.
13. "On the People's Democratic Dictatorship June 30, 1919", *Selected Works*, Vol.IV, op.cit., pp.411-23.
14. "Farewell, Leighton Stuart August 18, 1919", *Selected Works*, Vol.IV. pp.133-39.
15. *Diplomacy of Contemporary China* (Hong Kong: New Horizon Press, 1990), p.49.
16. Ibid., p.213.
17. Stanley Karnow, *Mao and China – From Revolution to Revolution* (New York: Macmillan, 1972), pp.92-109.
18. See Mira Sinha, "India China Confrontation – Re-Interpretation", *China Report*, Vol.VI (3), (May-June 1970), pp.1-15.
19. The Three Worlds Thesis was propounded in a speech to the General Assembly of the UN by Deng Xiaoping, leader of the Chinese Delegation, on 10 April 1974. For my analysis of this thesis see Mira Sinha. "Strategic Rediscovery of the Third World", *China Report*, Vol.X(3) (May-June 1974). pp.44-45.

11. Mao in Shaping China's International Personality

ABU NASAR SAIED AHMED

. . . Remember still
How, venturing midstream, we struck the waters
And waves stayed the speeding boats?

Changsha – *Mao Zedong*[1]

An adventurist as he was, Mao Zedong had infinite capacity to take recourse to calculated risk in deciding most of the major steps in his political life – viz. joining the communist party and then leading a mass revolution to a spectacular victory in establishing the People's Republic, cooperating with his arch rival Chiang Kai-shek in order to defeat the Japanese, making alliance with the Soviet Union and then confronting with it even militarily, challenging the United States ideologically and militarily more than once at the risk of nuclear retaliation by the most powerful state in the world and then forging a rapprochement with it. Although he was the prime mover of China's foreign policy, he was publicly less known as a foreign policy-maker till his death in 1976, as Zhou Enlai used to represent China in international affairs.[2] Mao usually refrained from public utterances except for a few instances of extending formal greetings or goodwill messages till the beginning of the cultural revolution. Yet, he played a decisive role in shaping China's international personality and in doing so he demonstrated a fascinating capacity to take grave risk on a number of occasions. It is well-known that China's domestic compulsions and ideological foundation had a role to play in Mao's policy moves.[3] At the same time it cannot be mistaken to brand him as a dogmatic nationalist, unaware of international commitments and obligations of a potentially important power. Almost a decade earlier than the proclamation of the People's Republic of China, Mao answered to his own question: "Can a

Communist, who is an internationalist, at the same time be a patriot?" by saying "Chinese Communists therefore combine patriotism with internationalism. We are at once internationalists and patriots".[4] What he dreamt long before 1949 to see China as a "prosperous and powerful"[5] became his primary goal in life, and therefore, he combined his nationalist objectives and ideological commitment with international obligations of an emergent power.

A patriot like Mao, a visionary leader, a warrior and a strategist, aspired to see his country powerful and prosperous occupying an important place in the community of nations. Like Napoleon, distant observers like Marx and Engels regarded China as a unique country among early non-western civilizations, potential as a revolutionary force.[6] Lenin too saw nationalism in China as a future ally against imperialism.[7] As a leader who had deep understanding of the history, the tradition and the people, Mao was aware of Chinese weaknesses as an underdeveloping country and also of its reserved strength with massive land, natural and human resources, and therefore, was conscious of its future role in international relations. At the dawn of the proclamation of the People's Republic of China, Mao and his associates had already acquired the rewarding historical experiences of national awakening of their people and were aware of the collapse of the traditional order and emergence of a revolutionary force having decisive role to play at least in the context of the third world.[8] Being reminded of frequent and devastating interventions in China by outsiders in past, Mao was definitely guided by a serious motivation to cleanse China from all imperialist vestiges and to secure a permanent and foolproof defence against future occurances of such interventions by accelerating its economic and industrial development along with building up a massive and modern military force. It is difficult to understand how could he convincingly argue that China's under development in all respects was an advantage like "a blank sheet of paper" on which the best poem could be written. He was confident that his country "shall be able to overtake other countries" in a few decades, even the United States after several decades. In September 1955 he said:

> It will probably in about fifty to seventy years, or roughly between the 10th and the 15th Five Year Plans, that we shall succeed in our efforts to catch up or overtake the United States.[9]

Three months later he again said:

> Our population is large and our position is favourable. . . *Chinese peasants are even better than the workers of Britain and America.* Hence, they can achieve greater, better and faster results in reaching socialism. We should not always compare ourselves with the Soviet Union. By being able to produce 24 million tons of steel after three Five Year Plans, *we will be faster*

than the Soviet Union.[10]

His prophetic statements are found to be valid in view of the break up of the Soviet Union and the recent economic prosperity of China though not on the line of classical Marxian economy.[11] Mao's statements were based on correct assessment of international situation of that time and on his sound vision of the future of his country. Long before in the period of 1944-47 when many of the Western journalists including American Foreign Service officials, who had met him, were highly impressed by his thorough grasp of international affairs, as recorded by Edgar Snow.[12] With such astounding grasp he wrote on 30 June 1949 his celebrated essay "On the People's Democratic Dictatorship" in which he set down the guidelines for the structure and policies of New China. He argued that China's history and experiences taught that "all Chinese without exception must lean either to the side of imperialism or the side of socialism. Sitting on the fence will not do, nor is there a third road." He defined China's international personality in the following manner:

> Externally, unite in a common struggle with those nations of the world which treat us as equals and unite with peoples of all countries. That is ally ourselves with the Soviet Union, with the People's Democracies and with the proletariat and the broad masses of the people in all other countries, and form an international united front.[13]

At the formative phase of the Peoples Republic of China, Mao had two preoccupations. His country suffered gravely from outside interventions and imperialism, and now time had come to fight against these and to ensure the security of his country against any possible outside interventions.[14] Simultaneously, if foreign policy was to serve national interests, he was to mould it to give China a distinct international personality and status, which did not carry the reflected glory of any great power.

The ideas and experience of a considerably long and arduous revolution under the leadership of Mao Zedong laid a definite and decisive impact not only in the internal situation of his country but also on the theory and the conduct of China's external affairs.[15] The pre-1949 China was the source of explaining its dealings in international relations. Consequently, Mao's concept of war and peace, his assessment of power, weaknesses and strength of his country and also of the hostile countries, his perception of imperialism and ideological positions of the major powers, and also the revolutionary situation in the world governed Chinese foreign policy till his death in 1976. Although the Communist Party of China in the pre-1949 era paid great importance to collective leadership and democratic centralism, in the post-1958 period a tendency of personality cult grew in China which eventually thrust upon Mao a kind of mystifying single leader's authority, an unassailable position from which he could play the historic role as a peasant organizer, military strategist, ideological spokesman and ruling statesman, The charisma of an undisputed leader superseded the impersonal organization, and it encompassed every aspect of the nation-building process in China including foreign policy making.[16] It is true that Mao was ambivalent on the issue of his continuation as the leader of the party on a number of occasions, and even prepared to give up his ceremonial position of the chief of the state in April 1959 in favour of Lui Shaoqi.[17] Maoism, however, withstood and outlived Mao's transitional desire to retire. The enigma of Mao's preponderant position is the result of the Chinese long struggle against imperialism and consequences of the dissolution of the comintern, an action that gave Mao an opportunity to consolidate fully his leadership in the party and act independently in matters of external affairs. The lengthy resolution of the Seventh plenum of the Communist party of China's Sixth Congress of 20 April 1949 gave Mao the historic authority to act as the undisputed leader of the party,[18] and definitely a free hand in dealing with both internal and external affairs of his country. Undoubtedly, Mao enjoyed this position almost unquestionably till his death.

II

As stated already that the relentless struggle against outside interventions in China was one of the main preoccupations of Chinese leadership headed by Mao Zedong. In this context, he gave credence to prudence over principles when he collaborated with Chiang Kai-shek against Japan,[19] taking the grave risk of being overwhelmed at the end of the war by greater human and material resources of his principal political opponent. It was a calculated move to master his support base and also to come in touch with the West.[20] President Truman's decision not to take recourse to military intervention "to influence the course of China's internal strife"[21] in favour of Chiang Kai-shek and the meeting between Mao and General George C. Marshall in Yenan bore significant prospects of meaningful dialogue between the Chinese communists and the United States.[22] But the US assistance amounting to $2.8 billion in the period of 1945 to 1949 to the incompetent and corrupt Government of Chiang pushed Mao and his party to the Soviet fold.

Mao's decision to cultivate friendship with the Soviet Union under Stalin was also a calculated risk. It was definitely a well-planned strategy to lean to the Soviet side despite the fact that Mao had deep-rooted distrust in Stalin. There are historic reasons for Mao's ambivalent position in praising and criticizing the Soviet leader.[23] He was aware of Stalin's desire to see latter's confident Wang Ming to take the leadership of the party from Mao.[24] There was bitterness between the Chinese and the Soviet side on Manchuria. In 1946, in full connivance of Kremlin leadership, the Soviet dominated People's Republic of

Mongolia conspired to slice off Inner Mongolia from China, the move was frustrated by Mao's forces.[25] Even the US policy-makers, who were unprepared to view China independently of Moscow, privately expressed the hope that conflict would arise between Mao and Stalin.[26] Mao later on recalled his bitter experience with Stalin in his speech on 25 April 1956:

> At the time of the War of Liberation Stalin first enjoined us not to press with revolution, maintaining that if civil war flared up, the Chinese nation would run the risk of destroying itself. Then when the fighting did erupt, he took us half seriously, half sceptically. When we won the war, Stalin suspected that ours was a victory of the Tito type, and in 1949 and 1950 the pressure on us was very strong indeed.[27]

On 18 March 1958 he spoke on this matter again:

> In 1950 I argued with Stalin in Moscow for two months. On the questions of the Treaty of Mutual Assistance, the Chinese Eastern Railway, the joint-stock companies and the border we adopted two attitudes: one was to argue when the other side made proposals we did not argue with, and the other side was to accept their proposal if they absolutely insisted. This was out of consideration for the interest of socialism.[28]

Mao and his associate Liu Shaoqi, knowing it fully the unsympathetic attitude of Stalin, took the risk of leaning to the Soviet side in order to reassure the countrymen against outside intervention, particularly by the United States, at the same time convince the Sovict leader that China would remain as an important part of the anti-American camp. Left almost isolated in 1949, Mao's China had no option but to cement its special relations with Moscow by concluding Sino-Soviet Treaty of Mutual Assistance in February 1950. In his important essay entitled "On the People's Democratic Dictatorship" he dismissed the possibility of accepting aids from the West and confirmed his party's affiliation with the Socialist camp. With the emergence of new China in 1949, Mao needed desperately economic assistance from a major power, and the Soviet Union was the only country which was willing to offer substantial aid, besides providing a protective shield to China against any possible attack from the United States, Mao's eight week visit to the Soviet Union from 16 December 1949 produced the most natable result: Article 1 of the Treaty of Alliance and Mutual Assistance signed on 14 February 1950 which deterred the possibility of US military action against China at least on two occasions – one during the Korean War and the other in August 1958 when China launched long-range artillery shelling on Quemoy and Matsu. The treaty, however, was the result of hard bargaining and struggle, as Mao recorded once again at the Tenth Plenum of the Eighth Central Committee on 24 September 1962. It will be relevant to quote a long passage of his statement:

> They did not permit China to make revolution: that was in 1945. Stalin wanted to prevent China from making revolution, saying that we should not have a civil war and should cooperate with Chiang Kai-shek otherwise the Chinese nation would perish. But we did not do what he said. The revolution was victorious. After the victory of the revolution he next suspected China of being a Yugoslavia, and that I would be a second Tito. Later when I went to Moscow to sign the Sino-Soviet Treaty of Alliance and Mutual Assistance, we had to go through another struggle. He was not willing to sign a treaty. After two months of negotiations he at last signed. When did Stalin begin to have confidence in us? It was at the time of the Resist America, Aid Korea campaign from winter of 1950. He then came to believe that we were not Tito, not Yugoslavia.[29]

Nevertheless, the treaty paved the way for the massive Soviet aid to China amounting $300 million over five years, of course, at the cost of granting the Soviet Union a special sphere of influence in Sinkiang and Manchuria. The treaty and the two subsequent agreements signed on 27 March and 19 April 1950 boosted Chinese economy and industrialization.[30] Mao was aware of the benefit that China derived out of his policy of leaning to the Soviet side, and therefore, was liberal in paying tribute to Stalin in his characteristic style. As the CPSU began de-Stalinization campaign since the 20th Congress of February 1956, the Communist Party of China regarded him as a legitimate "continuator" of Marxism-Leninism and as an outstanding statesman who displayed remarkable resolution and praiseworthy restraint in the struggle against "imperialism" than his successors.[31] While criticizing Stalin for his mistakes and praising him for his contributions towards consolidation of socialism, Mao demonstrated independence. That is why much before the 20th Congress of the CPSU, Mao had already embarked upon a Chinese course in national and international affairs with a spirit of self-confidence and freedom of action.[32] To quote one of his statements:

> When we lean to one side we are with the Soviet Union and on equal footing with her, we won't encounter problems such as those Poland and Hungary have faced. We are followers of Marxism but we do not blindly copy Soviet experience.[33]

The Politburo of the Communist Party of China disapproved the personality cult indulged by Stalin but recorded its appreciation of the Soviet leader:

> Stalin expressed the will and wishes of the people and proved himself to be an outstanding Marxist-Leninist fighter. The reason why Stalin won the support of the people and played an important role in history was primarily because he, together with the leadership of the Communist Party of the Soviet Union, defended Lenin's line on the industrialization in the Soviet Union and collectivization of agriculture.[34]

It was quite natural for Mao not to divulge his independent line of thinking in the national affairs and also not make the rest of the world known the different course of foreign policy till the death of Stalin for a valid reason. He had genuine fear of Stalin's suspicion that Mao was another Tito in making. Mao could not afford to incur Stalin's displeasure by showing his independent approach to domestic issues and international relations at the critical moment of Chinese participation in the Korean war which carried high probability of opening an American backed war-front on the mainland in view of President Truman's decision on 27 June 1950 to intervene afresh in China by interposing the Seventh Fleet between the mainland and Taiwan. It was a desperate situation, as Mao decided to participate in the Korean war when the consolidation of the revolutionary victory of his party was incomplete and when the Chinese leadership was not unanimous over the decision to participate in the war.[35] It was undoubtedly a risky decision in the face of the possibility of US military assault on China. But he was sure that no American military action against his country was forthcoming considering the existence of Article 1 of the Treaty of Alliance and Mutual Assistance. At any rate, his risky decision served the purpose of disabusing Stalin's suspicion of another Tito in making and also guaranteeing the flow of much needed Soviet aid to China.

The Sino-Soviet dispute, however, might be ideological or personal, played its historic role in shaping China's independent personality which retained its hidden character till the death of Stalin, once again at a high risk of pushing itself to an insular life in world politics and stalling the completion of 211 major industries and also of Soviet withdrawal of about 10,000 experts and workers from China.[36] Mao's difference with Soviet leadership had personal, ideological and national perspectives. After the death of Stalin, Mao appeared to have claimed the status of "continuator" of Marxism-Leninism[37] which, however, was not recognized by the Soviet leadership. Apparently, Mao did not formally stake the leadership of the socialist world and continued to refer to the Soviet Union as the "head of the socialist camp" down to the Moscow conference of 1960. Keeping his personal dislike of Khrushchev still hidden, Mao chose an indirect and tactful way of criticizing Soviet revisionism by attacking Tito,[38] describing Yugoslavia as a mirror of revisionism. In the midst of the Chinese criticism of Moscow on theoretical issues, Mao found another ground to be unhappy with Moscow in its handling of Middle East situation, more particularly, its failure to prevent the United States and Britain from intervening in Lebanon and Jordan in July 1958.[39] The Soviet backing of Defence Minister P'eng Tehuai, who spearheaded criticism of the failure of the Great Leap Forward and that eventually cost his position after the Eight Plenum of the party (2-16 August 1959),[40] added fuel to Mao's distrust of the Soviet leadership. His famous idea of "East wind prevails over West" received unexpected jolt when Khrushchev visited the United States and held Camp David talks with President Eisenhower. He probably felt isolated and betrayed, and made up his mind to accelerate his anti-Khrushchev campaign directly and vigorously. He had no hesitation to state in January 1962 that the Soviet leadership had been "usurped by revisionists".[41]

The U2 incident of 2 May 1960 not only added fuel to Mao's belligerent position against the United States but also offered an opportunity to remind Khrushchev of his wrong assessment of President Eisenhower as a great lover of peace and also of the disastrous consequences of his revisionist policy of peaceful coexistence.[42] He, therefore, pledged to continue his struggle against revisionism knowing it fully that his action would entail hardship to China and adversely affect its development projects. He saw no alternative to relentless campaign against the two superpowers as he felt more and more cornered and encircled at the Soviet economic and military aid to India in 1959-62.[43] Close on the heels of these developments, Chinese leadership felt hard to bear a barrage of blows from the Soviet Union, such as, Soviet conclusion of an agreement with the United States on non-proliferation of nuclear weapons which was considered as "an attempt to deprive China of the right to possess nuclear weapons to resist the US nuclear threat",[44] the conclusion of the Nuclear Test Ban Treaty of 1963 which the Chinese considered to be the end of "any of the Soviet leaders in developing its own nuclear strength to resist the US nuclear threat",[45] and the Soviet intervention in Czechoslovakia and the proclamation of the Brezhnev doctrine which carried the dangerous implication of self-ordained Soviet right to do to China what had been done to Czechoslovakia.[46]

As the ideological difference between China and the Soviet Union began to unfold itself in early 1960 in unmistakable terms, Mao probably was not sure of the dependability of the security system in his country in view of the absence of its nuclear deterrence capability, notwithstanding the fact that China had been maintaining since 1949 the most powerful armed forces of any Asian state. The Soviet refusal to transfer nuclear technology to China, while continuing its massive aid to build up Chinese military infrastructure,[47] did not stop China to explode a nuclear test on 16 October 1964 almost coinciding the fall of Khrushchev.[48] Once confident of China's nuclear capability, however, limited and fragile it might be at that point of time, Mao was aware of the fact that China could become a target of nuclear attack as it did not possess a second strike capability. These abstract considerations were more or less strategic issues which provided the strong rationale for Chinese nuclear programme. During the 1960s a surgical attack on China's nuclear positions was there in American thinking, and in 1969 in the Soviet mind for a pre-emptive strike. But Mao correctly considered atom bomb as a "paper tiger", an unusuable weapon. He never thought of using it against any country after China had acquired it, yet "in developing nuclear weapons, China's aim is to break the monopoly of the nuclear powers and to eliminate weapons."[49]

It may be noted that Mao correctly assessed the global strategic scenario and had the firm opinion that China had bitter enemies like the United States and the possibility of a limited nuclear war on China could not be ruled out. Even then he ws definite that China was not at all the target of any nuclear attack from anybody, including the United States. He did not see any rationality of a nuclear war even by the imperialists:

> Exploitation means exploiting people: one has to exploit people before one can exploit the earth. There's no land without people, no wealth land. If you kill all the people and seize the land, what can you do with it? I don't see any reason for using nuclear weapons, conventional weapons are better.[50]

Mao faced more than once the threat of nuclear blackmail, and therefore, wanted to counter it with nuclear deterrence. His analysis of atomic weapon as "paper tiger" was based on correct understanding of the limits of strategic deterrence, and hence, he refused to be deterred by nuclear blackmail of imperialists – whether socialist or capitalist. Not being frustrated by the Soviet refusal to share the knowledge and technology of nuclear weapons, Mao inspired his nuclear scientists to develop the deterrent bomb.[51]

There are several implications of China's nuclear programme in the 1960s. The acquisition of nuclear weapons and thus the status was a constant factor in China's international relations, although China's nuclear capability without a massive second strike capability was overwhemingly inferior in the context of Mao's two superpower adversaries. Therefore, Mao was aware of the fact that the acquisition of nuclear weapon would expose his country's vulnerability to a surgical first strike by either of the two adversaries. But once the first step towards strategic deterrence by testing a nuclear bomb was undertaken successfully, that would eventually lead to the development of China's second strike capability, i.e. ability to absorb an initial nuclear strike and still have enough fire power to hit back the enemy inflicting unacceptable damage. China accomplished this objective in the life time of Mao Zedong.[52]

At any rate, Mao's "paper tiger" thesis appeared to be theoretically sound. Even in the worst case either of the superpowers refused to resort to a nuclear strike in a huge and over-populated country whose conventional military strength was considerable and important safeguard against any nuclear strike.

Therefore, China's official statement on the occasion of its first testing of the nuclear weapon was significant. It recorded: "On the question of nuclear weapon, China will never commit the error of adventurism nor the error of capitulationism. The Chinese people can be trusted."[53] The acquisition of nuclear weapon, therefore, was a calculated risk; at the same time it was an important objective to prove that China refused to be treated shabbily by the rich and powerful enemies. It provided the people with a resurgence of national pride, military security, however debatable and obsecure it might be at that given point of time, and also proved the correctness of ideological commitment to an assiduously planned national policy. This was also an example to be followed by other third world countries aspiring to join the exclusive nuclear weapon power club.[54]

The acquisition of nuclear weapon gave China some kind of self-confidence which eventually prompted it to take another grave risk of a military confrontation with a superpower, this time its former ally, the Soviet Union, on 2 March 1969 on a frozen and disputed island in the Ussuri river.[55] Mao was philosophical in explaining China's position of 2 March incident: "we will not attack unless we are attacked; if we are attacked we will certainly counterattack", Mao said, "as far as our own desire is concerned we don't want to fight even for a single day."[56]

III

China's military conflict with the Soviet Union drew it closer to the United States. As the sporadic clashes eruptted along the 4650 mile long Sino-Soviet border President Nixon and National Security Adviser Henry Kissinger publicly moved to deter a possible Soviet massive retaliation, and thereby signalled their interests in detente with China.[57] Mao presided over China's opening to West taking the March incident as the turning point of China's role in international relations and thus initiated steps to end the long two decades of profound hostility.

It is not difficult to understand why did Mao at the fag end of his life turn to the United States, which was considered to be the most pronounced enemy. Mao and Zhou Enlai in January 1945 expressed willingness to go to Washington DC to meet President Roosevelt.[58] Had this historic desire been fulfilled, the course of international relations would have been different. It is a matter of history that with the death of Roosevelt, change of the Presidency and the onset of the Cold War left the USA with no option but to deny the People's Republic of China the legitimate recognition and to block its entry into the United Nations with a special status in the Security Council, a right denied to China till 1971.

It is argued that China's participation in the Korean War was an "unmitigated disaster" in the Sino-American relations.[59] It forced the Truman Administration to adopt a hard line placing the Seventh Fleet in the Taiwan strait. Mao embarked upon a risky course of provoking US retaliation on the assumption that a military confrontation with the United States was inevitable, and if it was to come it should come in area strategically advantageous to China.[60] Mao's risky calculation did not go wrong, as the Truman Administration rejected McArthur's suggestion to start a land and air assault on mainland China to force the Chinese volunteers' withdrawal from Korea. The Administration did not want to enlarge the dimension of the War by involving the Soviet Union directly in view of the Sino-Soviet Treaty of February 1950.

Mao's approach to the United States and his steps to dare a military confrontation with the superpower at least twice in 1950s – during the Korean War, and Quemoy and Matsu incidents of 1958 can be explained in the framework of his "paper tiger" thesis, whcih he first started to define imperialism as a superficially terrifying force needed to be despised from the strategic point of view, while respected at the tactical level.[61] Mao did not think that the US would unleash a nuclear war against his country, but the possibility had to be considered seriously. Recalling his interview with Anna Louise Strong in August 1946, Mao once again tried to convince his countrymen that all imperialists were paper tigers, and therefore, they could be defeated.[62] He disagreed with Nehru and Khrushchev, who believed and argued that a nuclear war would be a total catastrophe and annihilate the mankind. "In reality such talk amounts to saying that there is no alternative to capitulation in the face of imperialist blackmail."[63] He was uniquely accustomed with such types of veil threats at least seven different occasions by the end of 1955 and an eighth in 1958.[64] Another fundamental reason apart from "paper tiger" thesis for not being cowed down by imperialists is that Mao believed that the West was always divided and contradiction always wrecked their so-called unity. While the United States did not accord recognition to the People's Republic of China, its strongest ally the United Kingdom did recognize, of course, to protect Hong Kong and to continue its trade relations with China. Similarly, for him the Suez War of 1956 signalled an important configuration of contradiction, as he explained:

> From this incident [Suez War] we can pinpoint the focus of struggle in the world today. The contradiction between the imperialist countries and the socialist countries is certainly most acute. But the imperialist countries are now contending with each other for the control of different areas in the name of opposing communism.[65]

He concluded in the following manner:

> In short, our assessment of the international situation is still that the embroilment of the imperialist countries contending for colonies is the

> greater contradiction. They try to cover up the contradictions between themselves by playing up their contradictions with us. We can make use of their contradictions,a lot can be done in this connection. This is a matter of importance for our external policy.[66]

It is an irony of history that the Brezhnev doctrine, the Sino-Soviet military conflict of March 1969 and Brezhnev's vague proposal of June 1969 for a "collective security"[67] system in Asia which carried implicit anti-China overtones notwithstanding Soviet denial, produced probably the most spectacular and unexpected political and diplomatic result – Mao's quick move towards rapprochement with the United States, responded to favourably by Nixon and Kissinger.[68]

It is relevant to refer to one of the characteristic but philosophical explanations of Mao's move towards the USA. On 18 December 1970, much before Kissinger's historic secret visit to China in July 1971, while talking to Edgar Snow, the Chairman expressed high hope on the peoples of United States and his country. Snow records:

> If the Soviet Union wouldn't do [point the view], then he would place his hopes on the American people. The United States alone had a population of more than 200 million. Industrial production was already higher than in any other country, and education was universal. He would be happy to see a party emerge there to lead a revolution, although he was not expecting that in the near future.
>
> In the meantime, he said, the Foreign Ministry was studying the matter of admitting Americans from the left, middle, and right to visit China. Should rights like Nixon, who represented the monopoly capitalists, be permitted to come? He should be welcomed because, Mao explained, at present the problems between China and the USA would have to be solved with Nixon. Mao would be happy to talk with him, either as a tourist or as President.[69]

Besides, the highly publicized but obscure skirmishes of March 1969 as the fundamental rationale behind Mao's move towards his one time arch enemy for improvement of relations to counter Soviet hegemony, Mao found certain positive changes in US foreign policy. At the global scenario he believed that the USA was preparing itself for a retreat from its interventionist role, while the Soviet Union was pursuing a hegemonist policy, and this paved the way for Sino-American cooperation to contain Soviet hegemony. President Nixon's visit to China in February 1972 can therefore be seen as a move to that end, besides of course, as a vindication of Mao's prediction in 1958 somewhat in a different tone. He said in unmistakable terms:

> Though we have a large population, we have not yet demonstrated our strength. One day when we catch up with Great Britain and the US, Dulles will respect us and acknowledge our existence as a nation. Our policy is that we will not invite him as a guest, but if he should knock on our door, we will entertain him.[70]

Nixon's visit was an explicit recognition of China's great power role in international relations. Although China had been regarded as an important factor in international relations for its distinctive role in the Geneva Conference in 1954 and then in the Bandung Conference in the next year,[71] but the visit of the US president thrust upon China an internationally acclaimed diplomatic role commensurate with its importance in world politics. China's opening to the West entailed the fulfillment of at least two national objectives: (i) the People's Republic got its permanent seat in the UN Security Council which was denied to it for two decades, and (ii) the President of the USA, the most powerful country in the world, had to come to China and accord an explicit recognition of China's great power status, to be subsequently reinforced by a serial visit of President Ford, President Carter and President Reagan. Within four years, from 1969-1972, China took recourse to a breathtaking speed of transformation from revolutionary isolation to a fully recognized great international personality. It normalized its relations with most of the third world countries, including India in April 1976, without sacrificing any national interests. It did not shed any degree of its national sovereignty, self-reliance and ideological foundation of a socialist state while trying to and eventually accomplishing its task of playing the role of a formidable international personality. So long as Mao was alive China's economic and political system remained intact supporting its foreign policy goals.

Notwithstanding China's newly acquired important international personality in 1972, Mao did not disassociate his country from the fraternity of the third world. On 22 February 1974, on the occasion of the visit of the Zambian President Kenneth Kaunda to Beijing, Mao made certain important statements which eventually constituted the core of a leading article of *People's Daily* on 1 November 1977 entitled "Chairman Mao's Theory of the Differentiation of the Three Worlds is a Major Contribution to Marxism-Leninism."[72] Mao stated:

> In my view , the United States and the Soviet Union form the first world. Japan, Europe and Canada, the middle section, belong to the second world. We are the third world. The third world has a huge population. With the exception of Japan, Asia belongs to the third world. The whole of Africa belongs to the third world, and Latin America too.

Then he concluded in unequivocal terms:

> China belongs to the third world. For China cannot compare with the rich or powerful countries politically, economically, etc. She can be grouped only with the relatively poor countries.[73]

Mao's theory of three worlds and China's self-proclaimed status among the third world countries continues to be highly relevant and guiding factor in present day Chinese foreign policy.[74] Many of Mao's internal policies have been criticized and rejected by the present generation of Chinese leadership, but his fundamental contributions to Chinese foreign policy in shaping its full grown personality in international community largely its own terms have been revered and appreciated. The statement of Jiang Zemin, the General Secretary of Chinese Communist Party, on the occasion of celebration of Mao Zedong's birth centenary on 26 December 1993 may be quoted:

> Fundamental changes took place in China under the leadership of the party and Mao Zedong. It was transformed from a country plundered and enslaved by imperialism into an independent and sovereign state; from a fragmented country into a unified country with the exception of Taiwan and some other islands; from a country of oppressed people into a country where people are their own masters and enjoy democratic rights; from a country with a backward culture and economy into a country with a prosperous economy and rapid progress in all fields; and from a country looked down upon by the world into a country enjoying the respect of the international community.[75]

Pointing out Mao's contributions as the mainstream, and mistakes in his late years as secondary, Deng Xiaoping acknowledged the fact that Mao had played his unique role in building modern China and its socialist foundation.[76] At any rate, Mao's contribution in giving China a distinct international personality overshadows his mistakes in the internal front. The history of modern China is therefore, inseparably interwoven with the life and activities of Mao Zedong. The foreign policy making was one such activity which cannot be discussed without understanding the part played by him. To conclude the present paper with two lines of Wang Fuzhi is a too strong temptation to resist:

> If the nation is to be governed, there must be a leader
> who will establish the laws and institutions.

NOTES

1. *Mao Tse-tung Poems* (Peking: Foreign Languages Press, 1976), p. 2.
2. John Gittings, "The Statesman" in Dick Wilson (ed.), *Mao Tse-tung in the*

Scale of History (London: Cambridge UP, 1977), p. 246.

3. Franz Michael, *Mao and the Perpetual Revolution* (New York: Barron, 1977), pp. 146-157, Jurgen Domes, *The Internal Politics of China: 1949-1972* (London and New York: C. Hurst & Co., 1973), pp 220-21.
4. *Selected Works of Mao Tse-tung*, Vol.II (Peking: Foreign Languages Press, 1975), p. 196, henceforth referred to as *Selected Works.*
5. Ibid., Vol. III, p. 229.
6. Maurice Meissner, "The Despotism of Concepts: Wittfogel and Marx on China", *The China Quarterly*, October-December, 1963, pp 99-111.
7. Allen S. Whiting, *Soviet Policies in China: 1917-1924* (New York: Columbia UP, 1954), ch.II.
8. For one of the fascinating accounts of this period, see Wang Gung-wu, *China and the World since 1949: The Impact of Independence, Modernity and Revolution* (London: Macmillan, 1977), pp. 1-26; also C.F. Fitzerald, *The Chinese View of Their Place in the World* (London: Oxford UP, 1969).
9. *Miscellany of Mao Tse-tung Thought*, Vol.I (Washington DC: Joint Publications Research Services, 1974)p.14.
10. Ibid., p. 29.
11. Vincent Cable and Peter Ferdinand, "China as an economic giant; threat or opportunity?" *International Affairs* (London), Vol. 70, No. 2, April 1994, pp. 243-61.
12. Edgar Snow, *Scorched Earth*, Vol.II (London: Left Book Club, 1941) pp. 270-71.
13. *Selected Works*, Vol. IV, p. 415.
14. Allen S. Whiting and Shen Shih-Ts'ai, *Sinking, Pawn cf Pivot* (Michigan: Michigan State University Press, 1958).
15. For a thought provoking analysis, see Tang Tsou and Morton H. Halperin, "Mao Tse-tung's Revolutionary Strategy and Peking's International Behavour", *American Political Science Review*, Vol. 59. No.I (March: 1965) pp. 80-99.
16. Helmut Martin, *Cult and Cannon: The Origins and Development of State of Maoism* (Armonk, New York: ME Sharpe, 1982). For an interesting psychological analysis of Mao's greatness in successfully mobilizing public emotions in shaping the destiny of his country, see Lucian W. Pye, *Mao Tse-tung: The Man in the Leader* (New York: Basic Books, 1976), also his "Mao Tse-tung's leadership Style", *Political Science Quarterly* (Summer: 1976) pp. 219-235.
17. Roderick MacFarquhar, *The Origins of the Cultural Revolution: Contradictions among the People 1956-1957* (New York: Columbia UP. 1974), pp. 105-107; 152-56.
18. Richard C. Thornton, *China: A Political History, 1917-1980* (Boulder, Colorado: Westview Press, 1982), p. 170.
19. For details of the famous Chunking negotiations, see *Selected Works*, Vol. IV, pp.53-63.
20. Richard C. Thornton, ch. VI.
21. Ibid., p. 186.

22. For details see, *Foreign Relations of the United States – China*, IX, pp. 444-46.
23. For details see, Manoranjan Mohanty, "Mao's Portrait of Stalin", *China Report*, July-August 1975, pp. 19-29.
24. Charles B. McLarne, *Soviet Policy and the Chinese Communist, 1931-1946* (New York: Columbia UP, 1958), pp. 119-23.
25. John Gittings, *Survey of Sino-Soviet Dispute* (London: Oxford UP, 1968), ch. 1 and his *The World and China: 1922-72* (New YorK: Eyre Methuen, 1974), pp. 148-50.
26. John Gittings, *The World and China*, ch. 8.
27. *Selected Works*, Vol. V. P.304, for a slightly different version see, Stuart Schram (ed.), *Mao Tse-tung Unrehearshed* (Penguin, 1974), pp. 61-83.
28. For details of Mao's speech of 10 March, 1958 at the Chengtu Conference see Schram, *Mao Tse-tung Unrehearshed*, pp. 101-2.
29. For Mao's speech on 24 September, 1962 see ibid., p. 191. For a slightly different wording of a similar statement made in the 12th Plenum on 9 March1967 see John Gittings, *Survey of Sino-Soviet Dispute*, p. 15. Khrushchev shares similar views and commented that Mao was "under the lock and key", see *Khrushchev Remembers*, Vol. 2, (Penguin, 1974) pp. 287-88.
30. For the text of the Treaty and Agreements see O.B. Von der Sprenkel (ed.), *New China: There Views* (New York: John Day, 1951) pp. 227-35.
31. Lewis S. Feur, "Marxism . . . How many?", *Problems of Communism* (March-April 1960), p.50.
32. Abu Nasar Saied Ahmed, "Chinese Response to Soviet Interventions: Hungary, Czechoslovakia and Afghanistan", *Indian Journal of Political Science* (January-March 1968), pp. 43-44.
33. *Miscellany of Mao Tse-tung Thought*, Vol. I, pp. 37-38.
34. *People's China*, 16 April 1956, pp. 4-12, p. 7.
35. For details of Chinese decision to intervene in the Korean War see Allen S. Whiting, *China Crosses the Yalu* (Michigan: Michigan State University Press, 1960).
36. *Peking Review*, 29 April 1958, p. 23 recorded the enormity of Soviet assistance to China up to December 1957.
37. Harold C. Hinton, *Communist China in World Politics* (London: Macmillan, 1966) pp. 86-87 and 95-96: also Vidya Prasad Dutt, *China's Foreign Policy: 1958-1962* (Bombay: Asia, 1964), pp. 62-63.
38. Donald S. Zagoria, *The Sino-Soviet Conflict, 1956-1961* (Princeton: Princeton UP, 1961), pp. 176-78, John Gittings, *Survey of the Sino-Soviet Dispute*, pp. 85-86. It may be noted that as late as March 1958 Mao still praised Khrushchev, Schram, *Mao Tse-tung Unrehearshed*; see Introduction p. 27 and the text p. 114.
39. Vidya Prasad Dutt, *China's Foreign Policy*, pp. 69-71.
40. For details see David A. Charles, "The Dismissal of Marshal P'eng Teh-huai", *The China Quarterly* (October-December 1961) pp 65-70.
41. Stuart Schram, *Mao Tse-tung Unrehearshed*, p. 192.
42. See Mao Tse-tung's *Important Talks with Guests from Asia, Africa and Latin*

America (Peking: Foreign Languages Press, 1960) and *Peking Review*, 17 May 1960, pp. 5-7.

43. John Gittings, *Survey of the Sino-Soviet Dispute*, pp. 110-11, Arthur Stein, *India and the Soviet Union: The Nehru Era* (Chicago: University of Chicago Press, 1969) p. 125.
44. *The Polemic on the General Line of the International Communist Movement* (Peking : Foreign Languages Press, 1969), p. 96.
45. *Peking Review*, No. 33 (1963), pp. 7-15, p. 15.
46. Premier Zhou Enlai reacted to the Soviet action in Czechoslovakia in August 1968 by condemning it as a socialist imperialist. See *Peking Review*, 23 August, 1968, pp. III-VIII of the Special Supplement, also authors's article, op.cit., for the text of the Brezhnev Doctrine, see *The Current Digest of the Soviet Press*, 4 December 1968, pp. 3-5.
47. Raymond L.Garthoff, "Sino-Soviet Military Relations", *The Annals of the American Academy of Political and Social Science* (September 1963), pp. 81-93.
48. See "China Successfully Explodes its First Atom Bomb", Special Supplement, *Peking Review*, No. 40 (1964). The long statement in the Supplement carries the Chinese determination not to be humiliated by richer and powerful adversaries.
49. Ibid.
50. John Gittings, *The World and China*, p. 231.
51. Allen S. Whiting, "Mao, China and the Cold War" in Yonosuke Nagai and Akira Iriye (eds.), *The Origins of Cold War in Asia* (New York: Columbia UP, 1977). For an interesting analysis on China and the nuclear question, see Alice Langley Hsieh, *Communist China's Strategy in the Nuclear Era* (Englewood Cliffs, N.J.: Prentice-Hall, 1962), Morton H. Halperin, *China and the Bomb* (New York: Praeger, 1965).
52. *Asian Age*, 21 April 1995 reported quoting a reliable Australian source that China will acquire the capability of deploying ICBM with 12,000 km range and massive second strike capability by 2000 AD.
53. *Peking Review*, No. 40 (1964) special supplement.
54. President Nasser's request to China for the transfer of nuclear technology was rejected with the advice "If the Egyptians wanted to step into the atomic field they would have to do themselves. This was the way the Chinese did it and it was the best." Mohammed Heikal, *Nasser, The Cairo Documents* (London: New English Library, 1972), p.283.
55. Thomas W. Robinson, "The Sino-Soviet Border Dispute: Background, Development and the March 1969 Clashes", *American Political Science Review* (December 1978), Harlod S. Hansen, *The Bear at the Gate: Chinese Policymaking under Soviet Pressure* (Stanford, Calif: Hoover Institute Press, 1971).
56. For the full text see *Peking Review*, 30 May 1969, pp.3-9.
57. Seymour M. Hersh, *The Price of Power: Kissinger in the Nixon White House* (New York: Summit Books, 1983), pp. 357-359.
58. Barbara Tuchman, "If Mao Had to come to Washington: An Essay in

Alternatives", *Foreign Affairs* (October: 1972), pp. 44-64; also see Admiral Leahy, *I was There* (London: Gullancz, 1950), p. 100.

59. Nancy Bernkopf Tucher, "China and America: 1941-1991", *Foreign Affairs* (Winter, 1991-92), pp. 75-92, esp. p. 80.
60. For a recent analysis on the issue see Zhai and Hao Yufan, "China's Decision to Enter the Korean War: History Revisited", *The China Quarterly*, (March, 1990), pp. 94-115.
61. For the details of Mao's definition of imperialism while talking to Anna Louis Strong in August 1946 see *Selected Works*, Vol. IV. pp. 98-109, and for his further comments see *Selected Works*, Vol. V. 308.
62. Ibid., Vol. V, p. 517.
63. John Gittings, *Survey of Sino-Soviet Dispute*, pp. 82-83, p. 83.
64. For a detailed list and related documents see John Gittings, *The World and China*, p. 203.
65. "The Talks of January 27, 1957", *Selected Works*, Vol. V, pp. 361-62.
66. Ibid., 362-363.
67. Brezhnev made the proposal in a speech before the International Conference of Communist and Workers' Parties in Moscow on 7 June 1969, p. 16, for the Chinese reaction see "Trap is the word for so-called Asian 'Regional Economic Cooperation'," *Peking Review*, No. 29 (1969), pp. 23-24.
68. Henry Kissinger, *White House Years* (Boston: Little Brown and Co. 1979), ch. 6, pp. 18-19, 24, also Marvin Kalb and Bernard Kalb, *Kissinger* (New York: Dell Publishing, 1975), pp. 272-323.
69. Edgar Snow, *The Long Revolution* (New York: Random, 1972, pp. 171-172.
70. *Miscellany of Mao Tse-tung Thought*, Vol. I, p. 115.
71. George McTurnin Kahin, *The Asian-African Conference* (Ithaca: Cornell UP. 1956).
72. For details of the translated version of this long article see *Peking Review*, No. 45 (1977). It is noteworthy that Mao's statement and thinking on China's fraternal relations with the third world appeared in the Chinese press more than three-and-a-half years after he had made. The inordinate delay in the publication of such an important statement leaves a scope to doubt its credentials.
73. Ibid., pp. 11,28.
74. Xie Yixian, "China's Foreign Policy: A 1980s Tune-up", *Beijing Review*, 13-26 February, 1989, pp. 112-17.
75. Ibid., 10-16 January, 1994, pp. 9-10.
76. Idem.

12. Mao Zedong's Military Thought A Perspective

GIRI DESHINGKAR

Until the military thought of Deng Xiaoping emerged recently, Mao Zedong remained the only comprehensive writer on military doctrine and other aspects in China. Neither Sun Yat-sen nor General Chiang Kai-shek had much to say on such matters. Even Mao's Military colleagues like Zhu De[1] and Peng Dehuai[2] wrote largely about the tactical aspects of warfare and Lin Biao in his published writings, echoed Mao's military thinking to the last detail; his only contribution was to make Mao's thinking as the guiding star for all revolutionaries in the Third World.[3] (In his private writings, however, Lin was supposed to have written on the role of coups d'etat in history.)

Mao wrote on every aspect of the military; the philosophy of war, strategy, tactics, organization, logistics, the importance of man in warfare, the relationship between the army and the society, between the party and the army and so forth.[4] Yet, Mao was never attracted to the soldierly profession. His introduction to warfare or "armed struggle" came when he concluded that that was the only way to respond to the repression of the Chinese peasants by the Guomindang. Later, his Red Army also fought many engagements with the Japanese Army. But once he took to it, he learned the craft very fast. It was a very special craft, one of leading poor unarmed peasants to wage a war against vastly superior enemies both in terms of numbers as well as the variety and quality of weaponry. In this war, Mao accumulated enormous experience. He raised that experience to the level of theory,[5] a theory which fused politics and warfare in the actual conditions of China at that time.

Mao rarely took charge of battlefield operations; it was mostly Zhu De and others who did that. But he excelled at summarizing the experience of operations in different theatres and drawing larger conclusions from it. He was not a battlefield hero like Rana Pratap or Shivaji. He was more in the tradition of traditional Chinese military heroes like Sun Zi or Zhuge Liang who were strategists not battlefield commanders. But Mao went beyond grand stratagems and counter-stratagems to prescribing tactics on the battlefield.[6]

When Mao's military thinking was evolving, experience on the ground was his sole guide. It is doubtful if he had any access to foreign military writings, even Soviet ones; these were simply not available in Chinese translations. He had, of course, read the popular Chinese classics like *Zanguozhi Yanyi* and *Shuihu Zhuan* and stories about the exposits of Zhuge Liang but he said that he had not read Sun Zi's *Bingfa* until *after* he had finished his most seminal military writings. When he wrote, he wrote with concrete situations in China at that time in mind and his writings were specifically intended to apply to Chinese situations. They do contain time-tested universal truths about strategy, war and tactics but he came to those truths independently.

Most of Mao's military writings, the published ones, are of the period between the Zunyi Conference of 1935 when his military "line" became the Party's line and the end of the civil war in 1949.[7] During that period, he developed several seminal concepts: of war as a social product, not a product of inherent human nature (here he departed not only from European thinkers but also from Confucius, Mencius and the Legalists); war as a form of politics – with bloodshed (a concept similar to that of . . . but turned on its head) the necessity for the weak to engage in a "protected war" with a powerful enemy; the establishment of "red' bases where the entire population could be mobilized for a total war; the concentration of superior force to attack the enemy's weak-points; treating the enemy as a supplier of weapons; treating enemy soldiers humanely and giving them political education; Party control of the armed forces which were geographically widely scattered; the three strategic phases of the protracted war: strategic defensive to conserve one's strength → strategic consolidation to build up strength → finally, the strategic offensive to completely annihilate the enemy and achieve victory – and he prescribed the styles of war for each, i.e. guerilla war during the phase of strategic defensive, conventional war of movement or mobile warfare during the consolidation phase and then stand-up warfare by units of divisional strength and above during the strategic offensive phase. During all these phases, Mao emphasized man over weapons: which he was later to call the "spiritual atom-bomb".

Although Mao charted out the theory of development of the protracted war, until the Japanese surrender in 1945, his Red Army, with local exceptions, remained in the first phase, i.e. of strategic defensive. After that, the intermediate stage of consolidation was quickly by-passed and his army, now the People's

Liberation Army (PLA) went on the strategic offensive until the victory of 1949.[8] It was during the Civil War of 1946 to 1949 that the enemy became the major supplier of weapons to the PLA.

But the availability of new weapons, chiefly artillery but also tanks and some aircraft, does not seem to have made Mao rethink about the role of modern weapons in war. He also does not seem to have studied the role of weaponry in the Second World War or the Korean War.[9] And his thinking – man is primary, not weapons – changed little even when China began to acquire modern weapons and military technology from the Soviet Union during the 1950's.[10] But there was one exception: nuclear weapons. It is said that he asked the available experts in China to make a study of the impact of atom-bombs dropped over Hiroshima and Nagasaki and the hydrogen bomb exploded over the Bikini atoll. His initial reaction given to Anna Louise Strong in 1946 was: "Atom bombs are paper tigers".[11] They are used by imperialists to frighten people. He was to modify that conclusion after ten years by admitting that nuclear weapons were indeed very destructive. But he went on to say that if there were to be a nuclear war, the whole of humanity would not be destroyed; the survivors would thereafter establish a glorious socialist civilization and imperialism would be buried for ever.[12] This is a crude summary of a sophisticated argument Mao further held that the imperialists were only threatening the revolutionaries not to press forward with revolutions. The revolutionaries should not be frightened and should proceed to engage in wars of liberation. He obviously saw the importance of nuclear weapons delivered at long range by missiles because soon after the launching of Sputnik, he declared that the "East Wind" was prevailing over the "West Wind".

Mao's military theories did not become obsolete after 1949, even after revolutionary armed struggle for seizure of power (except in Taiwan) had come to an end, partly because they had become completely internalized by the PLA rank and file and largely because they were still considered applicable in a situation where the Chinese PLA was weak and the enemy (then it was the United States allied to the Guomindang on Taiwan) was strong. The Chinese threat perception was of an all out protracted war fought on Chinese territory by a combination of GMD and US forces for overthrowing the CPC. The doctrine maintained that the PLA would still counter that with a protracted people's war. But there was one modification. China would seek to deter such a war by developing a strategic nuclear deterrent: long-range missiles with nuclear and thermonuclear warheads.[13] Only if the deterrent failed, would China engage in a people's war. China expected that its limited deterrent could fail to deter America and hence a continuous preparation for fighting a China-wide people's war was necessary.[14]

I see some peculiar incongruencies between theory and practice in the period after 1949. Despite the total dominance of the people's war doctrine, neither in the Korean War nor in the India-China war did the PLA fight a people's war. Both wars were fought by a regular, standing army, albeit with revolutionary indoctrination, that the Chinese PLA had become. It did not use the strategy of trading space for time or of sucking in the enemy to annihilate him bit by bit; they were frontal engagements on a wide front. These wars were not conceived as protracted wars either. Mao did not draw – or did not seem to draw – any lessons from this experience; Peng Dehuai did.[15] As a result of his rethinking, Peng wanted a professional regular army patterned after the Soviet Red Army but his kind of thinking was repudiated. In fact, in the late 1950's Mao proceeded to deliberately deprofessionalize the PLA and to boost the importance of the people's militia.

He intensified political education at the expense of combat training, increased the decision-making powers of the political Commissars over those of the commanders and later abolished ranks in the PLA.[16]

Another incongruity was that while Mao thought that US imperialism intended only to frighten others with nuclear weapons, in the Taiwan straits crisis of 1958, he backed down in the face of an American nuclear threat.[17] Of course, a countervailing nuclear threat against American forces from the Soviet Union was not available to China at that time (Khrushchev did not want a nuclear war in support of a more-revolutionary-than-thou-ally) but all the same the fact is that American nuclear threats deterred China from completing its revolutionary war against the Guomindang on Taiwan.[18]

The protracted Vietnam War which in many ways followed Mao's military doctrine,[19] revalidated the theory of people's war; this may be why it was no longer challenged from within the Communist Party of China. The military confrontation with the Soviet Union which had several new features, e.g. massing of troops along the entire border also seems to have produced no new military thinking on Mao's part. It was just assumed that the Soviet Union would get into an all-out war of aggression with China if the Chinese nuclear deterrent failed and China would respond to it with an all-China people's war, every Chinese becoming a soldier, digging tunnels deep and storing grain everywhere. Mao's theory that all wars have a class-nature was kept alive by saying that the Soviet Union had become "social imperialist" and even "social fascist". The Soviet Union could have used tactical nuclear weapons in a war with China – it had the capability – but we heard nothing from Mao about how to fight a peoples war in a nuclear environment. Major PLA formation did include anti-nuclear and anti-chemical units but these were to protect regular combatants, not "people". Although China's military confrontation with Vietnam began in Mao's time, no theoretical explanation for this phenomenon of two Marxist states fighting with each other was offered; the Vietnamese leaders were not declared "class enemy".

When Japan invaded China, it occupied the most urbanized and industrialized parts of China and then halted its advance.[20] The defeat of Japan in China came against the background of the Allies fighting Japan on other fronts in the Pacific in S.E. Asia and air attack on Japan itself; Japan's defeat was not the direct outcome of a successful people's war. But in the context of a possible war with the Soviet Union, Mao does not seem to have considered the possibility of less than an all out war despite some serious fighting over disputed parts of the borders. If the Soviet Union had done what Japan did, i.e., occupation of only some territories along the border, in the absence of powerful allies outside China, how effective, would a people's war by the Chinese people would have been ? As in the case of the Korean War, others like Deng Xiaoping seem to have considered the question differently. In fact, such thinking seems to have started during Mao's last years in the 1970's.

All these statements of mine-must be tentative because apart from the spotty disclosures made during the Cultural Revolution by the Red Guards, we really do not have writings by Mao himself on military matters after 1949.[21] What were Mao's views on "national defence" as opposed to fighting a revolutionary war? Since the Cold War between the United States and the Soviet Union continued even after the Sino-Soviet split, would a war between the two superpowers have been a "just war" or an "unjust war" by Mao's definition? During the 1950's, did Mao agree to link China's defence policy with that of the Soviet Union? Did he agree to become dependent on Soviet military technology? That was very definitely the trend in the 1950's. Was the declaration of "no first use" of nuclear weapons made in 1964 Mao's handiwork? He was then in the "second echelon". After saying that nuclear weapons in the hands of revolutionaries was a good thing, why did China not provide them to say Albania, North Vietnam, Cuba or North Korea? In Mao's thinking, did the concept of war as "Politics with bloodshed" include the use of nuclear weapons? In *Sixiang Wansui*, Mao is quoted saying that the imperialists would not use nuclear weapons on others because that would limit the possibility of economic exploitation.[22] Why then did China need to deter them? There are many such questions waiting to be asked but we will probably get no answers for them in the absence of authentic documentation. Unfortunately, none is forthcoming.

Deng Xiaoping and his colleagues must know the answers to such questions and they were obviously not satisfied with those answers. Hence they began to change Mao's doctrine after they came to power but without explicitly repudiating Mao's military theories. There are, of course, continuities but there are many changes.[23] But this paper is not the place to discuss Deng's military thinking and the changes he brought about.

Mao's military thought was emulated with success only in Vietnam and may be partly by the Communists in North-Burma. Elsewhere his ideas failed and I can see no future takers for them except for the odd group in Latin America. In China, some of his ideas like absolute Party control over the PLA will continue into the foreseeable future. And, of course, the eternal verities about warfare which Mao expressed in pithy, easy-to-understand style will live on. Similarly, the Chinese cultural preference for strategy over "military science" is also likely to continue.

Mao's military thinking was a brilliant exposition of many facets connected with war, from philosophy at one end to hygiene in the barracks at the other. But much of his thinking which has come to us in published form is situation – and time-bound. Since he formed his ideas and put them in the corpus of Mao Zedong's military thought, unprecedented technological changes have almost revolutionized the nature of warfare and nuclear weapons have changed the philosophy of war. After nuclear annihilation, there can be no politics, with or without bloodshed.

Today, in the outside world, Mao's image as a strategist and military thinker has already faded. Even in China, he is quoted selectively on military matters to support some current military thinking or, of course, when discussing the revolutionary war in China's past. His military writings continue to occupy an important place on the syllabi of military academies in China but I suspect largely to reinforce the PLA traditions. Today, Chinese military academics study the strategies and tactics of foreign militaries, perhaps more zealously than Mao Zedong's military thought. Of course, Deng Xiaoping's military writings occupy the centre stage. So, in the foreseeable future, it will be modern international military thinking "with Chinese characteristics."

NOTES

1. See *Fifty Years of the Chinese People's Liberation Army* (Peking: Foreign Languages Press, 1978), pp. 80-1.
2. Jurgen Domes, *Peng Te-huai – The Man and the Image* (London: C. Herst and Co., 1985), pp.67-68.
3. "Long Livethe Victory of People's War", *Peking Review*, No.36, Sept. 3, 1965, p. 24.
4. See *Selected Works of Mao Tse-tung*, Vol. I (Peking: Foreign Languages Press, 1976), pp. 179-249' Vol. II, 1977, pp. 79-232; Vol. IV, 1969, pp. 141-55. Hereafter *Selected Works*.
5. *Mao Tse-tung – Six Essays on Military Affairs* (Peking: Foreign Languages Press, 1972).
6. See *Selected Works*, Vol. I, pp. 179-249; Also Vol. II, pp.79-114.
7. The first such work was written in December 1936, entitled "Problems of Strategy in China's Revolutionary War". See *Selected Works*, Vol. I. pp. 179-249. The last military writing came up on April 30, 1949 – a statement drafted by Mao for the Spokesman of the General Headquarters of the PLA

under the title 'On the Outrages by British Warships– Statement by the Spokesman of the General Headquarters of the Chinese People's Liberation Army'. See *Selected Works*, Vol. IV, pp. 401-2.

8. See *Cambridge History of China* (Vol. 13) *Republican China (1912-1949)*, Part 2. Edited by UK. Fairbank and Albert Feuerwerker (Cambridge: Cambridge University Press, 1986), pp. 774-82.
9. Mao, in his military writings or later speeches and writings, nowhere talked of the role of weaponry in the Second World War or the Korean War.
10. The Red Guard posters do not refer to any public pronouncement by Mao on Soviet military technology.
11. See "Talks with the American Correspondent Anna Louise Strong, August 1946," *Selected Works*, Vol. IV, p. 100.
12. See "The Chinese People Cannot be Cowed by the Atom Bomb", 28 January 1955, *Selected Works*, Vol, V, (Peking : Foreign Languages Press, 1977), p. 153.
13. See Giri Deshingkar, "The Maoist Strategic Doctrine", *The India International Centre Quarterly* 3(4), 1976, pp. 237-52.
14. Ibid.
15. David A. Charles "The Dismissal of Marshal Peng Teh-huai," *The China Quarterly*, No. 8 (Oct. Dec. 1961), p. 65.
16 Stephen Pan and Raymond J. de Jaegher, *Peking's Red Guards – the GPCR* (New York: Twin Circle Publishing Co., 1968), p. 52.
17. See Donald S. Zagoria, *The Sino-Soviet Conflict 1956-61* (Princeton, New Jersey: Princeton University Press, 1962), pp. 213-17.
18. Ibid.
19. William J. Duiker, *Vietnam-Nation in Revolution* (Boulder, Colorado: Westview Press, 1983), pp. 88-9.
20. The areas occupied by Japan were Shanxi, Hubei, Shandong, Jiangsu, Anhui, Jiangxi, Zhejiang, Guangxi and Guangdong. The unoccupied ones included Gansu, Sichuan, Guizhou etc., – the inner provinces.
21. See No. 8.
22. See John Gittings, "New Light on Mao – His View of the World", *The China Quarterly*, No. 60 (Oct.- Dec. 1974), pp. 758-79.
23. The emphasis has been more on combat and less on ideological linkages with military thought.

13. Influence of Mao's Thought on Indian Students (1967-71) Looking Back

TILOTTOMA MISRA

Mao Zedong and his revolutionary ideas had influenced the radical elements in the Indian Left as early as the 1950's. During the Telengana Movement, the younger group of the Andhra communists has stated in the "Andhra Letter" (1949): "Mao, the leader of the historic Chinese liberation struggle, from his unique and rich experience and study, has formulated a theory of New Democracy. This is a new form of revolutionary struggle to advance towards socialism in the colonies and semi-colonies". The impact of Maoism on the leadership of the Naxalbari uprising was therefore not a new phenomenon. For almost twenty years Indian communists had been debating about the relevances of Mao's line in the Indian context. Yet during these twenty years, the impact of Maoism in the Indian campuses seemed almost marginal. The sudden enthusiasm for Maoist ideas displayed by a significant section of Indian students soon after the Naxalbari uprising, therefore, must be studied in the context of the international political scenario of the 1960s.

The years 1964-70, witnessed student militancy on an unprecedented scale in different European and American university campuses. In 1964, the students of the University of Berkeley in USA staged a protest against the American war in Vietnam. This protest was in reaction against a government ban on the spread of any political or social ideas not approved of by it. The students of Berkeley displayed exemplary courage in defying this ban on freedom of thought and expression. "The ensuing struggle", according to Gabriel and Daniel Cohn-Bendit, "taught them [the students] a few fundamental truths about the nature of the State, and in particular about the relationship of the University with the world of business, local politics and the police" (Cohn-Bendit 1969, 23). The idealism and militancy of the Berkeley students was displayed a few years later in Europe by the students of Berlin University who not only demonstrated against the

American atrocities in Vietnam but also challenged the whole German system of education. The model of Berkeley and Berlin was soon followed in many other European campuses like the Sorbonne and Nanterre in France, Turin, Pisa, Milan and Rome in Italy and in the Madrid University of Spain. Everywhere the students defied the state machinery, demonstrated against all forms of authoritarianism and bureaucratization, demanded liberalization of university rules, greater participation of students in university bodies and changes in the curriculum and the examination system. This wave of student movements which is generally referred to as the New Left movement, was basically an expression of anger and disillusionment by the post-war generation against the "Ideological State Apparatuses" (Althusser's notion) of bourgeois democracy. The main thrust of the attack was on the university because it was considered the backbone of "the cultural apparatus" (Carl Davidson 1968, 348). The student revolutionaries attempted to turn the tables on the whole socio-political system of the modern capitalist state "by using the universities and colleges as base areas from which to undermine other key institutions of the social order" (Blackburn 1968,17). The campus revolutionaries were impatient with the leadership of the established communist parties for their policy of appeasement and compromise with Capitalism in order to survive within the system of bourgeois democracy. Alexander Cockburn, in the Introduction to his anthology "Student Power" hits out vehemently against all those who have chosen the bourgeoise parliamentary path: "In exchange for their political passivity bourgeois democracy offers people ballot papers every five years. In exchange for this quinquennial 'participation' people surrender control over their everyday existence. The revolutionary student movements have denounced this capitalist bargain as the graveyard of any hope of transforming society. The stated aim of the student movements of the sixties in Europe was to "renew" revolutionary politics by creating "an extra-parliamentary opposition" which would seize power from below, that is, reestablish people's power over all the social institutions including a general social control of the economy (Cockburn and Blackburn 1969,7). The demand of the students for university autonomy, which would mean the ability of the students to share university power and the freedom of the whole academic community from government control (Halliday 1969, 289), the assault on the bourgeois system of education which makes knowledge a fortress of capitalist ideology (Anderson 1969, 214) the demand for change of curriculum and methods of examination, the demand for liberalization of the archaic and repressive rules in the halls of residence – all these were part of the greater objective of "seizure of power from below".

Another aspect of the New Left movement was its struggle against imperialism which revealed its worst faces in Cuba, Vietnam and Algeria. Almost in every university where the students were in revolt, anti-Vietnam war rallies were held and solidarity with the struggling masses of those countries expressed.

Students declared themselves as "the internationalist social group par excellence" and drawing their lessons from international experience, recognized the necessity of uniting with workers and peasants (Halliday 1969, 324).

While the students in the European university campuses were waging their battle against "academic philistinism" (Cockburn 1969, 9) and asserting the force of "student power", a movement of another nature had taken Communist China by storm – the Cultural Revolution. Not only the theoretical foundation of this movement but also its tactical line and goal had a significant impact on the student movement of the West. The famous "Resolutions on the great Cultural Revolution of the Eleventh plenum of the CCP" of August 1966 highlighted the importance of repudiating the authority of persistent bourgeois ideology in the centres of education: "At present, our objective is to struggle against and crush those persons in authority who are taking the capitalist road, to criticize and repudiate the reactionary bourgeois academic 'authorities' and the ideology of the bourgeoisie and all other exploiting classes and to transform education, literature and art and all other parts of the superstructure that do not correspond to the socialist economic base . . ." (Jerome Ch'en 1970,118). According to this Resolution, the main target of the movement was not "the ordinary bourgeois academic ideas", but "the reactionary bourgeois scholars, despots and 'authorities'" (Che'n 1970, 121). Inspired and guided by such ideals propounded personally by Mao, Chinese students during the Cultural Revolution, like their counterparts in the American and European university campuses, assaulted the bourgeois system of education that had survived in the Chinese universities even after 1949. Whatever may have been the excesses committed by the students during the course of the Cultural Revolution, the anti-traditionalist zeal displayed by the students was to a certain extent spurred on by the spontaneous reaction against the rise of a privileged elite in the universities. The leaders of the New Left movement were aware of the significance of the Cultural Revolution for the radical students of the world over: "Its potential importance in preventing the rise of a privileged caste . . . is evident. So too is the valuable reminder that the need for vigilant and independent revolutionary students does not cease with the attainment of revolution" (Halliday 1969, 302).

Caught between the turbulent currents of the East and the West, the Indian campuses also experienced a wave of student insurgency in the 1960s. Though the nature of the movement, its course and extent were qualitatively different from both the New Left movement and the Chinese 'Red Guard' movement, yet some of the basic issues involved in it were strikingly similar to both these movements. The radical students voiced their disapproval of the opportunistic parliamentary line taken by the established communist parties of India. They rejected the Soviet system under the Stalinist bureaucracy and considered Maoism to be a more suitable model for the Indian revolution. In their urge to identify with the masses all over the world struggling against imperialistic aggression and to express solidarity with the armed struggle of the peasants and workers against the Indian State, the Indian students were a part of the world-wide student movement. However, the ideological orientation of the movement was closer to the Maoist line than to the New Left model set by leaders like 'Danny the Red'. How far the New Left movement itself had been inspired by the thoughts of Mao Zedong may be a separate matter for discussion, since the Maoist orientation of many a key figures in the radical intelligentsia of France and Germany of that time was well-known (Gottilieb 1994, 292).

An attempt would be made in this paper to trace these ideological moorings of the student activism in some of the Indian university campuses in the years 1967-75, based on the concrete instances of two of the metropolitan universities and of a relatively new university in a small town. The universities have been selected not on the basis of greater or more significant student activism but to emphasize the different levels of such activism. Nor is this a detailed chronological account of the events that took place during those turbulent years in the campuses, rather, it is an attempt to focus attention on the changes wrought by Mao's 'Thoughts' on the plane of ideas and how these ideas steered the students towards political action which they considered meaningful at that time. In all this, there was certainly a strong streak of idealism no doubt, bordering often on romanticism; but it is the young who will always dream of a future millennium and Mao himself was a dreamer when he spoke those impassioned words about a hundred flowers blooming. In 1967, Calcutta was torn by violent student demonstrations which at first appeared to be just another phase of militant student activity that were sporadic in Bengal right from the days of the food movement of 1952. What began apparently over a minor issue of confrontation with the University authorities soon assumed unprecedented dimensions with the students waging pitched battles with the police in the streets, picketing examination centres, making bonfires of examination scripts, barricading hostels and indulging in other forms of expression of their total rejection of authority.

These violent demonstrations, mildly termed as instances of "student indiscipline" were different in nature from earlier movements led by the college unions because this time the students did not appear to have in view any short-term solutions to their problems which could be achieved through dialogues with the authorities. The majority of the students appeared confused by the reign of chaos in the campus and many were resentful of the academic losses incurred because of the disruption in classes and examinations. The picture gradually became more clear when the theoretical questions involved in the Naxalbari uprising of 1967 became the subject of widescale discussion in the political circles and in the media. It was then that the thoughts of Mao received widescale publicity amongst the students and slogans from the Red Book began to adorn the walls of the campus as well as those of the suburban towns. The

Hsinhua News Agency at this time brought out a series of articles in support of the Naxalbari movement and one such report, under the heading "Indian people Love Chairman Mao", discussed the popularity of Mao's Thoughts amongst the students of a small town in West Bengal (Dasgupta 1974, 264).

The practical experience of the Naxalbari uprising and the armed movements of the tribals and peasants of Srikakulam together with the theoretical base provided by the writings of Mao Zedong gave the initial impetus to the radical student politics of Bengal in the late 60s and early 70s. When news about the Cultural Revolution of China of 1966 began to trickle in and the literature dealing with the theoretical foundation of the movement became available, an unprecedented enthusiasm was generated amongst the politically conscious section of Bengali students in its support. It was then that Mao became almost a cult figure amongst a section of the students and the Thoughts of Mao as compiled in the Red Book became a gospel of revolution. Mao's portraits hung from walls, songs were composed and set to popular folk music in praise of the path shown by Mao and the controversial slogan "China's Chairman our Chairman, China's path our path" gained currency amongst the students. The impact of the Cultural Revolution and the ideas of Mao Zedong that spearheaded this movement affected the views of a whole generation of Indian students. An analysis of the contents of the Presidency College magazine of the year 1968-69 provides an index to the impact of the Thoughts of Mao on the radical students of Bengal. The front cover of the journal spoke out eloquently about the nature of the contents. It bore a sketch of an angry young man smashing his pen. Below, a slogan in Bengali read "Destroy the Yankee culture". On the back cover was the Bengali version of the Internationale. Inside, there were a number of photographs of the martyrs of the Naxalbari uprising and of Charu Mazumdar. But occupying the pride of place on the first page of the journal was the portrait of Mao Zedong with the caption 'Ajker Juger Lenin' (Lenin of the present times). Below the portrait were the famous words of Mao addressed to the Chinese students in Moscow in 1957: "The world is yours as well as ours, but in the last analysis it is yours. You young people, full of vigour and vitality, are in the bloom of life, like the sun at eight or nine in the morning. Our hope is placed on you."

There were also several other Mao quotations occupying prominent places in the journal besides sketches of the leader drawn by students. A cartoon depicting a revolutionary honing his indigenous weapon, with the caption "The enemy is sharpening his weapons, let's sharpen ours", seems to be frought with tragic irony today. But in the context of the mood of glorious optimism reigning amongst the radical students at that time, the words merely summed up a general attitude. The articles in the journal also contained optimistic assertions of a glorious future for Indian revolutionaries. The role of the youth in the Chinese Cultural Revolution, the history of the militant peasant movement in India and critiques of Gandhism featured prominently in the journal.

During this period another significant change took place in the student politics of Bengal as well as of several other states. Whereas in the earlier times, students' union elections used to generate mass enthusiasm, now the radical Maoist students gave the slogan for boycotting college elections. The students of the Presidency College once more took the lead in this by making an editorial statement in the above-mentioned issue of the college magazine that "from henceforth our revolutionary tactic would be to boycott college elections and to take up the path of armed people's war by integrating ourselves with the workers and the poor landless peasants." This position must have been taken as an immediate reaction to a call given by Charu Mazumdar to the students to boycott college union elections because "they destroy the revolutionary talent of the students." But the criterion set by Mao to judge the revolutionary credentials of the students was the guiding force behind the call. Mao had said in 1939: "How should we judge whether a youth is a revolutionary? How can we tell? There can only be one criterion, namely, whether or not he is willing to integrate himself with the broad masses of the workers and peasants and does so in practice." (Mao Zedong, 2, 246).

The role of the Bengali students in disseminating the message of armed revolution amongst the peasants of West Bengal and the neighbouring states in the post-Naxalbari period has been widely discussed in the political writings dealing with that phase. The peasant uprising of Debra and Gopiballavpore in the Midnapore district of West Bengal in 1969 was "much more disciplined and planned" according to one opinion (A. Sen 1970, 88) because it was organized strictly according to the strategy put forward in Naxalite journals by students from Calcutta and other parts of West Bengal. However, this intellectually advanced section of student leadership also became the first to criticize some of the strategic lines put forward by veteran leaders like Charu Mazumdar. Mazumdar's line of "annihilation of class enemies" and the tactic of forming little conspiratorial groups of killers who should "dip their hands in blood" in order to prove their revolutionary bona fides (Mazumdar 1970), repelled many a sensitive young student who realized the deviation of this line from that put forward by Mao in his famous essay, "The Role of the Chinese Communist Party in the National War". Rejecting the tendency of party workers to form conspiratorial groups, Mao had said: "Communists must never separate themselves from the majority of the people or neglect them by leading only a few progressive contingents in an isolated and rash advance, but must forge close links between the progressive elements and the broad masses." (Mao Zedong, 2, 201).

The fierce debate that ensued following the break-up of the Naxalites into rival splinter groups, reveals a sincere urge on the part of the students and intellectuals to understand the philosophical and strategic base of Mao's Thoughts as an addition to Marxism-Leninism. (For details of this debate refer to Samar Sen, ed., *Naxalbari and After: A Frontier Anthology*, 2, 1978.)

A discussion of the Naxalite student movement in Bengal in the 60s and early 70s will not be complete without a reference to the phase of "urban red terror" and the terrible repercussions that followed. In their attempt to bring about a so-called "Cultural Revolution", the Calcutta students boycotted examinations, organized raids in schools and colleges, decapitated and disfigured statues of national leaders as well as of leaders of the Bengal Renaissance. The justification for such action was given in a language that resembled that of the New Left leaders: "This smashing of the idols raised by the imperialists and domestic reactionaries, by the revolutionary youths helps in restoring class outlooks and in raising the revolutionary consciousness of the people. Without demolishing these models, new models – those of the heroes of the people, cannot be created." ("Revolutionary Youths and Students Wage a Valiant Struggle", *Liberation*, August 1970). The second phase of this "red terror" was however bloodier than the European student movement ever was. Blessed and supported by leaders like Charu Mazumdar, the "urban guerillas" of Calcutta soon took to the line of "annihilation", killing police constables, suspected informers, petty traders, bureaucrats, trade unionists and even educationists. The ruthlessness displayed in these attacks on individuals horrified and bewildered even those sections of the public which had initially sympathized with the Naxalite cause (Prabhat Jena, 1973).

Why did such an intelligent, self-sacrificing, idealistic section of the students indulge in such apparently senseless violence that ultimately brought about their own annihilation in the hands of the state machinery? This question has confused and embarrassed many a political analyst who wishes to adopt a sympathetic stand towards the student revolutionaries of the Naxalbari period. According to one opinion, majority of the brilliant "elite" students who were dubbed as "doubtists" by the party bosses because of their critical attitude towards the Charu Mazumdar line, were marginalized during the "urban red terror" phase by the lumpen elements in the party consisting mostly of school drop-outs (Dasgupta 1974, 77). Such an approach seems to support the standpoint adopted by parties like the CPM which offered tacit support to the brutal and systematic extermination of Naxalites by the state machinery and its hired agents, in the name of getting rid of "anti-socials". According to several reports on the planned witch-hunting carried out against the Naxalites in Calcutta in 1970-71, the nefarious role of the lumpen elements in the CPM also could not be discounted. In the bloody encounters that often took place between the CPM and the Naxalite groups, the former allegedly received support of the government (B. Bose, *Frontier*, 16 May 1970).

There were charges and counter-charges galore on either side; but no political party could evade responsibility for the enormity of violence let loose in those days. Whether the "brilliant students" were involved in the terroristic attacks or not, the sensitive sections of the Maoist intellectuals expressed their distress and bewilderment at the turn of events through their writings. Many of them considered it futile to shield the "boys" from the charge of "unreasonable murders" that had taken place in Calcutta. A contributor to *Frontier* writes: "Why do so many fear us. Why whenever there is an unreasonable murder do all of us tremble and hope that it was not the work of "our boys?" (S. Roy 1971, *Frontier*).

It was evident from the bitter tone of the Naxalite intellectuals and students who opposed the Charu Mazumdar line at this time that the resentment was not against Maoism but against the distortion of Maoism by a few demagogues. An impassioned letter written by one such intellectual on the death of Sushital Roychaudhury, the editor of the Naxalite journal *Deshabrati*, reveals such an attitude: "Those who accepted this theory [of individual assassination] failed to see that by making conspiracy the only method of organization, by placing the conspiratorial organization outside the control of the party unit and by narrowing the definition of 'annihilation' to mean only the slitting of throats – this 'theory' was fundamentally against Mao Tse-tung Thought," (S. Roy 1971,96-97). According to this opinion, it was not the Maoist theory of revolutionary violence but the distortion of it by leaders like Charu Mazumdar that wrecked a revolutionary party like the CPI(ML) and a whole generation of dedicated youth who were passionately committed to a cause. The dilemma of these young people who were loved, admired, respected and hated at the same time can be aptly summed up by the following lines from a poem by Brecht quoted by Ravindra Ray in his book:

> And yet we knew well:
> Even hatred of vileness
> Distorts a man's features.
> Even anger at injustice
> Makes hoarse his voice. Ah, we
> Who desired to prepare the soil for kindness
> Could not ourselves be kind.

The impact of Maoism on students during the period 1967-70 was not confined to the students of Calcutta alone. There were rumblings of the "spring thunder' in the other Indian universities too, though the nature and the extent of it was not the same in all the universities. In Delhi university, around the year 1967, a small group of students and teachers formed the nucleus of a Maoist unit which was to exercise considerable influence on the university life during the next few years. In the beginning, the group worked under the cover of a cultural front named "Yugantak" which organized discussions and staged plays with revolutionary themes. There was at that time at least one more Marxist student group in the university known as "Sankalp"comprising of leftist students and intellectuals who supported the parliamentary line. The Yugantak however soon shed its cultural mask and the Maoist students of the group formed an organization known as the Student-Youth Federation with the aim of carrying forward the cause of an armed struggle of workers and peasants guided by Marxism-Leninism-Mao Zedong Thought. Although there was always a conscious attempt on the part of the students to follow the Maoist path of "integrating with the masses", yet the fact remained that right from its inception the SYF continued to have an elitist character because the leadership was in the hands of a group of students from an elite campus college. These students, mostly boarders, came from affluent families in different parts of the country and could boast of brilliant academic records. Significantly, most of them belonged to the social science stream. Referring to a similar phenomenon in the student composition of the New Left movement, Robin Blackburn says that since student movements always entailed "a searching critique of the dominant ideas about politics and society," so it is not surprising that "social science faculties are usually so heavily involved in student revolt" (Blackburn 1969,163).

Amongst the radical Maoists of Delhi University in the sixties, besides the "elites', there were also some local students drawn mostly from lower-middle class localities of the city. These students suffered from an intense sense of frustration with the education system that left most of them unemployed at the end of their university career. The contradiction between the two groups of students remained one of the main contradictions with the Students Youth Federation (SYF); but there were always attempts to solve problems arising from this latent contradiction, in the truly Maoist method of "criticism and self-criticism" put forward in the 'Red Book'. It was a common practice amongst the SYF members to hold solemn meetings in which erring members were openly lambasted for having committed one or the other of the eleven types of "liberalism" identified by Mao as dangerous for a revolutionary party in his essay "Combat Liberalism" (Mao Zedong, 2, 31). Often in these sessions, the over-zealous students would cross the practical and humane limits set by Mao in his advice to his party men: "Our aim in exposing errors and criticizing shortcomings, like that of a doctor curing a patient, is to save the patient and not to doctor him to death." (Mao Zedong, 'Quotations', 262).

The elitist character of the SYF continued to prevail with more students from affluent background joining in, whose commitment to the revolutionary cause was often skin-deep. However, these students, with their romantic notions of a revolution, added colour and glamour to the group. Many of them were highly talented and displayed remarkable creativity in whatever they did. Wall writings, political skits, musical compositions and posters were executed with considerable artistic skill. Perhaps one of the finest such productions by this group of Maoist students was the staging of a political satire named 'India 1969' in one of the campus colleges. The spontaneity of the production, the analysis of the political situation of the country from the point of view of a firm ideological position and the impassioned assertion of faith in the revolutionary change that was believed to have been imminent, made the production a great success amongst the students. It not only enthused a large number of students to join the Naxalite group but also created a sort of history as one of the earliest such productions in the capital. In later years, street-plays made effective use of this mode of political satire.

Besides these activities on the cultural front, the SYF members were also eager to "integrate with the masses" by holding small group meetings in working class localities of the city with the purpose of disseminating Maoist ideas of a revolution in a semi-feudal, semi-colonial situation. Inside the campus, a significant aspect of their political activities was the attempt to storm the bastions of intellectual authority, or, in their favourite Maoist vocabulary, "to bombard the Headquarters". Like the New Left radicals in the West and the Red Guards of the Cultural Revolution in China, the radicals in the Delhi University campus too sought to transform the system of education that perpetuated uncritical attitudes which were inculcated through the traditional university system. They organized sessions in which heated discussions took place between the leading intellectuals of the university and the students on different issues relating to the curriculum or the interpretation of the economic and political situation of the country. The ultimate purpose of these meetings was to demolish what Louis Althusser had termed "the true fortress of class influence in the university" (Blackburn and Cockburn, 1969, 214). Following Mao Zedong's views on the role of the intellectuals during a revolutionary struggle, the SYF members not only exhorted the university intellectuals to "throw themselves into the heat of the struggle "but also to revise the whole concept of knowledge in the light of the dialectical materialist theory of knowledge. A short essay by Mao named "Where do Correct Ideas Come From" (Mao Tse-tung, *Selected Works*, Calcutta 1967, 726-27) was a constant source of inspiration to the radical students in their struggle against the outmoded system of education. They also received constant guidance and encouragement form a few teachers who were either supporters or sympathizers of their cause. Amongst the other activities of these students were holding of demonstrations against US aggression in Vietnam and garnering support for the people's struggle against the forces of imperialism in different parts of the world.

The SYF activities gradually started undergoing a change with the political developments in West Bengal, Bihar, Andhra Pradesh and other parts of the country. Underground literature of the different Naxalite organizations began to be circulated amongst the students which emphasized the need to abandon over-ground activities in the campus and to move out to the countryside to organize the peasants. Earlier, the Delhi students, in their attempt to increase the level of political consciousness amongst the workers of the organized sector, had failed to generate much enthusiasm because they did not display much interest in trade union activities or in the economic demands of the workers. So at a meeting held in 1969, a decision was taken that the SYF members should start moving out into the rural areas where Naxalite activities were already on. Thus fired by revolutionary zeal, a group of students and young teachers of the university gave up their careers and jobs in order to "integrate with the masses". But, since none of them at that time was a member of a revolutionary party, there was great deal of uncertainty about the exact nature of the work to be undertaken. It is not the purpose of this paper to analyse the reasons for the failure of that group to achieve its ultimate goal. Much has already been written on the reasons for the failure of the Naxalite movement of the sixties and the seventies. Whatever may have been the shortcomings of the student revolutionaries, the sincerity and the dedication of at least a handful of them evoked respect even from their critics. There was immense hope and optimism amongst the students at that time which steered them forward and steeled them against all kinds of adversities.

It would not be irrelevant to mention here the basic difference between the Maoist student groups in Calcutta and those in the Delhi University. The Calcutta students displayed a greater propensity for violence than their counterparts in Delhi, even before the phase of "urban red terror". The Delhi University Maoist appeared to have been more contained and disciplined, their show of violence being confined mostly to staging of demonstrations that were by and large peaceful, with occasional slogan-shouting during a meeting or a convocation or the display of anger against the education system by tearing up degree certificates during a convocation. The difference between the Naxalite activities in Calcutta and the other Indian cities has become the subject of much political speculation in several recent studies. Rabindra Ray, one of the original members of the SYF who had left his studies to "preach revolution in the country-side", attempts to relate the Naxalite movement in Bengal to the existentialist ideology of European nihilism and finds this ideology peculiarly suitable to the Bengali temperament. He says in his book: "The categorical import of violence is embedded in a situation that is distinctively Bengali". (*The Naxalites and Their Ideology*, OUP 1988, 229.) Such a view may be unacceptable because it imputes the cause of certain political phenomena to subjective considerations like a "national temperament." But the fact remains that the students of Bengal responded more readily to the line of political violence than their counterparts elsewhere. One reason for this may have been that the political and the economic scenario in Bengal at that time generated a greater degree of anger and frustration amongst the students. Also, the tradition of revolutionary politics which was a legacy of the Bengali students, was absent in the case of Delhi University whose student composition was also more cosmopolitan in character. The different groups of students coming from different states of the country had problems peculiar to their own regions. Though all of them rallied together under the banner of one revolutionary student organization, yet it was a temporary phenomenon. Despite the internationalist outlook of the group, the students could not relate the political problems of their home states to those affecting the campus. That was why there was a sincere eagerness to leave the metropolis and study the concrete situations of their own regions. The student community of Bengal was more homogeneous in this respect and therefore could react more immediately to the political situation around them. This probably was the reason too why those Naxalites who survived the great Calcutta killings of 1970-71, continued to play a meaningful political role in later years while most of the Delhi University Naxalites after their frustrating experiences in the country-side, gradually drifted away from the political scene.

The student activism of the sixties was not confined only to the metropolitan universities. There were militant student activisms in campuses situated in and around areas that were politically in the eye of the storm, like the North Bengal University. But, even in places that were politically less turbulent at that time, mild waves were created by the induction of revolutionary theories of Marxism-Leninism-Mao Zedong Thought into the campuses. Dibrugarh, for example was a relatively uninteresting place from the political point of view in the 1960's and the new university that had come up in this tea-town was considered to have been safely tucked away in a secluded corner. But, the new radical ideology that had transformed almost half the world at that time, had its impact on the life of this university too, primarily on the plane of ideas. The small discussion group that functioned under the name of Dibrugarh University Marxist League, was formed by a handful of students, young teachers and office employees of the university with the purpose of disseminating Maoist ideas of a social revolution. For almost five years, till the declaration of Emergency in 1975, when many of its members were thrown behind the bars, this small group kept itself active by holding discussions on various relevant political and social issues. Though the Marxist League as an organization never contested university students' union elections, its members exercised considerable influence in mobilizing students' opinion on matters like democratization of the university structure. Amongst the other activities of the group to raise the level of political consciousness of the students was the celebration of May Day every year with the holding of meetings to celebrate workers' unity and singing of revolutionary songs. Meetings were also held to express solidarity with the people of Vietnam in their struggle against US aggression. These activities of the students had their impact on the areas around the university and there was a sudden spurt of activity amongst different organizations that began to display a new social awareness. Existing cultural organizations chose revolutionary themes for their publications or for their dramatic productions. The Marxist League of the university also began to publish its own mouthpiece, an Assamese journal named '*Angikar*', which played a pioneering role in setting a certain trend in political journalism in Assam. This journal was the first in Assam to publish translations of Mao's writings. The journal was in circulation for almost ten years, and during this period it made significant contributions towards moulding public opinion on issues that greatly affected the lives of the people of this region. Some of the views expressed through this journal which had their impact on the politics of the region in subsequent years were: the rejection of the parliamentary path and emphasis on militant peasant movements as a means of uniting the different ethnic groups of the region; extending support to the struggle of the Nagas and the Mizos formulating the thesis of the Centre's colonial exploitation of the North-East. Thus the small group of students and intellectuals of Dibrugarh University played a role which had its own historical significance in the context of later developments in the region.

Looking back, the general mood of the Indian students in the sixties and the seventies was one of dissatisfaction with the prevailing socio-political system and the "instruments of state apparatus". This mood of anger and frustration impelled the students to seek a new political alternative that was better suited to the needs of a country like India. The armed uprisings of the peasants in different parts of the country at this time under the leadership of organizations that had rejected the policies of the established left parties, gave a new impetus to this new students movement of this period. However, no discussion of this period can overlook the inherent weaknesses in the organization and functioning of the Maoist student groups. Some of these could be ascribed to the wrong understanding of the national and the international situation and some to the adoption of a tactical line not suitable for this country. Both these weaknesses, however, applied to the whole Naxalite movement of which the students were only a part.

One of the reasons for the frustration experienced by some of the students in their sincere attempt to identify with the masses was the general anti-intellectual attitude of some of the veteran leaders who were in command of the movement. They were suspicious of the "elite" students from the cities some of whom displayed a snobbish highbrow attitude in their dealings with others from a less privileged background. This conflict was inevitable in a situation where there was a vast gap in the level of political consciousness between the intellectually advanced section and the peasant leaders whose understanding and analysis of situation were based primarily on immediate practical knowledge of their surroundings. The Naxalite students, despite their avowed commitment to a dialectical theory of knowledge that stresses the need to combine theory and practice, often succumbed to a weakness common to all Marxist intellectuals for whom the reading of theory was often, as Mao described it, like "shooting arrows without a target and not at the target" (Mao Zedong 'Rectify the Party's Style of Work', Quotations, 308). It was probably because of this attitude that many of them were repelled by what they termed as the "rural idiocy" of some of the semi-literate peasant leaders. Charu Mazumdar's "annihilation line" which was a total distortion of the Maoist concept of a war of annihilation, finally struck a death-blow on the revolutionary student organizations, literally and figuratively. It not only exposed the students in the urban areas to the worst kind of state-terrorism but also shook the very foundations of their faith in the vision of a more humane world-order.

The idealism, the heroism, the sacrifice as well as the weaknesses that marked the nature of student politics of the period discussed in this paper, have left a deep mark not only on the political history of post-Independence India, but also on the literature and art of the past two decades. The impact of Maoism on the Indian intellectual world in general was therefore undoubtedly a significant one. Whether the majority of the intellectuals, including the students, were truly Maoists in practice remains a debateable issue. The rejection of the mass line, the policy of individual killings, the failure to make creative adaptation of Mao's theories to the Indian situation and above all, the tendency to turn Mao into a demi-god by using slogans like "China's Chairman Our Chairman", exposed the Thoughts of Mao to much adverse criticism and slander in India. Mao himself was more than aware of the dangers of such a "dogmatic line" being adopted by over-enthusiastic or fanatic followers. In his characteristic homespun style Mao had warned his young comrades against such a tendency common to all communist movements; "Now, there are two different attitudes towards learning from others. One is the dogmatic attitude of transplanting everything, whether or not suited to our conditions. This is no good. The other attitude is to use our heads and learn those things which suit our conditions, that is, to absorb whatever experience is useful to us. This is the attitude we should adopt" (Mao Zedong, "On the Correct Handling of Contradictions among the People", 1957, Quotations, 305).

REFERENCE

Blackburn, Robin, *A Brief Guide to Bourgeois Ideology, Student Power*, Ed. Alexander Cockburn and Robin Blackburn, London, 1969.

Ch'en, Jerome (ed.), *Mao Papers, Anthology and Bibliography*, London, 1970.

Cockburn, Alexander, Introduction, *Student Power*, London,1969.

Cohn-Bendit, Gabriel and Daniel, *Obsolete Communism, The Left-Wing Alternative,* trans, Arnold Pomerans, London, 1969.

Davidson, Carl, "Campaigning on the Campus", *Student Power*, London, 1969.

Dasgupta, Biplab, *The Naxalite Movement*, New Delhi, 1974.

Gottlieb, Freema, "From Mao to Moses", *Partisan Review*, Vol. 61, No.2, 1994, 292-302.

Halliday, Fred, "Students of the World Unite", *Student Power*, Penguin, 1969.
Jana, Prabhat. "The Main Danger", *Naxalbari and After: A Frontier Anthology*, ed. Samar Sen et al., Vol. 2, 137, Calcutta, 1978.
Mao Zedong, *Selected Writings*, Calcutta, 1967,
— Selected Works, Vol.1 & 2, Calcutta, 1973;
— Quotations from Chairman Mao Tse-tung, Peking, 1968.
Mazumdar, Charu, "A Few Words about Guerilla Action", *Liberation*, Feb. 1970.
Ray, Rabindra, *The Naxalites and Their Ideology*, New Delhi, 1988.
Ram, Mohan, *Indian Communism: Split within a Split*, Delhi, 1969.
Sen, Abhijnan, "Naxalite Tactics in Cities", *Frontier Anthology*, 2, 88.

14. Amilcar Cabral and the Liberation of Guinea Bissau

NEERA CHANDHOKE

When in 1960 Amilcar Cabral visited China and had become acquainted with the philosophy and strategy of Mao Zedong, the liberation struggle in Guinea Bissau against Portuguese colonialism was almost four years old. The PAIGC had been formed in 1956 by Cabral and six others. From 1956-58 Cabral was away except for two brief visits in 1958 and 1959. The party started with a small membership of about 20-30 and the core of the party from 1956 to 1960 comprised what Cabral was to call the petite bourgeoisie-dock workers, civil servants, salaried workers. In the first three years the party tried to root the ideas of the movement in the minds of whatever elites existed in the social strata. The party had difficulty in mobilizing the people, because few were prepared to take the risk of joining the party. But the activists managed to infiltrate the legal trade union. The first phase of mobilization had led a massacre of striking port and dock workers on the 3rd of August 1959. The authorities viewed these events with a great deal of unease and responded with the usual brutality which the Portuguese had become famous for. With a toll of 50 dead and 100 wounded on the Pidjiguiti quay, the PAIGC, the party set up by Cabral and other leaders suffered a major setback. Later as Cabral was to remark on the sixth anniversary of the massacre, the Pidjiguit event was a historic lesson. It showed that the path to liberation lay not in the cities. Faced with Portuguese armed weapons the only way out would be armed struggle. The transition from political action to armed struggle was proclaimed on the second anniversary of the Pidjiguiti massacre, after a period of profound reflection.

This had major consequences for the movement and totally altered the course of the movement. The previous policies of nationalist agitation in the urban centres and the infiltration of existing legal organizations were abandoned. The original emphasis on the proletariat taken under the influence of the Portuguese PCP was rejected. The decision was taken to shift the focus of attention from the urban centres to the country-side and to prepare for liberation by all means including war.

It is here that acknowledging the influence of Mao's thoughts on the strategy of the liberation movement, Cabral said that "it was in 1961 that I came to know the works of Mao Tse Tung." "A lack of experience had led us to think that we could struggle in the cities by means of strikes and other activities, but we were mistaken and the reality of the time proved to us that this was not possible." It was the period when Cabral came into contact with Mao, that the original strategy of an orthodox Marxist movement with a view of the working classes as the principal social base of the struggle gave way to an emphasis on the peasantry.

The party was totally transformed when Cabral came back in 1960 to take charge of a party preparing for war. He admitted the earlier mistakes thus: "At the beginning of the struggle we were convinced that if we were able to mobilize the workers of Bissau, Boloma and Bafata to strike, to demonstrate in the streets the Portuguese would change and grant us independence. It was false. From the economic standpoint, wage labourers are not a sufficient force in our country; the main economic force is in the countryside. . . . We therefore had to adopt to the conditions of the country". He concluded that a nationalist armed struggle could only be developed in the country-side. He had gone to China, he had also learnt from the Algerian war of Independence and from the Cuban Revolution. The subsequent development of the strategy of the national liberation struggle in Guinea Bissau revealed the influence of the thought of Mao Zedong, and the strategy Mao had adopted in a predominantly peasent society, his emphasis on building a national bloc to fight Imperialism, his insistence on the predominance of the political and his experiments in alternative ways of social and political arrangements in liberated zones. It testifies to the relevance of Mao's strategy and ideology in rural societies and technologically underdeveloped countries who become the subjects of Imperialism.

Whether his thought falls into the classical mode of Marxism-Leninism or Maoism is, however, debatable because he insisted that "national liberation and social revolution are not exportable commodities, they are, and increasingly so every day, the outcome of local and national elaboration". Our model, he said in 1971, in a meeting in London, is to be found in the liberated areas here today. "People here (in Europe) are very preoccupied with questions – are you or are you not a Marxist? Are you a Marxist-Leninist? Just ask me please whether we are doing well in the field. Are we really liberating our people, the human beings in our country from all forms or oppression? Ask me simply this and draw your own conclusions." The question whether Guinea Bissau was moving towards socialism was to Cabral a practical not a theoretical question.

It is not as though Cabral was a stranger to Marxism-Leninism. He had come into contact with the Portuguese Communist party during his days as a student in Lisbon. The party was the dominant influence in opposition politics, and many African students had become members of the party. Cabral supported the many activities of the party, but he was not impressed by the position of the communists on issues of national self-determination. At the time the Portuguese opposition had little to say about decolonization or African emancipation. The country had not taken part in the second world war, it was not a member of the United Nations till 1955 and it watched with disbelief the decolonization of Asia and Africa., The Communist Party likewise did not question the fact of the Portuguese Empire, and it was more concerned with the development of communist parties in the colonies rather than national parties.The first reference was made by the Party to independence only in 1957. Only in 1960, was it to state its support for complete and immediate independence in the colonies.

For Cabral the foremost question was the liberation of Africa, whereas for the Communist Party the main concern was the overthrow of fascism. Cabral did not believe that the demise of fascism would lead to independence for the colonies because decolonization was accepted neither by the Portuguese people nor by the democratic opposition. Marxist theory in its Soviet Stalinist version said little to inspire Cabral, it provided the activists with a theory of history, but it had little to say about decolonization. Cabral and the other students rediscovered themselves through what they called Reafricanization. Using the intellectual tools of the West, these students challenged the ideological and cultural rationale of colonial rule. And armed with these modes of analysis, these activists under the leadership of Cabral set out to wage a revolutionary war in the Portuguese colonies in Africa.

In order to understand the significance of the victory of the liberation movement in Guinea Bissau, and the particular accomplishment of Cabral in orchestrating the struggle, we need to know a little about the structure of society in that country. Portuguese colonialism has been described as ultra colonialism by Perry Anderson. Portugual, itself, a semi feudal country used the most primitive methods of colonial rule. Using the classic methods of divide and rule the colonial authorities segregated the local population into the natives and the assimiladoes. Those who could speak, read or write Portuguese, those who owned property, those who possessed some skills, profession, occupation, or who showed good behaviour, and did not practice the usages and customs common to their race were granted the status of assimiladoes (Article 2, decree 16.4 73, of 6th February 1929). Cabral belonged to this class, but even the assimiladoes did not possess any political rights. The Portuguese colonies were marked by rank discrimination, brutal methods of torture to repress the inhabitants and exploit them economically.

Economic exploitation was mainly commercial in nature and did not destroy the existing system of production. The barter system survived in many areas, in others areas where groundnut cultivation had been introduced some amount of monetary bargaining had begun. Since the Portuguese did not colonize the land, the share cropping system was maintained, and the peasantry resisted social and economic innovation. The most significant exception was the Fulas who allied with the colonizer through their chiefs.

The peasantry not subjected to appropriation of land or forced labour as in other parts of the Continent, were resistant to foreign ideas and outsiders. During the course of the struggle Cabral was to say that "We know from experience what trouble we had in convincing the peasantry to fight. The conditions of the peasantry in China were very different. In Guinea except for certain parts of the country and among certain groups where we found a very warm welcome, even right at the start, we unlike the Chinese Communists, had to win support by tenacious efforts" (1976-77).[1] Cabral's knowledge of the peasantry stemmed from his knowledge of the country-side. In 1953 Cabral was asked by the Governor of Guinea Captain Alvim whether he would undertake a survey of the country. This was the outcome of a promise made by Portugal to the FAO in 1947, and since Portugal was seeking admission to the UN, this promise was translated into policy.

Cabral who had been trained as an agronomist and his group undertook an exhaustive survey of the country, by the end of 1954 the report was ready. The report was pessimistic about the possibility of developing Guinean agriculture without improving the condition of the peasantry. The opportunity to travel and meet the villagers, to comprehend the predicament of the villages proved to be a major turning point for Cabral.This experience was to be a valuable one for him as it brought him into close contact with the socio-economic conditions of Guinea Bissau, and the trip gave him some idea of what would be involved in the organization of a nationalist movement in the country. The next step was the setting up of the party Partido africano da independencia e uniao dos povos da Guinea e Cabo Verda in 1956 when Cabral was visiting Guinea.

After a period of reflection following the Pidjuiti massacre he came to the conclusion that whereas the peasantry was the main physical force, it was not per se a revolutionary force. The nature of the peasantry in the country defied the processes of radicalization. In the rural areas, according to Cabral, there were two extremes. On the one hand were the feudal elements among the Fulas and it would be unrealistic to expect the peasants who worked for the chiefs to cooperate. Their social and ideological bonds with the chiefs were stronger than their loyalty to nationalism. The artisans who were dependent on the chiefs also opposed nationalism. The Dyulas the merchants, he stated, had to be rewarded in order to work for the PAIGC.

On the other hand there was a group without any defined form of state organization the Balantes. The Balantes and other stateless groups, the Fula chiefs and the Mandigas and Manjacas cooperated with the nationalists, because their more egalitarian and democratic political and social structure led to a belief in nationalism. Since production was carried on a communal and family basis made the producers more aware of the exploitation of colonialism and the disruption of their structure of production. Colonial attempts to make these groups comply led to resistance and resulted in the imposition of imposed chiefs.

The existence of a peasantry was not enough to forge a revolutionary class. "It must be realized that it is not the degree of suffering and hardship involved that matters. Even extreme suffering in itself does not necessarily produce the price conscience required for the national liberation struggle. In Guinea the peasants are subjected to a kind of exploitation equivalent to slavery, but even if you try to explain to them that they are being exploited and robbed it is difficult to convince them . . . whereas it is easier to convince the workers and the people employed in the town that they are subjected to massive exploitation because they can see it."[2] The leadership and impetus for the struggle came from a small section of the petite bourgeoisie. This was due to their ambiguous position. This was a new class created by colonialism and indispensable to the system. It was located between the working masses of the country and of the cities on the one hand and on the other the local representatives of the foreign ruling classes. The petite bourgeoisie tries to emulate the colonial masters and reduce the distance with its own people, but it can never become integrated. "It is prisoner of the cultural and social contradictions imposed on it by the colonial reality which defines it as a marginal or a marginalized class. It is this marginality experienced both by the local petite bourgeoisie and by those of its members which belong to the diaspora living in the colonial metropolis which constitutes the socio-cultural drama of the indigenous petite bourgeoisie".

This class became nationalist not because it is a politically conscious proletariat but because it is made conscious of the limits of the privileges it can enjoy in colonialism. This was the weakness of the colonial system, it engendered nationalism among the very people it had used as collaborators since assimilation was impossible. In his analysis of the declasses, he distinguished between the migrants from the rural areas and the lumpen proletariat which Fanon has credited with political awareness. These suggested Cabral acted as the informers of the colonial power, and the former were more likely to join the struggle. Whereas Fanon had seen the lumpen proletariat as the spearhead of the peasantry's thrust into the cities, Cabral conceptualized their role in different terms. To him these young men and women would become the cadre to carry the party's message to the country-side. The lack of ideological dogmatism and rigidity contributed to this, a durable unity of purpose was created because he created a common bond of ideas deriving from the experience in Guinea, this facilitated the maintenance of cohesion in the partly, the creation of a language which was easily intelligible to the masses and this partly explains the success with which the militants managed to convince the villagers. As Cabral said in a message that has become famous: "Always remember that the people are not fighting for ideas, not for what is in men's minds. The people fight and accept the sacrifices demanded by the struggle in order to gain material advantages, to live better and in peace, to benefit from progress, and for the better future of their children. National liberation, the struggle against colonialism, the construction of peace, progress and independence are hollow words devoid of any significance unless they can be translated into a real improvement of living conditions." Political mobilization meant visiting one village after another to gain the confidence of the people and then to organize support to initiate armed action in the area. This was the most difficult because political conditions were not favorable for this. Portuguese colonial rule had little effect on the rural people. Land had not been appropriated, forced labour had not been the norm, population had not been displaced and effect of the colonial economy had not been to create ethnic and regional disparities. The diversity of ethnic groups required different arguments and persuasions.

The party cadres first sought to win the support of the homen grand and other traditional authorities and then they explained the relevance of the nationalist struggle by focussing on the day to day problems of the villagers. "We never mobilized our people on the basis of the struggle against colonialism. It does not work, to speak of the struggle against Imperialism simply does not work here. Instead we used a simple language. We had to avoid giving the peasants the impression that we were strangers who had come to teach them lessons. We placed ourselves in the situation of someone who has come to learn and slowly the villagers discovered by themselves, that there is exploitation."

The avoidance of ideological dogma and the construction of an ideology which was closely related to the conditions in Guinea Bissau lent a certain creativity and flexibility to the movement. In 1964, Cabral said in a speech in Rome that "We are not a Communist or a Marxist-Leninist party. The people leading the peasants to a struggle in Guinea are mostly from the urban milieu and connected with the wage earning group. When I hear that only the peasantry can lead the struggle, am I supposed to think that we made a mistake? All I can say is that at the moment our struggle is going well."

He decided that young people had to be trained and mobilized in the school at Conakry, so that vanguard party could be forged. "A successful national revolution demanded that political mobilization be carried out by a modern, effective and politically conscious party." Many of these young people were sent to China, and Morroco, Tunisia and Algeria to be trained so that they could acquire a working class mentality. His training of these party workers was based on the belief that mobilization would require the integration of these militants into the villages and that they would be able to convince the rural people of the necessity of nationalism. Very many of them were recent migrants and were familiar with the social customs of the villages. He realized the difficulty of convincing villagers many of whom distrusted outsiders and foreign ideas.

Displaying great political acumen, he sought to temper the political activism of these activists by making it clear to them that successful mobilization would require cooperating with rather than ousting the chiefs. In this way the upper ranks of the party were drawn from those who had been trained in Conakry and who had shown their political skills in the rural areas.

From 1960-62 attempt was to intensify political mobilization in the country-side. Mobilization was not easy and the forces had to suffer many setbacks. The colonial regime was prepared to use force and extreme violence against any form of resistance. Military reinforcements were brought in any repression was greatly increased in Guinea to forestall any uprising. By September 1962 the party was convinced that a full scale armed struggle must be launched as early as possible. Armed struggle started in the south of the country and spread to the north in mid 1963. The pattern of armed action was in the nature of Maoist guerrilla warfare. Small groups of armed men attacked Portuguese patrols and transport bridges were blown up, roads were cut, ferries were destroyed and convoys were attacked, at the same time the first assaults on Portuguese barracks and garrisons were mounted. Guerrilla attacks were designed to paralyse means of communication and to force the Portuguese to retreat to their fortified camps. Further sabotage and harassment of the troops prevented the chances of a counter attack. By 1964 the island of Como of crucial strategic significance to the Portuguese was secured by a face to face confrontation, in which 900 Portuguese troops were killed. The southern areas were firmly in the hands of the liberation forces.

The impact on the Portuguese forces was apparent and in 1963 the strength of the military went up from 1000 to 13,000. By 1963, the Defence Minister General Gomes de Araujo admitted that numerous well armed groups operating in the southern part of the country had penetrated a zone equivalent to 15% of the province. By the early 1970's he was forced to admit that his forces had reached the edge of neuro physical exhaustion.

By 1963 PAIGC reports spoke of liberated areas where political mobilization was most successful, south of the river Geba and some northern and central parts of the country. Chaliand remarks of the struggle in Guinea Bissau that "Cabral patiently built up a political support structure within the population, and notably animist sectors more sensitive as they were to the issues and easier to mobilize. The case of Guinea Bissau is in this respect comparable to the Chinese and Vietnamese strategies" (1977, p. 115).[3] This was a major achievement, because Cabral drawing from his experience as an agronomist was aware of the problems in mobilizing the peasantry. The peasantry in Guinea, he said was not a revolutionary force "which may seem strange, particularly as we have based the whole of our armed liberation struggle on the peasantry. A distinction must be drawn between a physical force and a revolutionary force. Physically, the peasantry is a great force in Guinea; it is almost the whole of the population, it controls the nation's wealth, but we know from experience what trouble we had convincing the peasantry to fight . . . . The conditions of the peasantry in China were very different; there the peasantry had a history of revolt, but this was not the case in Guinea, and so it was not possible for our party militants and propaganda workers to find the same kind of welcome among the peasantry in Guinea for the idea of national liberation as was the case in China."[4] His own concern, he was careful to point out was with his own country and not with the problem of the revolutionary peasantry per se.

The focus on the petite bourgeoisie was to become Cabral's signature tune and perhaps his most famous and controversial contribution to the theory and practice of armed struggle. Colonialism, he said, had brought an end to the history of the people of the country because it had stripped them of control over their means of production. Revolution was the assertion of the right of the people to have their own history, that is to free the process of development of the national productive forces through a struggle against neo-colonialism. The people who would take over the state power in Guinea and fight neo-colonialism was not the peasantry which cannot read or write, there was neither a working class nor a proletariat, what could be found was a stream of people who had learnt to manipulate the colonial state apparatus, "it is this class which is the inheritor of state power – though I wish I could be wrong."

It is the situation of the underdeveloped countries which endowed the petite bourgeoisie with a function, that grants it a revolutionary rule. It is here that the gap between Cabral's analysis of the social structure of Guinea Bissau and the classical Marxist dictums becomes apparent. But this position posed a problem. To hope that this class will become a revolutionary class is hope for a miracle. The contradiction is clear, the petite bourgeoisie cannot carry out a revolution and yet it must. It does not possess the economic base, it has to transform itself into a bourgeoisie, and thus it negates the revolution. In order not to do so it only has one choice and that is to strengthen its revolutionary consciousness, to reject the temptation of becoming more bourgeois, and the natural concerns of its class mentality, to identity itself with the working classes. It must commit class suicide to be reborn as the revolutionary workers completely identified with the deepest aspirations of the people to which it belongs.

This is one of the most frequently cited statements of Cabral, and it reflects his pragmatic approach to the issue of independence. Revolution was necessary to overcome the phenomena of neo colonialism but it is by no means inevitable. There were compelling reasons why the national petite bourgeoisic should wish to avoid this. During the period of revolution, a national class based on unity could be forged but at independence internal contradictions were likely to break out again. Class, ethnic, urban vs rural contradictions would break out again. The party must, therefore, acquire a well defined sense of direction during the liberation struggle, so that it could distinguish between real and fictitious independence. "Only a revolutionary vanguard, generally an active minority, can be aware of this distinction from the start and make it known, through the struggle, to the popular classes. This explains the fundamentally political nature of the national liberation struggle and to a certain extent makes the form of the struggle important in the final result of the phenomena of national liberation."[5]

The dilemma of the petite bourgeoisie is to betray the revolution or commit suicide as a class. "The positive solution in favour of the revolution depends on . . . the development of revolutionary consciousness. This dependence necessarily calls our attention to the capacity of the leader of the national liberation struggle to remain faithful to the principles and to the fundamental cause of this struggle. This shows us, to a certain extent, that if national liberation is essentially a political problem, the conditions for its development give it certain characteristics which belong to the sphere of morals."[6] Party members, he stressed, had a responsibility which not only extended to following party rules, or fulfilling their historic mission, but displaying the qualities of goodness and honesty which the revolution demanded. Socialism was desirable because it created a better society, not simply a more honest one. And this could not be achieved at the expense of men's personal and political liberty. This meant that during the peoples war politics not militarism had to be in command.

Politics in Command

Cabrals strategy rested on two principles. One that national liberation was a political not a military struggle. And the second was that the war had to be fought in the country-side. In 1964 at the Cassaca Congress of the party it was made clear that the militarist tendencies could be counterveiled only by civilian organizations in the liberated areas. The military aspect was secondary, more important was the need to improve the daily conditions of people's lives and decentralization of power to the village level. The Cassaca Congress proved to be a turning point for the policies of the party, after a year of armed struggle admitted Cabral the party was already sick. The main problem analysed by Cabral was that of militarism. Militarism led to grave abuses by the guerrilla groups in areas where they had achieved military success. Military successes had led to personalized political power and this assumed dangerous proportions in liberated areas. A few guerrilla commanders installed themselves as Chiefs and gathered courts around themselves. This posed a very real threat to the party because it was contrary to the principle of politics in command, and the local population was withdrawing its support altogether. Some of these local self-styled leaders came to the Congress with armed escorts.

All the guerrilla fighters were disarmed and they were instructed to respond to the complaints made against them. Those who were found guilty were taken prisoner and others who had not come to the Congress were liquidated. By the end of the Congress the leadership of the party had been put in the hands of the most politically conscious leaders. Cabral crushed what he called the militarist faction of the party. The Congress had turned into a power struggle between military commanders and Cabral's supporters. "A tendency towards militarism had begun to appear" wrote Cabral, "It seemed from the fact that fighters as well as some officials have forgotten that we are armed militants and not militarists. This was a direct consequence of inadequate political work within the armed forces."

The document written by Cabral after the Congress reemphasized the two principles underlying the party's political strategy – "the party is the driving force of the revolution, but its strength lies with the masses; the masses, which constitute the main force of the struggle will only remain loyal to the party if there aspirations, initiatives and criticisms are taken into account by the party leadership." Cabral in rethinking the party's policy realized that the only adequate alternative to the militarization of nationalism was the development of a social and political infrastructure in the liberated areas. Along with other leaders Cabral took charge of the liberated areas. Society was reorganized in these areas and the subsequent period saw the development of a party state. This involved two tendencies – one was a stronger and more centralized party organization and other was greater political participation in the control and reconstruction of the liberated areas.

The elected village committee in the liberated areas became the political and the administrative nerve of the village. Each of the five members of which two were to be women had specific functions, by 1970 there were 400 village committees in the liberated areas. These areas moved away from cash crops to food production. By 1970 groundnut exports were stopped, and the Portuguese were reluctant to force the villagers to grow cash crops, or pay taxes for fear that they would flee to the liberated areas. The commercial system set up by the Portuguese became unprofitable. Though agriculture was not modernized, there was an increase in the output of rice and the party was able to export rice coconuts and kola nuts to Guinea. People's stores were created as means of distribution, these were trade centres where people could exchange their surplus for other things. Lars Rudebeck gives this example – in 1970, 25 sheets of writing paper were exchanged for one kilo of rice and 3 meters of cloth for 10 kilos of rice.

It was in the social achievements in these areas that Cabral was justifiably proud. Insisting that the war was to improve each villager's life, Cabral initiated primary education programmes, health care system, hospitals and dispensaries.

A new judicial system was set up with a village peoples' tribunal at its core. The final authority rested with the supreme court. Social changes included attention being given to the status of women and the institution of marriage.

By 1973 the PAIGC could declare itself independent, because it controlled three quarters of the territory. The UN special mission validated this in 1972. It confirmed that the party did not only control but administer the zones and that it enjoyed unquestioned supremacy and legitimacy in these areas. The UN mission recommended that the forthcoming declaration of Independence should be recognized. The PAIGC held national elections in the second half of 1972 with an extremely high turnout. By October 1992 Cabral felt that the party was in a position to declare the independence of the country and set up a government. He was assassinated in January 1973, but it speaks of the high degree of institutionalization of the party initiated by Cabral, that independence was declared on 24 September 1973. Within three weeks sixty states recognized the new government. As Basil Davidson said of the armed struggle waged under the leadership of Cabral "It may be questioned whether the world had previously seen a success to compare with this one. Enormous modern armies, of a general toughness and tenacity never in doubt until the near end, were outpaced and outmatched by fighters who came from populations whose technological level, whose initial command of any aspect of modern science, whose starting point of literacy or any other education preparation were always far lower than had been the case, for example, in Cuba or Vietnam. In technological terms those were very backward populations. And yet they were able to win."

NOTES

1. A Cabral, *1976-77 Unity and Struggle Speeches and Writings* (New York: Monthly Review Press).
2. *A Cabral 1969 Revolution in Guinea* (London: Stage One), pp. 52-53.
3. G. Chaliand, *1977 Revolution in the Third World: Myths and Prospects* (Sussex: Harvester).
4. *Revolution in Guinea*, op. cit. p. 50
5. Ibid., p. 89.
6. Ibid., pp. 89-90.

15. Mao's Literary Views and His Poems

NAGEN SAIKIA

Mao Tse-tung, now called Mao Zedong (1893-1976) was a great political thinker and a revolutionary-statesman of the twentieth century. No doubt, his 'time' is no more there in today's China to surcharge the air with a spirit of emotion to the cause like that of 'Big Lip Forward' in a changed situation. The younger generation of China today is coming away so far from him that most of them do not feel at all any attachment to him so much so that they could easily remove the big statue of this maker of Red China from the campus of the Beijing University a few years back. But still, the human civilization cannot ignore this personality so easily, for his immense contributions towards the growth and implementation of Marxism-Leninism in the soil of China with new dimensions. Under his leadership, the communist party of China made new interpretations of Marxist theory to fit the Chinese situations. He was a visionary, a philosopher, a teacher and a creative personality too.

He had a total view of life, based on Marxism-Leninism. This total view included naturally his literary view also. This view is more close to Leninism than to Marxism. A question may arise immediately whether there is any difference between Marxism and Leninism. The clearly loud answer is that there is not at all. Because what was theory in Marx, had been practised in reality by Lenin. To implement the theory of dialectical materialism of Marx, Lenin creatively developed it in new conditions. He raised Marxist philosophy qualitatively to a new stage, generalized the latest achievements of science, comprehensively developed materialist dialects by applying it in new conditions of social life.[1] Mao in the new conditions of his own country gave it a new working dimension to fit it with the life of the peasantry of China. When we try to analyse Mao's literary view, this point of distinction should not be missed.

Mao, like Lenin, gave more importance to the message and total effect of literature so that literature can help people to be inspired to work for the change of the society from feudalism to socialism. Anything which was not adapted to the needs of the peasants, was not acceptable for Mao. As for example, though, mythology has been charming people for last thousands of years, yet Mao observed that "Mythology is not based on the specific conditions of actual contradictions, and therefore does not scientifically reflect reality.[2] Of course, this view of Mao to some extent was identical to the view of Marx who hoped that 'All mythology masters and dominates and shapes the forces of nature in and through the imagination; hence it disappears as soon as man gains mastery over the forces of nature.[3]

Mao's literary view was an integral part of his total political view. He emphasized the study of the theory of Marx, Engels, Lenin and Stalin, not only by the party cadres, but by all as the science of revolution. At the same time he had a total view of the growth of the human civilization and with this view he analysed the history of several thousands years of China and its rich cultural heritage with an aim to utilize the resources of the past in building up neo-democratic culture.[4] He was very much against subjectivism and sectarianism and was very much critical about the ignorance of the history of one's own country. He was very much concerned with the need of continuous working for the change of society and therefore he wanted all thoughts, imaginations and actions to be directed accordingly. He instructed his party cadres to follow the Bolshevik law where it is said, "When writing or speaking, always have in mind the rank and file workers who must understand you, must have in mind those for whom you write, to whom you speak."[5] He also wanted that the rules laid down by Lu Hsun for young writers should be strictly followed. Some of Lu Hsun's directions were – (1) Pay close attention to a great variety of things; observe more and do not write if you have seen only a little; (2) Do not force yourself to write when you have nothing to write about; (3) Read over your article at least twice after you have finished writing it, and do your best to strike out ruthlessly redundant words, sentences and paragraphs. Rather condense the material for a novel into a sketch than spin out the material for a sketch in to a novel; (4) Do not coin new-angled epithets or the like that are intelligible only to yourself.[6]

Mao, finally at the 'Yenan Forum on Art and Literature' made his observations more clear and direct. He stated unequivocally that the writers should take the standpoint of the proletariat and the mass of the people. He asked "Are there any of our artists and writers who still lack a correct or clear understanding of this point?"[7] He wanted to make art and literature a component part of the whole revolutionary machine. At that time Japanese force was there as the target of attack. Mao on several occasions referred to this need. Moreover, he emphasized heavily that the writers must know the common people, must know their socio-cultural heritage, must love them and should identify themselves with the people. He referred to the summon made by Lenin in 1905 to the writers to "serve the millions upon millions of working people."[8] Lenin discarded at that time the non-party literature which was of no use to the fighting people. Mao too discarded the pure literature, which, according to him, can serve only the exploiters and oppressors. So he pleaded that art and culture should be created for four classes of people, namely, the workers, the peasants, armed workers and peasants and the working people and the intelligentsia of the urban petty bourgeoisie who are also taken to be allies of the other three classes. Mao's view sometimes echoed the view of Lu Hsun that he recorded in his essay, "My view on the alliance of left wing writers."[9]

Mao took artistic or literary work to be the ideological expressions of the human mind reflecting the life of a given society. Why art and literature attract people more than the real life is also a question that he wanted to meet with. He summed up that "Although both are beautiful, life as reflected in art and literature ought to be on a higher level and of greater intensity than real life, in sharper focus and more typical, never the ideal, and therefore more universal."[10] But at the same time he did not forget to say that art and literature are subordinate to politics, and he opposed the Trotoskian view that "Politics is Marxist, art bourgeois."[11]

Mao's literary views are very much rigid and strictly associated with the political ideology. But a pertinent question arises, can a writer be directed to write something in accordance with the party-line and at the same time to make his/her writings universal? The literary view of Marx himself was rather different from that of Mao on this point. Marx always gave emphasis on aesthetic value of literature. Heine and Gothe of German, Aeschylus of Greece and Shakespeare of England were his most favorite writers. He took Aeschylus and Shakespeare to be the greatest of the greats.[12] Inspite of being materialistic in regard to the life and the universe, Marx very well identified the inner man in the context of the universe; but Mao, and to some extent Lenin also, stood for immediate social need. They sometimes overlooked the fact that party-literature cannot be compared with those time-tested literatures created by the most celebrated writers at different times of the history of human civilization. No doubt, the cultural life of man, his intellectual, aesthetic and spiritual life, his ideologies, nothing is independent from his material life.[13] Marx clearly stated that "It is not the consciousness of man that determines their being, but on the contrary, their social being that determines their consciousness."[14]

Whether idealist or materialist nobody can eliminate the society, and its spirit expressing itself in terms of literature from the literature of a given period. The sense of aesthetic value and beauty is also related to life itself. But at the same time it will also have to be kept in mind that literature is created by the individual creative ability of the writers, not by cooperative efforts of the society nor by any ideology which is current in some given time. Therefore, mechanical implementation of the political view would cause harm to the literature itself.

The intrinsic aesthetic merit of a book cannot be created by mere dictation of policies.

However, Mao himself also was a poet.Whether his poems can be judged by his own literary views is also a question of great importance. We have in our hand an English translation of 36 poems of Mao Tse Tung (published by Foreign Languages Press, Peking, 1976). Yes in some poems Mao is singing the warring youths and their spirit:

> How bright and brave they look
> shouldering five-foot rifles
> On the parade ground lit up by the
> first gleams of day.
>
> (Militia Women)

Sometimes he sings of the flags and banners flying above the hill tops of the warring people standing against their fow (Ching Kang Shan). In his "Reply to Comrade Kuo-Mo-Jo" he draws a picture of a boiling earth with a few words:

> The four seas are rising, clouds and
> waters raging,
> The five continents are rocking, wind
> and thunder roaring.

But, in most of his poems we hear the lone voice of a poet whom the nature with beautiful landscape and the country with its rich heritage appeal greatly. In these poems of Mao, we can also hear the voices of his predecessors of long long ago. We know during the period of the Tang dynasty the Chinese poetry flourished colourfully. Tu Fu, Li Po, Bai Jai are some poets who left indelible prints in the history of Chinese poetry. When Mao writes:

> Alone I stand in the autumn cold,
> On the tip of orange island,
> The Hsiang flowing northward;
> I see a thousand hills crimsoned through
> By their serried woods deep-dyed,
> And a hundred barges vying
> Over crystal blue waters.

We hear a nostalgic voice of the poet. In his "Yellow Crane Tower", "Three Short Poems", "Loushan Pass", "Rcply thc Doublc Ninth", "Ode to the Plum Blossom", Reply to Li-Shu-Yi", etc. are some of his poems which cannot be judged by his own literary theory. When he says "The lonely moon goddess spreads her ample sleeves", we do not hear the voice of a political teacher, we then listen to a lone poet. A political poet awakens when we hear him saying "The Red Army fears not the trials of the Long March" or "The Red Flags stream in the wind in a blaze of glory". These writings will remain as memories of some important historical events. But when he says "The yellow crane is gone, who knows whither? Only this tower remains a haunt for visitors", we feel sadness at the passing away of time and the beauty. It appeals to our heart, not to the thinking faculty of the brain directly. Mao's thirty six poems are enough to show that the personality of a political thinker and leader and the personality of a poet, both the personalities dwelt in him. And it is also proved that his literary views which he tried to propagate through his talks and prose writings, failed to guide his own soul when it was at work of writing poetry.

NOTES

1. Frolov, I. (ed.), *Dictionary of Philosophy*, pp. 245-46., (Revised edition 1984).
2. Mao Tse-tung, *On Contradiction in 'on Art and Literature'*, 11.
3. Marx, *A Contribution to the Critique of Political Economy*, 1904, pp.310-11.
4. Mao Tse-tung, *New Democratic Culture* in *New Democracy*, p. 3.
5. Mao Tse-tung,*On Art and Literature*, p. 63.
6. Ibid., pp. 63-65.
7. Ibid., p. 68.
8. Ibid., p. 76.
9. *Complete Works of Lu Hsun*, Vol. 17.
10. *Talk at the German Forum*, 1942.
11. Ibid., p. 93.
12. Paul Lafarque and WhielmLei Knecht, *Karl Marx; His Life and Work*, pp. 10-12, 16-20.
13. Karl Marx, *Selected Writings*, p. 90, Editors P.B. Bottmore and Maxlailen.
14. Ibid., pp. 96-97.

Index